MUTES *&*
EARTHQUAKES

MUTES & EARTHQUAKES

Bill Manhire's
Creative Writing Course
at Victoria

VICTORIA UNIVERSITY PRESS

Victoria University Press
Victoria University of Wellington
PO Box 600 Wellington

© *Introduction, editorial material and*
this selection, Bill Manhire 1997
© *Contributors 1997*

ISBN 0 86473 318 6

First published 1997

Designed by Margaret Cochran
Printed by GP Print, Wellington

Contents

Bill Manhire

Introduction

A couple of pieces of advice:

1. Write what you know, and

2. Write what you don't know.

Write what you know is easy. If you want to write a novel set in an Icelandic fish factory, you had better know something about Iceland and fish factories. Write what you don't know is a bit harder, but much more rewarding. I started teaching writing at Victoria University twenty years ago. I had no idea what I was doing.

The course began in 1975 as a sort of undergraduate thesis paper, giving recognition to students' own writing.[1] There were no formal classes, but the students—who had to be third-year English majors to enrol in the first place—were able to submit a folio of original writing and receive credit towards their degree.

The next year, the students who were enrolled in the course, half-a-dozen of them, began to feel lonely and I was asked by the department chairperson, Stuart Johnston, to arrange some informal meetings where they could share problems and discuss their work. It proved a good place to be, the shabby prefab room where we all gathered. To start with, everyone actually wanted to be there, which was never something you could safely say of tutorials on *Richard III* or the nineteenth-century novel. And the students were interesting,

---

[1] In fact the teaching of creative writing began at Victoria in 1969, with Christine Cole Catley's University Extension workshops, which were also conducted by Michael King and Fiona Kidman.

too. They talked about literary texts, their own, without having to worry about what the approved, time-honoured judgements might be.

Somehow or other the idea of exercise work began to develop. It was interesting to see what each writer did with the same set of challenges, and as we went along I began to get adventurous. I introduced cranky constraints, strange systems of chance. For instance: 'Write a haiku using only the words you can find on the racing page of the *Evening Post.*' And so, in 1977, Helen Gabites wrote this:

> A tamed life moored in
> shifting dark horizons, this
> quiet lady.

My memory is that we were all surprised by the quality of the work this exercise produced. But of course we shouldn't have been. New Zealand's best words are there on the racing page: much of the nation's most strenuous creative endeavour has gone into the task of naming horses.

We were beginning to enter the gaming halls of the imagination. Soon I was asking people to make large cardboard dice, write words on them and throw short poems:

> Stones in distance, or
> just blue stones. As you touch them
> they attach their wings.

Then I was asking students to 'find' poems and bring them to class (see p.292). I was asking for riddles, for spells.

By the early 80s I began to have some sense of what was going on. I didn't know what I was doing; but somehow I did know, sort of. The course had changed in certain ways. It had moved to 200-level, and was available not just to English majors but to anyone. The prerequisite was now 'any twelve credits', along with something even vaguer: 'a required standard of writing'. This was simply a way of coping with admissions. There was space in the workshop for twelve students only, and many, many more were applying. Students submitted poems and stories, as samples of their wares. By 1996 there were over 150 applications for the course each year, and we were turning away large numbers of talented writers.

Still, the exercises had become more formal, a key part of the early stages of the course, and I had begun to understand more clearly what I was doing with them, and just how they might be useful to new writers meeting in a group. Creative writing workshops depend on their members behaving in certain ways. They have to read their work aloud; they have to be willing to listen to a dozen other people making comments on it. In turn, they have to be willing to make comments on the work of everyone else in the workshop; they have to be honest (or honest enough) without being damaging, and they have to be encouraging without being false or fatuous. Students also have to let their work be published. By this I mean that they bring a dozen copies of their work to class, then two or three hours later watch the other members of the workshop leave the room, taking copies of all the poems or stories with them. This can be a hard moment. Not only have you had to listen to comments a little less gratifying than those your mother might offer, you also have to watch your work departing into the universe. Now anyone might read it.

For a range of reasons like this, it helps if the first pieces of course work produced are exercises—and, in some respects, the sillier the better. If you are forced to write a story that somehow incorporates a child standing in water and the *Oxford Dictionary of Saints* (see p.286), and several people express disappointment with the second-last paragraph, you needn't feel personally hurt or deflated. After all, it's not the heartfelt poem you wrote about your last disastrous love affair, or the meditation on your pet budgie's death, that evocative piece which mattered so much to you but you never quite got right. So the exercises give us conversational practice. People learn to talk about one another's work in—I hope—civilised ways. Eventually we move on to discuss the 'real' work that people have been getting on with, and which will be in their end-of-course folios.

Of course, the exercises are real work, too, and often the results find their way into course folios and, in many cases, into books and literary magazines. For me, one of the great satisfactions of the Victoria workshops has been to see, year after year, the amount of surprise and pleasure people get from producing work that copes with—and often transcends—the arbitrary demands of an exercise idea. Our culture has inherited the dangerous assumption that the only work which matters—and, by extension, can be any good—is the stuff which is sincere, which springs from something deep within the writer, which is, indeed, somehow *inspired*. But how can you be inspired or sincere when you are made to write an exercise?

Well, Stravinsky is supposed to have said that inspiration is what happens when you are working really hard. I'm sure this is true for writers. The hopeful writer who waits for inspiration may end up waiting forever. This is one of the big reasons why writers should write what they don't know. If you know too much before you begin, you won't find your way to characters or stories which you yourself find interesting, or—especially if you are a poet—you will write in the stale phrases we've all heard somewhere else, rather than letting the words be instruments of exploration, part of the actual process of discovery. The need for creative ignorance is something which all kinds of writers seem to agree on. Poems are like dreams, says the American poet, Adrienne Rich; in them you put what you didn't know you knew. Or, as the Australian novelist David Malouf says, 'You have to fall out of that part of your mind where you know too much, into an area where you don't know anything before the best writing can happen.' And here is the great New York short-story writer, Grace Paley, making the same case:

> Lucky for art, life is difficult, hard to understand, useless and mysterious. Lucky for artists, they don't require art to do a good day's work. But critics and teachers do. A book, a story, should be smarter than its author. It is the critic or teacher in you or me who cleverly outwits the characters with the power of prior knowledge of meetings and ends.
> Stay open and ignorant.

Exercises are a way of encouraging new writers to stay open and ignorant, to write what they don't know. Constraints seem to prompt inventiveness; we use our imaginations because we need to solve problems; we don't simply put on paper the things we knew we knew already. And, in the Original Composition exercises, quite a bit of genre-jumping goes on. Poets are made to try prose fiction, fiction writers, poetry. (It's the fiction writers who get most anxious about this.) There is another advantage here. Writers who are made to jump the tracks imaginatively can develop a broader sense of what they might be able to do. Occasionally a poet walks into the course, and a novelist walks out—or even a playwright.[2]

I get a perverse pleasure from the range of things some of the Victoria graduates are able to do. Vivienne Plumb has published highly successful fiction and poetry, as well as drama. Anthony McCarten isn't just the co-author of *Ladies' Night*; you can also find his poetry quoted admiringly in the *Oxford History of New Zealand Literature*, while a collection of his short fiction has been published in both the UK and New Zealand. Barbara Anderson was writing poems and stories when she did Original Composition; then she became a successful writer of radio plays; now she's a novelist.

My greatest pleasure comes, however, from watching new writers find and begin to explore their own voices. This is a slightly different thing from finding the genre that they write best in, though that can be part of it. Voice is simply the unmistakable, distinctive sound that a writer makes on the page: an almost unanalysable combination of effects—tone, cadence, texture—of language and of subject matter. We each have our own voice as a writer, just as we have our own voice on the telephone or tape recorder. The problem is to find that voice, and to speak in it, in a world filled with noise.[3]

Creative writing is big business in the United States. There are over 400 degree courses, and they say that some American publishers can pick 'the Iowa voice' or 'the Stanford voice' when a new manuscript

---

[2] I am puzzled by all the playwrights—Jeff Addison, Allen O'Leary, Vivienne Plumb, Ken Duncum, Kerry Jimson, Jo Randerson, Anthony McCarten, David Geary and Evan Watts among others—who have passed through the Victoria workshop. How on earth did that happen?

[3] Oddly enough, Alison Glenny's story, 'Mutes and Earthquakes', which gives this book its title, takes up the question of finding a voice in several ways. See especially p.79.

thuds onto their desk. The implication is that teachers of writing busy themselves producing clones. I can see that this is a danger, but an even greater danger would be for a workshop teacher simply to keep quiet, and avoid expressing opinions. I'm pleased by the variety of voices and writing styles which can be heard on the far side of Victoria's Original Composition course. Elizabeth Knox does not sound like Chris Orsman who does not sound like Forbes Williams who does not sound like David Geary who does not sound like Gabrielle Muir who does not sound like Jenny Bornholdt who does not sound like John Macdonald—and so on.[4]

One explanation for this is my decision to keep my own workshop role separate from the assessment processs. There are three examiners for each end-of-course folio (a little like publishers' readers); they write reports, which often differ from one another and which may or may not make individual writers happy. Equally, students simply pass or fail: there are no grades like B- or C+ or straight A. All this means that I am free to say what I think in workshop sessions. No one need feel pressured—at least in terms of grades—to take particular account of what I say. If they have found what they can do, they can go on doing it.

Voice shouldn't be confused with originality, another of those big ideas like inspiration and sincerity. We all learn to speak by mimicking the adult figures around us. We hear a noise and copy it. We are shown approval, or not. When we grow up we can hear our parents inside the sounds we make, and yet we are still ourselves—distinctive, and distinctively different from the voices which shaped us. The writing voice is like this, too.

This is why imitation can be very useful for a writer. You find your way to your voice by being influenced, by copying. The twelve-year-old Frank Sargeson started copying out Sir Walter Scott's *Ivanhoe*

---

[4] If I'm to be honest, I think that a couple of things which I emphasise are sometimes apparent in writers who have attended the Victoria workshop. One is the element of *play* to which Dinah Hawken refers (see p.41). The other—which may spring from the diversity of exercise work—is hybrid writing which hovers (like the contributions here from Louise Wrightson and Paola Bilbrough) somewhere between poetry and prose, or texts which explicitly mix poetry and prose (as happens in the work of writers such as Jenny Bornholdt and Emily Perkins).

into an exercise book, which is going a bit far; but the idea has a strange sort of merit. Poets, especially, can be silly about this. I have met plenty who declare that they never read other poets: their own pure, original voice might somehow be contaminated. People who talk like that aren't writers. They simply like the idea of calling themselves writers. If you read a hundred poems by Seamus Heaney and write in his influence for a month or even a year or two, that's fine. It may be part of the process of finding out what to do. I don't imagine there are many aspiring screen writers who decide not to go to films on the grounds that the experience may destroy their art. The only person who will never become a writer is the one who doesn't read. Concert pianists listen to music. Great chefs like to eat.

So I encourage people to read widely. We talk—sometimes formally, more often informally—about the people we are reading. We recommend writers to one another the way some people recommend restaurants. Have you tried Lorrie Moore, Raymond Carver, Beth Nannestad? Carol Duffy can make a good night out; or Donald Barthelme, if you're in the mood.

I hand out sheets—thoughts by writers about writing. I pass around an essay by Ursula Le Guin, called 'Why Are Americans Afraid of Dragons?', which emphasises the importance of fantasy and the imagination. Or I distribute a sheet of advice from Grace Paley, which includes various pieces of genuine wisdom. There is the piece about ignorance quoted above. Or this:

> Literature has something to do with language. There's probably a natural grammar at the tip of your tongue. You may not believe it, but if you say what's on your mind in the language that comes from your parents and your street and your friends you'll probably say something beautiful.

Or this:

> It's possible to write about anything in the world, but the slightest story ought to contain the facts of money and blood in order to be interesting to adults. That is—everybody

continues on this earth by courtesy of certain economic arrangements, people are rich or poor, make a living or don't have to, are useful to systems, or superfluous. And blood— the way people live as families or outside families or in the creation of family, sisters, sons, fathers, the bloody ties. Trivial work ignores these two FACTS and is never comic or tragic.

May you do trivial work?

I also have a sheet I occasionally distribute called 'Two Works of Art'. This contains Homer's astonishing description of the shield of Achilles from Book 18 of *The Iliad*:

Next [the artist] depicted a large field of soft, rich fallow, which was being ploughed for the third time. A number of ploughmen were driving their teams across it to and fro. When they reached the ridge at the end of the field and had to wheel, a man would come up and hand them a cup of mellow wine. Then they turned back down the furrows and toiled along through the deep fallow soil to reach the other end. The field, though it was made of gold, grew black behind them, as a field does when it is being ploughed. The artist had achieved a miracle.

and Wallace Stevens' deliberately flatfooted poem, 'Anecdote of the Jar', whose opening suggests the way in which a work of art can bring the messy natural world to order:

> I placed a jar in Tennessee
> And round it was, upon a hill.
> It made the slovenly wilderness
> Surround that hill.

Then there is a sheet containing poems by children from Elwyn Richardson's wonderful book, *In the Early World*:

The Tea

The Tea makes you funny as can be
It is a hush tea; it goes for you
Hush a bye on the tree top,
Goodnight tea.
Makes yourself as good as gold,
The gold.
The gold is a wonderful thing;
It is a happy gold.
Gold go to sleep.
He bites all the little dogs' feet.

Telephone Wires

In the far away distance
I can hear the telephone wires
Singing in churches
Like pakehas.

Untitled

The frightening of a flower:
Bees' muscles singing.

The idea with poems like this is to indicate a standard that we might all aspire to. If we can do half as well, we'll be doing extremely well. But in fact I don't discuss this sheet or others like it in class. They simply get carried home in the writers' bags. But my hope is that they will supply contexts and points of focus which will help students as they set about their work.

❖

Most writers I know have had the experience of recklessly answering the question, 'What do you do?' with the words, 'I'm a writer', only to be faced with the follow-up question, 'Yes, but what do you *really* do?' Aspiring writers enrol in workshops for a range of reasons, but one reason must be that a workshop legitimises the desire to write; at last that novel can be given priority, and not simply be the thing you are going to do 'one day', when everything more pressing is finally out of the way. Workshops *make* you write, too. There are regular deadlines. If you don't produce work week by week, you are failing in a social obligation, one you may also be paying for. Writing is a solitary business—you work in what Eudora Welty has called 'a kind of absolute state of Do Not Disturb'—but all the same you belong to the curious community of the writing group, and you have responsibilities within it. After a while, you also begin to feel that you belong to a larger community of writers. Some of them, like Maurice Gee or Patricia Grace, actually visit the workshop, as do figures from the literary marketplace, from radio, film, television, magazine and book publishing. Some of them, like Ursula Le Guin and Grace Paley, live elsewhere; others, like Homer and Wallace Stevens, are dead. But everyone is somehow in the same big house of words. Maybe this, rather than mere self-absorption, is what the poet Richard Hugo means when he says that 'a creative writing class may be one of the last places you can go where your life still matters'.

A sense of community, if it is achieved, can be a key factor in whether students persist as writers. Whatever gets taught in workshops, I have never been much interested in describing it in terms of 'course objectives' or 'pedagogical outcomes'. It would be possible to teach the short story entirely in terms of technique: a workshop on beginnings, one on point of view, one on characterisation, one on dialogue, and so on. There are useful things to be learnt, of course, and learning them can save a lot of time (sometimes years). It helps the budding poet to be told plainly how disastrous it can be to fill poems with adjectives, or with abstract language, or with dozens of '-ing' words (which in practice are just adjectives trying to sound a bit poetic). It helps an aspiring story writer to be warned off all those elegantly various verbs which signal direct speech. Contrary to what they used to tell us at high school, it is a very bad idea to write like this:

> 'Darling, I'm home!' called Odysseus cheerfully.
> 'Just a moment,' Penelope fluted from the bedroom.
> 'I hope there's plenty of beer in the house,' snorted Odysseus, picking his way past the loom. 'I've brought all the blokes back for a drink.'

A formal understanding of technique will only take you so far. As Flannery O'Connor (whose thoughts I sometimes distribute to the class) says: 'Discussing story-writing in terms of plot, character, and theme is like trying to describe the expression on a face by saying where the eyes, nose, and mouth are.'

So technical things matter—just as taking the right creative risks or acquiring the right work habits matter—and we deal with them as they come up, in relation to exercise or folio work. But they do not constitute a set of goals or course objectives. I suppose the course objectives appear in what students go on to write after they have taken the Victoria workshop—in poems, stories, novels and plays, in the works which the course itself may never have contemplated.

A pretty good sampling of those works is printed in *Mutes & Earthquakes*. The anthology sets out to celebrate achievements, and I have chosen work to represent both the quality and the range of what has come out of the workshops at Victoria. However, I have made no attempt to choose the best piece of work by each individual writer (though I guess some contributors have been luckier than others). There is work here from a range of sources—from books published well after the course's conclusion, from end-of-course folios, from exercise pieces produced during the course, even (in the case of Eirlys Hunter) from the portfolio of work submitted with an entry application.

If this book is a celebration, it is also meant to be useful. I hope it will work as a stimulating prompt book for anyone who wants to write. Alongside the poetry and fiction and drama, there are commissioned essays on creative writing by Joy Cowley, David Geary, Dinah

Hawken, Fiona Kidman and Damien Wilkins, who have generously included a number of their own exercise ideas. A few secrets are being shared. There is also a chapter which outlines many of the exercises used in the Victoria course. Most of these exercises are cross-referenced to particular poems and stories. Thus the book itself behaves a little like a workshop. Writers present their work, while I link and interrupt and perhaps hold forth a little. If you read *Mutes & Earthquakes*, dipping in and out, flipping to and fro, you will find yourself eaves-dropping on a busy conversation. And if you are prompted to do some writing of your own, you may find you are participating in it.

❖

There are many names missing from these pages. There are writers I didn't have room for, some whom I haven't kept track of, others whose work has mostly been for stage or screen, and others who haven't (to my knowledge) carried on writing. I have not included writers like James Belich, Jane Westaway and Simon Wilson who took the course in its very early days when it was still, as it were, under construction; nor one or two, like Jean Watson, who were fully formed writers before they ever enrolled. To try and take credit for any of their achievements would be pretty cheeky. But then, to try and take credit for any of the writers in this anthology would be to get the emphasis wrong. Original Composition is something that everyone here did along the way to becoming a writer. For some, the experience of an audience, there in the room, will have been what made the difference; for others the workshop will have sped a few things up. It is not modesty, however, which makes me feel that none of these writers needed the workshop. People learn to be writers, and a little bit of teaching can be part of the learning process. But sitting down and reading your way through the whole of Dickens, like the young Maurice Gee, might work just as well. Reading and writing, and then reading and writing, and keeping on going—that in the end is what makes the difference.

❖

Many people have helped with the Original Composition course since 1975. Professor Don McKenzie was the prime mover in setting it up, and a long line of English Department chairpersons has encouraged and fostered it. Most of the university's writers-in-residence have visited the workshop, and there have been a large number of other visiting writers; Patricia Grace and Maurice Gee, especially, have been frequent and generous contributors. Radio New Zealand (particularly Fergus Dick and Carol Dee) and Learning Media (especially Brent Southgate) have been very good friends of the course. Folio readers have included Tony Bellette, Bede Corrie, Charles Ferrall, Linda Hardy, the late Frank McKay, Brian Opie, Colleen Reilly, Harry Ricketts, Heidi Thomson, Kim Walker, Lydia Wevers, Peter Whiteford, Damien Wilkins (who convened the 1995 workshop) and—in particular—Fergus Barrowman and Kathryn Walls; I thank them all for their often anonymous work in keeping the course afloat. Thanks also to Marion McLeod, who has had to live with the course and its various demands for rather a long time; to Rachel Lawson and Margaret Cochran for their work on this book; and to the Department of English for its grant to support publication.

Bill Manhire
Wellington
June 1997

Rachel Bush

Rachel Bush took the Original Composition course in its final year, 1996, as part of an MA in English. Her MA was awarded with distinction, and a version of her folio, *The Hungry Woman*, is being published in 1997. Rachel Bush lives in Nelson, where she works as a teacher.

How I Ate Them

I see the girl in the path on the track, daft and daffy with her basket just so and her smile, smile face and she walking hoppity, skippity, skip, sing a little tune, and wander this way and that and pick a bit of flower then add it to the natty basket and not touch a spotty toadstool, but maybe some slippery jacks, yellow in the pine needles.

So I hide and watch and hide and watch and then I leap out and hello my little one, but, 'Oh,' she screams and, 'Oh oh oh,' like she reads this line in a play. So, sweetly, 'Calm, be cool,' I say and smile so much it sends her worse and I have to say, 'No harm, no harm, little lady, pretty miss, and where do you be going?' Like that, I say it, where do you be going, making up a foolish funny syntax that will sound folksy and friendly and I say, 'Okay now how can I help you, little girl, a wee lass alone in the wood wandering under the dark firs?'

She says, 'I am going to visit my grandmama who is sick and take her this basket of things to eat.'

'A crook granny, oh dear oh dear,' and, 'How kind,' I say. 'Now where does she live, pretty thing, this grandma of the ailments, your granny of the sick bed?'

'In the cottage at the edge of the wood, right by the path,' she says, 'and now, sir, I must hurry on to see her.'

'Well little one, you keep safe and straight on the path and do not wobble and go astray.'

And she says, 'No sir, oh no sir and thank you and I will so keep safe, sir.'

Off I go, gallop, lirrupy, lollopy, not too fast until I am out of sight and then my four feet leap towards the house of granny which is all correct, flowers in the front and honeysuckle over the porch. I knock on the door and when she calls, frail and wavery, 'Who is it?' I make my voice small and high.

'Your granddaughter,' I say, 'in my red riding hood.'

'Lift the latch and come in,' she says. I see Granny in bed and I hope she has no bad disease but this I think most quickly, because then I eat her right up and whole. Granny, she is okay, but not her cotton bonnet with a frill. I pull this over my ears but it will not stay down. Her spectacles I put on and I snuggle down in the bed that is still granny-warmed.

When there is a knock I say, quiet old voice a-quiver and a-quaver, 'Who is there?' and when she says her name, her voice high sweet and girly, I tell her to lift the latch and push open the door. 'Come here, my dear, so I can see you better,' I say.

'What big eyes you have, Grandmama.'

'All the better to see you with, my dear.'

'And what big ears you have,' she says, for she has learned all her lines, this girl, is a good girl.

'All the better to hear you with,' I say.

'And what big teeth you have,' she says coming close, closer.

And I say, 'All the better to eat you with, my dear,' and I do. I eat her then and straight away, swillow swallow and straight away, gobble, gobble and quite whole she is going down the gullet and joining Granny.

I am trying to digest. There is a functioning, a ferment, but I am fearful, waiting for the strong woodsman to force his way into the house. How hard and strong is his axe, how fine honed the blade. He will chop open my gizzards and expose Granny and the sweet maid churning gently in my gut, being transmogrified and made into wolf.

Barbara Anderson

Barbara Anderson took the Original Composition course in 1983. Her first published book was a volume of stories, *I think we should go into the jungle* (1989), and this has been followed by several novels, including *Portrait of the Artist's Wife*, which won the 1992 Wattie Book of the Year Award. Anderson is brilliant at dialogue, and 'Up the River with Mrs Gallant' uses the device of 'committee dialogue', a sort of wry, distancing, reported speech which has been used by other writers, notably Donald Barthelme and Mavis Gallant (whose example is quietly acknowledged in the story's title).

Up the River with Mrs Gallant

Mr Levis invited them to call him Des. And this is Arnold he said.

Mr Kent said Hi Arnold.

Mrs Kent said that she was pleased to meet him.

Mrs Gallant said Hullo, Arnold.

Mr Gallant said Good morning.

Mr Borges said nothing.

Des said that if they just liked to walk down to the landing stage Arnold would bring the boat down with the tractor.

Mrs Gallant said wasn't Mr Gallant going to leave the car in the shade.

Mr Gallant said that if Mrs Gallant was able to tell him where the shade from one tree was going to be for the next six hours he would be happy to.

Mr Kent said that he was going to give it a burl anyway and reparked the Falcon beneath the puriri.

Mrs Kent told Mrs Gallant that she and Stan were from Hamilton.

Mrs Gallant told Mrs Kent that she and Eric were from Rotorua.

Mrs Kent said that she had a second cousin in Rotorua. Esme. Esme. She would be forgetting her own head next. And that she supposed she should wait for Stan but what the hell.

Mrs Gallant smiled at Mr Borges.

Mr Borges nodded.

At the landing stage Des said that he would like them to take turns sitting in the front and perhaps the ladies?

Mrs Kent remarked that the landing stage looked a bit ass over tip.

Arnold said that the landing stage was safe as houses and would the lady get into the boat.

Mrs Kent said Where was Stan.

Mr Kent said Here.

Mrs Kent asked Mr Kent where he had got to. She hopped across the landing stage, climbed onto the boat and into one of the front seats. She said that it wasn't too ladylike but that she would be right.

Mrs Gallant followed.

Mr Kent and Mr Gallant climbed into the next row.

Des said that Arnold was on the Access Training Scheme and doing very well but it was difficult to fit in the hundred hours river time in a business like this and that he hoped that the customers would have no objection if Arnold came with them and drove the boat back because of the hundred hours.

Mrs Kent said that she would be delighted anytime.

Mr Kent said Well.

Mr Gallant asked how many passengers the boat was licensed for.

Des said that it was licensed for seven passengers.

Mrs Gallant smiled.

Mr Borges said nothing.

Arnold said Good on them, climbed into the boat and sat in the back row with Mr Borges. Mr Borges smiled.

Des started the motor and picked up the microphone. He said that the river was approximately ninety miles long and had been called the Rhine Of New Zealand. It had been used as a waterway since the time of the first Maoris.

Perhaps the busiest time on the river, he said, was the end of the nineteenth century and the beginning of the twentieth until the Main Trunk was completed. River boats plied, freight and passengers were transported in thousands and in all that time there were only two deaths which must be something of a record.

Mr Gallant said that he hoped that it would stay that way.

Des invited him to come again.

Mrs Kent said that Mr Gallant was only kidding.

Mr Gallant said No he wasn't.

Mrs Gallant said Eric.

Des said that he was born and brought up on the river. He had lived on the river all his life and he knew the river like the back of his hand and his aim was for every one of his passengers to learn more about this beautiful river which was steeped in history.

Mr Kent said that Des would do him.

Mrs Kent said Hear Hear.

Mr Borges, Mr Gallant and Arnold said nothing.

Mrs Gallant said that it was a lovely day.

Des said that she wasn't running as sweet as usual, probably a few stones up the grille.

Mrs Gallant asked What did that mean.

Des said Stones you know up the grille.

Mrs Gallant said that she realised that.

Mr Gallant smiled.

Mrs Kent said that they had a lovely day for it anyhow.

Des said they certainly had and to take a look at the flying fox across the river. He explained that the alignment of the posts was very important indeed.

Mr Gallant said that it would be.

Des said that otherwise she could come across but she wouldn't go back. On the other hand if it was wrong the other way she would go back but she wouldn't come across.

Mr Gallant said Exactly.

Mr Kent said it was all Dutch to him Ooh Pardon.

Mrs Kent said that the young man wasn't Dutch and that Stan needn't worry.

Mr Kent said Then what was he?

Mrs Kent said that yes the day certainly was a cracker.

Mrs Gallant smiled.

Des said that the cooling system wasn't operating as per usual either. Usually she stayed at twenty. That was what he liked her at. Twenty.

Mrs Gallant said that it was at seventy now was it not.

Des said Yes it was.

Mrs Gallant said Oh.

Mr Gallant laughed.

Des said that they certainly would like Pipiriki.

Mrs Kent said That was for sure.

Des moored the boat at the Pipiriki landing stage. Everyone climbed out. Des put a large carton on an outdoor table and said they could help themselves to tea or coffee.

Mrs Gallant said that she and Eric would only need one teabag between them as they both took tea very weak without milk.

Des said that Mrs Gallant needn't worry as he had provided two teabags each per person as usual.

Mr Gallant said that she was only trying to help.

Mrs Kent asked if there was a toilet.

Arnold pointed up the path.

Des said that after lunch they should go up and look at Pipiriki. Pipiriki House had once been a world-famous hotel. It had burned down in 1959. He said to have a good look at the shelter and to go around the back as there were some flush toilets.

Mrs Kent said that now Des told her and they both laughed.

Mrs Gallant said What shelter.

Des said A shelter for tourists you know trampers, that sort of thing.

Everyone liked Pipiriki very much. After an hour they climbed back into the boat.

Mr Kent said that he wished some of those activists could see all those kids happy and swimming.

Mr Gallant said Why?

Mr Kent said to look at that one jumping there. That he hadn't a care in the world.

Mr Gallant said that that was hardly the point.

Mrs Gallant said Eric.

Mr Gallant said Hell's delight woman.

Mr Borges smiled.

Mrs Kent said that they used to live near Cambridge but that they had moved in to Hamilton when the boy took over.

Mrs Gallant said Was that right, and that she wished they had been able to land at Jerusalem.

Arnold said that he could go a swim.

Des said that he had been going to have a good look at her yesterday but that he hadn't had a break for so long and that he just hadn't felt like it.

No one said anything.

Des said that anyway he had had another booking in the end as things had turned out.

The boat leapt and bucked high in the air.

Mrs Kent said Ooops.

Des said that that showed you what happened if you let your concentration slip even for a second with a jetty. She had hit a stump.

Mr Gallant laughed.

Arnold asked if the Boss would like him to take over.

Des and Arnold laughed.

Mrs Gallant said to look at that kingfisher.

Mrs Kent said Where.

Mrs Gallant said There. That Mrs Kent was too late. That it had gone.

Des pointed out many points of interest and said that no she certainly wasn't going too good.

Mrs Gallant said that hadn't the temperature gauge gone up to eighty or was she wrong.

Des said that no she was not wrong and that he had better give her a breather and stopped the boat. He said it was probably the temperature of the water, it being a hot day.

Nobody said anything. The boat rocked, silent on the trough of its own waves. The sun shone.

Des said that that should have cooled her down a bit and started the boat.

The temperature gauge climbed to seventy.

Des said that that was more like it and that there had been a Maori battle on that island between the Hau Hau supporters and the non-supporters.

Mr Gallant wondered why they had chosen an island.

Des said that Mr Gallant had him there and swung the boat into a shallow tributary of the river. He told Arnold that they had better check the grille and how would Arnold like a swim.

Arnold said that that would be no problem. He climbed around onto the bow of the boat and said that they would now see his beautiful body. He removed his shirt and told Mrs Gallant and Mrs Kent to control themselves.

Mrs Kent yelped.

Arnold faced the vertical cliff of the bank, presented his shorts-clad buttocks and shook them.

Everyone laughed except Mr Gallant and Mr Borges.

Mr Borges stood up quickly, took a photograph of Arnold's back view, and sat down again.

Arnold jumped into the water and swam to the back of the boat. Des fumbled beneath his feet and handed the passengers various pieces of equipment for Arnold to poke up the grille. The male passengers handed the things on to Arnold with stern efficiency.

After some time Arnold said that he had found three stones up the grille.

Des said that that was good.

Arnold said that they were not big buggers though.

Des said Never mind.

Arnold handed the equipment back into the boat and did a honeypot jump from the shallow water into a deep pool.

Mr Kent said See?

Arnold swam to the bow of the boat and heaved himself into the boat.

Mr Borges took a photograph of Arnold's front view.

Mrs Gallant said that they were lucky that Arnold had come with them.

Mrs Kent said that Mrs Gallant could say that again and would the boat go better now that Arnold had removed the stones.

Des said that he hoped so.

Mr Gallant laughed.

They stopped several times on the return trip for the boat to cool down and as she was not going too well Des sometimes had to make several sweeps before she could pick up enough speed for her to lift up over the rapids. Des said that normally at this stage, when she was less than half full of gas he could fling her about all over the place no sweat.

Mr Gallant said that they must be thankful for small mercies.

Des swung the boat in a wide spraying circle and pulled into the jetty at the old flour mill. They climbed the hill, Des carrying the afternoon tea carton. After tea Des said that he would tell them about the old flour mill and the river in general. Everyone expressed interest. They trooped into the warm shadowy old building and Des began.

After half an hour Mrs Kent asked whether Des would mind if she sat down.

Des said that although perhaps it was technically more correct to call them river boats he still thought of them as steamers though strictly speaking they weren't steamers for long.

Mrs Kent sat down.

Mrs Gallant sat down.

Mr Kent looked as though he was going to cry.

Mr Gallant closed his eyes.

Arnold sat outside in the shade.

Mr Borges joined him.

After three quarters of an hour Des said that he hoped they had all learned something of the river.

They climbed down to the river in silence.

Des said that as she wasn't the best perhaps if Mrs Gallant and Mr Kent would like to sit in front.

Mr Gallant muttered something about sensible arrangement of ballast.

Mrs Kent asked Des why.

Arnold said it was because he liked the good-looking girls in the back with him.

Mrs Kent told Arnold to get away and climbed nimbly into the back seat.

Mrs Gallant said nothing.

They set off with Des at the wheel. The temperature gauge rose above eighty. Des asked the passengers to look around their feet for a tool which would enable Arnold to take another poke up the grille without getting out of the boat.

Mrs Gallant said that there was a pipe thing here if that was any help.

Mrs Kent gave a startled cry and said What was that smoke.

Mr Gallant said that that was steam.

Mrs Kent said that it was red hot that pipe thing there.

Mr Gallant said that he was not at all surprised.

Arnold said that she would be right.

Des said that she had better have another cool off and stopped the boat.

The boat limped to the original landing jetty two hours later than planned. The passengers collected their belongings without comment and trailed up the hill.

Des told Arnold that he could bring the boat up.

Arnold said that Des was the Boss.

Mrs Gallant remarked that it had been a very interesting day and that wasn't the river beautiful.

Mrs Kent said that yes it was but that she had felt so sorry for the poor chap.

Mr Gallant said God in Heaven.

Mrs Gallant remarked that she saw that Mr Kent's car was in the shade.

Mr Gallant said that it probably had not been for the first six hours.

Mrs Gallant said that that remark was typical absolutely typical.

Mrs Kent said that they used to have Jerseys but the boy had switched to Friesians.

Mr Kent said that he had been happy enough in Jerseys but that there you were.

Mrs Kent said that they just want to be different and that it was quite understandable.

Mr Kent said that he had never said it wasn't.

Mr Borges said nothing.

Arnold appeared on the tractor, pulling the boat on its trailer. He parked it in the shed and appeared with a Visitors' Book. He invited the passengers to make their crosses.

Everyone laughed except Mr Gallant and Mr Borges.

Des said that he would give her an overhaul tomorrow that was for sure.

Mrs Kent signed the book and wrote Lovely day under Comments.

Mr Kent signed and wrote Ditto.

Mr Gallant signed his name only.

Mr Borges signed and wrote Sweden.

Mrs Gallant missed the signing. She stumped across the bleached grass and stood gazing at the river.

It said nothing.

Forbes Williams

Forbes Williams took the Original Composition course in 1987. 'All Falls Still' was part of his workshop folio, which eventually grew into the fiction collection *Motel View* (1992).

All Falls Still

Today I ran over a dog. At first I thought it was a trivial thing—nearly didn't even bother to stop, though I did in the end, down the road a bit. I walked back and stood above it on the road, with my hands in my front pockets, while two children came and watched from under a tree by the roadside, silent. I picked it up, heavy thing, and it whimpered and half-struggled until I put it down in some long grass and it became still. I walked back to the car, rubbing my hands on my pants, knowing the children watched me, knowing the dog was not yet dead. And I drove off fast, revved the engine right up high before changing gears, so the children would be scared, maybe too scared to tell anyone till later.

Later, with friends, I laughed about the dog, and we made jokes about dogs dying in the grass, stupid dogs who never learn, and I pretended it was something inevitable, just the way life sometimes goes.

But now I am sad, and I wish it hadn't run out, sleek-haired thing, under the wheel. Maybe it spied a cat, or maybe a new bone had just gone down, I don't know, but I wish it hadn't stared at me, big brown eyes, sad dying eyes, quiet in the grass.

Another dog pads into the kitchen, stops by its bowl panting, pads on into the room with the fire. I'm on the couch—still rubbing my hands—remembering Anna the fire-eater, who swallowed fire for money and praise and who I loved for her audacity. It pads over to me, licking its face, climbs up onto the couch and curls up until it is Banjo, World Famous Circle Dog, who in her heyday could roll round and round the circus ring in ever-diminishing circles until the audience were hypnotised, so that Anna could come out from behind the rustling curtains and swallow fire while I beat a rhythm on the tom-toms with the same hands that today held a dying dog.

Hey, Banj. I rub her flank. We're okay Banj. She looks up at me, blank dog look, chews her tongue and sniffs the air. Tonight she has nothing to say to me, nothing at all, and together we sit in front of the dying fire, sinking through the couch towards sleep. With tired eyes and heavy arms I sink, only saved from drowning by Banjo, World Famous Circle Dog, who floats warm under my hand, snoring softly through her strings.

Eirlys Hunter

Eirlys Hunter is Welsh by ancestry, English by birth, and a New Zealander who lives in Wellington. Applicants for the creative writing course at Victoria are asked to submit samples of their work. Eirlys sent 'A Brief Autobiography' with her 1991 application—not at all the sort of document you could argue with. Her stories often involve people moving from one place or state to another; many have been published in magazines like *Sport* and *Printout*, and broadcast on radio.

A Brief Autobiography

1952	Mewler, puker
1953	Reluctant sister
1954	Garden grubber
1955	Psychoanalysis beginner
1956	Early reader
1957	Be-schooled
1958	Bewildered
1959	Remodelled
1960	Reduced
1961	Dancer
1962	Invalid
1963	Ecstatic dreamer
1964	Maths muddler
1965	Music lover
1966	Boyfriended
1967	Psychoanalysis completer
1968	Exam passer
1969	Theatre goer

1970 Solo traveller
1971 Cambridge student
1972 Actor
1973 Drug taker
1974 Degree scraper
1975 Clockwatcher
1976 Married woman
1977 Training teacher
1978 Passionate mother
1979 Campaigner
1980 Explorer
1981 Mourner
1982 Crisis survivor
1983 New New Zealander
1984 Chameleon
1985 Friend maker
1986 Domestic wallower
1987 School teacher
1988 Nipple woman
1989 House builder
1990 Researcher

1991 Writer
1992 Writer
1993 Writer
1994 Writer
1995 Writer
1996 Writer
1997 Writer
1998 Writer
1999 Writer
2000 Writer and writer, first and before
(or at least as well as) the rest
until the very last line.

Dinah Hawken

Dinah Hawken describes something of her own development as a writer in the following essay. She has published three books of poetry: *It has No Sound and is Blue* (1987), where 'Talking to a Tree Fern' appeared, and which won the Commonwealth Poetry Prize for best first book; *Small Stories of Devotion* (1991); and *Water, Leaves, Stones* (1995), which includes 'A New Word' as part of a larger sequence. On 'Talking to a Tree Fern', see 'Blackbirds' in 'The Exercise Chapter', p.281.

Making Arrangements

The Dream

Bill Manhire and I are in a gravel courtyard outside a small Spanish villa in rural New Mexico. On the gravel in the centre of the courtyard are four low trestle blackboards in a row. Bill and I are sitting cross-legged alongside each other facing two adjoining blackboards. There are words printed on their slanted surfaces. Bill is taking a single word at a time from his board and speaking it to me with such intensity and such care that I realise each word must be of extraordinary importance. I am receiving each word by repeating it with an equivalent degree of intensity and care.

Living in New York

I did the Original Composition course at Victoria in the first half of 1983, when I was forty, and left straight afterwards to live in New York for three years. Buoyed up by my experience in Bill's course, I enrolled in a seminar called Poetry at Present at the 92nd St Y run by Sandy (J.D.) McLatchy, a New York poet and critic. He was a sophisticated, colourful teacher and in the seminar I met some new contemporary American poets, a few British poets, and no Canadian, Australian or New Zealand poets. Looking back, my favourite new American poets were Elizabeth Bishop, James Wright, Louise Glück and Charles Wright. I also re-met Adrienne Rich and John Ashbery whose poetry had in a strange way attracted me to the US—though I'd actually gone because my husband had been posted to the United Nations. In Poetry at Present I also met Bob and Champ. And it was probably around that time, four storeys above a six-lane highway and the East River, that I had the courtyard dream.

The MFA

Buoyed up by the pleasure of learning and reading in Sandy McLatchy's seminar, and encouraged by Bob and Champ, I then joined a poetry-writing workshop Sandy was offering. After that I had the confidence to apply for a Master of Fine Arts programme in creative writing at Brooklyn College where John Ashbery was the writer-in-residence. For a month or so, before he won the McArthur prize, he was my individual tutor for poetry. For the rest of the two years, my main teachers were William Mathews, Ann Lauterbach and Joan Larkin, all of them excellent. One of the highlights of the programme was a term of part teaching (Yeats, Eliot, Pound, Auden, MacNeice) and part writing workshop with Stephen Spender. What I liked about Stephen Spender was his ability to bring poetry down to earth. He had a low-key, unpretentious teaching style and talked for example about small decisions he was trying to make revising some of his own poems for a collection, and what he liked and didn't like about *The Waste Land* as if Eliot was just another poet in a poetry workshop.

It's good I think to demystify greatness. Which reminds me of an embarrassing moment I had at a party Ann Lauterbach gave for students at her flat towards the end of the degree. She is a friend of John Ashbery and had invited him to the party to meet up with students again. At one point she took me over especially to reintroduce me and both he and I stood tongue-tied—truly it wasn't one of those fleeting moments, it was a long time, probably half a minute—until Ann intervened. Why am I telling you this? Perhaps because I think that self-consciousness in writing—caring too much what others think—is like self-consciousness in other social situations, it can make you lose your voice.

Words and Their Meanings

I wonder now as I write the dream down what those words Bill was giving me actually were? If I knew in 1983, I've forgotten now. I'm thinking though of a poem in my last book, 'Light is the Word for Light', which I couldn't have written in 1983. In the 80s I was interested in words mostly for their accuracy of meaning, i.e. finding the right word for the poem. Later I became intrigued with the roots of words, suspecting that an older root meaning might be a truer, more essential meaning. I wondered if meanings changed over time in a way that reflected and maintained the dominant values in a culture. In my second book I wrote, '. . . if words are ripped from their roots, / lose truth or become unlovable, how can we take their lift toward / what they could gracefully offer?' In the sensual 90s I'm enjoying the texture and tone of single words, their sound and sight meanings, and trying to get a feel of how well *those* meanings get on with the dictionary meanings and with what the words actually stand for. Phyllis Webb, a Canadian poet, is wonderfully sensual talking about texture in poetry:

> I used to think of texture in poetry as mainly a sound apparition produced by an intricate play of vocables whose plosives, dentals, labials, fricatives, hoots, whistles, yells and chuckles, sighs, murmurs, phonemic and syllabic inter-actions could scuff up or smooth out the surface of a poem. Cacophony, sonority, plain-song created by the way consonants keep company with riverine vowels—assonance, consonance, alliteration and their often mimetic effects— are also part of the microstructure. . . . And, of course, vocabulary swanning around managing a variety of rhythmic manoeuvres (mating with syntax) is major mover.

Clearly I don't know half of it yet. I don't know what a few of those words mean in the dictionary sense but I do seem to have an idea in the sense sense. If I had to choose a central insight I gained from Bill Manhire's course it is that *play* is central to writing well and that an ability to play (and work) with language is just as important as saying what you mean. Because I'm a serious creature, maybe it is a lesson I particularly needed to learn. Anyway, in the Collins dictionary 'to mean' means to say or do in all seriousness and I have absolutely no doubt that Bill meant those words in the dream, whatever they were. His seriousness was, and is, the beauty of the dream. As well, mean means miserly in a chiefly British way and bad-tempered and vicious in a chiefly US way. It also means skilful, excellent. It has a fine, clear sound and of course it means the middle way.

Exercises

When I was a physiotherapist in the 1960s, we talked about strengthening exercises and flexibility exercises. Both are important to keep fit or to get better. When I joined Bill's workshop, I was a bit stiff about poetry though not particularly aware of it. Gradually since then I have been isolating some of the stiff joints and working on loosening up. The exercises in Bill's workshop were excellent in beginning to break down my notions of what I thought—often unconsciously— poetry should be. Was it like the poetry I'd read at school? Did it have to be lofty—or lyrical? Did it have to be totally, inventively original? I actually thought it did and so I was liberated by learning that there was such a thing as a 'found poem' or one made from words from the racing page of the paper. Language can come from anywhere—you don't have to produce it all yourself! Since then I have been 'stealing' words, ideas, phrases, images, lines, rhythms, layouts from wherever I find them, and acknowledging the significant steals with respect. Who makes these 'rules' about poetry anyway? Are they man-made? Does good poetry have to be clever, or intellectually complex? William Carlos Williams gave *things* a renewed place in poetry and Jenny Bornholdt manages simply to be funny without needing to be clever at all.

Adrienne Rich and John Ashbery

There seems to be a rule in Western English-speaking countries (particularly strong in the US?) that poetry cannot be good and political at the same time. Thank goodness, Adrienne Rich's poetry breaks that rule. Hearing the commitment in her voice gave me strength to cope with the terrible underside of New York which at first overwhelmed me. Lines like 'when did we choose / to be lynched on the queasy electric signs / of midtown' accompanied me around while I went through the vital struggle of turning helplessness at what I saw in New York into some kind of direction or passion. During my last year there I worked as a social worker with homeless mentally ill people in my neighbourhood.

Adrienne Rich has talked about Walt Whitman and Emily Dickinson as 'a strange uncoupled couple', which is just how I felt about her and Ashbery while I was in New York. In fact my last paper for the MFA was an attempt to come to grips with their differences and to integrate into myself somehow the qualities that I liked most about their poetry. Here is the clarity and passion (strength) of Adrienne Rich in her poem 'Hunger':

> I stand convicted by all my convictions—
> you, too. We shrink from touching
> our power, we shrink away, we starve ourselves
> and each other, we're scared shitless
> of what it could be to take and use our love,
> hose it on a city, on a world,
> to wield and guide its spray, destroying
> poisons, parasites, rats, viruses—
> like the terrible mothers we long and dread to be.

Here is the open-ended acceptance (flexibility) of Ashbery:

> And the issue
> Of making sense becomes such a far-off one. Isn't this 'sense'—
> This little of my life that I can see—that answers me
> Like a dog, and wags its tail, though excitement and fidelity are
> About all that ever gets expressed? What did I ever do
> To want to wander off into something else, an explanation
> Of how I behaved, for instance, when knowing can have this

Sublime rind of excitement, like the shore of a lake in the desert
Blazing with the sunset?

'A Wave'

Audience

I remember showing Ashbery a poem of mine called 'Balance'—a
heartfelt poem about violence in the world and whether or not we
can do anything about it. There was a part that he seemed genuinely
not to understand, that follows this question in the poem: 'where /
are the women, where exactly are we?' It goes:

> . . . and [we know] that we,
> crouched, still, in the hills
> of our bodies, are most needed
> when we are most
> revolted.

He liked 'crouched in the hills of our bodies' but didn't understand
what I meant by being 'most needed when we are most revolted'. The
occasions in a workshop when someone has not understood what I
have written have always been valuable. Sometimes I know I have
been as clear as I can or want to be, as in the lines I showed to Ashbery,
but often I know I can be clearer or more precise. You are always
thrown back on to your own judgement, of course. Is clarity one of
the rules that can't be broken? I'm not sure. I think there is a place for
almost everything in writing except sloppiness and neglect.

Bill Mathews, who was my main poetry teacher at Brooklyn
College, once said, 'You'll never again have such an attentive and
generous audience as you have in this workshop. Make the most of
it.' It was true. The American students and poets that I worked with
had a wonderful willingness to speak out. (New Zealanders can be
mean in a chiefly British kind of way.) As well, they were generous in
their appreciation and had, at times, dauntingly high standards. I was
often surprised and pleased that they thought both what I'd done was
good and that it could be better. So I went away to arrange and
rearrange.

Arranging and Rearranging

Once I've written something, it's inclined to get stubbornly settled in its place and I can't imagine it being anywhere else. Excluded altogether for example! Or the beginning might be better at the end? Sometimes a poem of mine has only worked when it has had this kind of structural rearrangement, or a book worked because of the added strength a certain arrangement of poems has given it. When it's hard to be flexible, or to see, other readers are a great help. Or going away for an hour or a week or two and coming back as 'another' reader yourself, i.e. less critical, less gung-ho, etc.

Arranging and rearranging is part of the work and practice of writing, it's strengthening exercises. The workshops I did in the US put more emphasis on looking together at students' work in progress than on set exercises. On the whole the exercises that Bill Manhire set were more inventive and enjoyable than the ones I did in NY but I remember one or two that were important. Mostly they were to do with using form. Sandy McLatchy set both a sonnet and a sestina writing exercise. I had discovered that I enjoyed working with form (Bill had set a pantoum and syllabics) and that to my surprise the constraints seemed (a) to stimulate a problem-solving energy that occasionally burst into creativity and (b) to produce more, rather than less, inventiveness with language. But a traditional sonnet and a sestina were hard. Adrienne Rich says: 'It's a struggle not to let the form take over, lapse into format, assimilate the poetry; and that very struggle can produce a movement, a music, of its own.' I remember walking home down 79th St when the solution to the sestina came out of the blue. I'd write a sestina with only *one* word in each line and by the time I got home I knew what the six end words would be. Then the fun of arranging and rearranging. 'Sestina' got into my first book. So did four poems written in syllabics and a long sonnet sequence. There is something special about fourteen lines without the effects of rhyme, etc. Another exercise poem in my first book which took much arranging and rearranging is called 'The Romantic Entanglement'. It was an exercise set by Ann Lauterbach. She gave us Ashbery's poem of the same name, and we were to use all (and only) the words in his poem to make a poem of our own. I was pleased with mine. It forced me to use language and sentence structure that I wouldn't naturally have used and yet somehow the voice was still my own.

Bob and Champ

Sometimes the very best thing about classes and workshops is the people you meet there. Bob befriended both Champ and me in Sandy McLatchy's seminar and from then on we met together almost once a week. An odd trio: Bob, a friendly Italian from a working-class background, Paterson, New Jersey; Champ, an English teacher in an exclusive boys' school who dressed like a Canterbury farmer; and me, a lonely New Zealand diplomat's wife. Bob worked on a computer in the New York tax department by day and was totally dedicated to poetry by night. He suggested that we go to the regular readings at the 92nd St Y, which we did, usually having a meal or drink together afterwards. Would I have gone to Sandy McLatchy's workshop without Bob's company and enthusiasm? There I met Mary-Stewart (her first name), a highly strung Southerner from a respectable religious family who wrote irreverent breathless poetry and got it published, when she dared to post it, in the *New Yorker*. She invited me to join an ongoing group who met regularly to discuss each other's work and from time to time we arranged for a teacher to come in. They were a great lot— sophisticated, serious about poetry, and very funny—I couldn't have struck it luckier. I met with them for the next two years until I left New York. Mary-Stewart, David, Elizabeth, Dina, Harriet and John.

An Exercise for You

Bill Manhire and I are in a gravel courtyard outside a small Spanish villa in rural New Mexico. On the gravel in the centre of the courtyard are four low trestle blackboards in a row. Bill and I are sitting cross-legged alongside each other facing two adjoining blackboards. Opposite Bill, sitting cross-legged on the other side of the small blackboard, is Bob. Opposite me and next to Bob is Jenny Bornholdt. On my right is Adrienne Rich and opposite her is John Ashbery. Next to John Ashbery is Louise Glück and opposite Louise Glück, you. There are words printed on the slanted surfaces of all the blackboards except yours. And now Bob is giving you welcome. Bill is giving you jalopy. Jenny is giving you Sophie. I am giving you stone. John is giving you meander. Adrienne is giving you eye. And Louise is giving you oblivion. You are taking these words, and arranging them with words of your own to make a story, or poem (or is it a prose poem?), in three parts on your own blackboard. In each part you are using, once, each of the words we have given you.

Postscript

I finished this essay and didn't look at it again for two weeks. When I did I panicked, lost my nerve, in fact all the nerves to the judgement area of my brain. Eventually I remembered what I'd just written here, i.e. 'when it's hard to see, other readers are a great help', and I asked three friends to read it for me. One of them was Jenny Bornholdt and just this hour I have had a note from her.

Dear Dinah,

As I said last night—I really enjoyed this & don't think you should change anything.

Last night I had a dream which I'm sure came about because of reading your piece and seeing you at Andrew's last night—I was in a *big* hall—like a church hall, and Bill Manhire was there with a paint brush & he'd just finished painting the ceiling (which was very high & steep—shaped ^) & I was going to help paint the walls, which he'd started painting in squares, like scrabble tiles—each square containing a beautifully painted letter of the alphabet, decorated.

They were really beautiful, like illuminated manuscripts, but plainer—in soft colours a bit like mohair (if this makes sense). We were going to paint all the walls like this.

I've just remembered, while writing this, that on my way into the hall, I was attacked by a dog. I guess the hall was some kind of refuge.

Love Jen x

Talking to a Tree Fern

I

You're not ashamed of your past.
It hangs there in rust-coloured layers
and you curve out of it
fully at ease.

2

Behind you the bay
sports expensive speed boats. More and more
they force their vibrations right up
your root-tips.

3

You used to live here with other natives.
Now willows and poplars flickering gold
have proudly established themselves.

4

I've heard you discussed as an item
of our international trade. They
conceive of you standing in each
pebble garden of suburban Los Angeles.

5

The man at the back
has asked how much I care about you.
He says you impede his view.

6

In the bush near here
you gather in tight bunches
your pasts hanging down and spreading
over the ground like soft mats.
I want to crawl under there.
I need to know what you're chatting about.

7

Rowing out as usual
to the calmest part of the lake
I hear a chain-saw preening itself
and sense the spikes stiffening on your trunks.

8

Once I saw you at a Marist Centre
stiff and brittle like an empty erection,
no fronds, no flow.
Mary was cramped into a grotto nearby
totally into pleasing God.

9

I was just wondering whether
Christ had risen again this year or not
(Good Friday was April Fool's Day)
when I saw three fantails fooling around
in your fronds, in the rain.

10

Under your dark arms
that night with no moon
I decided to let my life
climb up quietly
like the rata on your trunk.

11

It leans so superbly
your long black trunk
perhaps it is frightening
the man at the back.

12

Suddenly, in the city,
staked into a neat fence
you poke out your black tongue.
Keep coming and coming
back into my life.

A New Word

I have a new presence inside me.
You. It is a pale still day.

The tuis are really here,
I have seen them, three of them.

Thrush, tui—which is the more mellifluous?
A word I learned from Phyllis Webb.

'Drunken and amatory, illogical, stoned, mellifluous
journey of the ten lines.' If I could sing

like you, like her, tui, like spring water and
far off a rock falling.

Jenny Bornholdt

Jenny Bornholdt was a member of the 1984 workshop. Her books are *This Big Face* (1988), *Moving House* (1989), *Waiting Shelter* (1991) and *How We Met* (1995), while *Miss New Zealand*, a selected poems, will be published in 1997. She is also co-editor of the new *Oxford Anthology of New Zealand Poetry in English*. The selection of poems which follows is a quick chronological sampling of her work. 'On Seeing Ian Jamieson in Lower Hutt' is an unpublished piece from her workshop folio, and plays with the fact that Ian Jamieson—then on the staff of Victoria's English Department, and a charismatic if self-deprecating teacher—is an expert in medieval English literature.

On Seeing Ian Jamieson in Lower Hutt

saw you walking
your dog today

you middle english man you
you middle english man

god eht gniklaw
god eht gniklaw

walking the dog
walking the dog

Make Sure

Make sure you fall in love with a man who you know will survive
in the bush.
This way, when he is three nights overdue from his trip and the
search and rescue team is out looking for him and the helicopter
has been called back because the weather is closing in and they're
interviewing you on television in a close-up camera shot, asking
you what you think his chances are—hoping you will cry and your
lip will tremble—you can look them straight in the eye
and say you *know* he will be all right, he has had plenty of
experience and he knows what to do, he was carrying plenty of
food and warm clothing and he is strong.
Even if he is hurt, you know he will be all right.
He's a fighter, you'll say. He won't give in.
But the weather is closing in, you must be worried, they'll ask.
You keep your resolve. He will be all right, you say.
I know he will.

The Bathers

Les Grandes Baigneuses—Cézanne
(begun about 1898 or 1899 and finished 1905)

Left for eight years amidst
the intense green and blue
of trees   pleased Cézanne
abandoned them in such a
pleasurable landscape.
Bodies slanted towards trees,
water, a dog asleep on the
ground. They sighed, over those
eight years, talked amongst
themselves quietly, each morning

a small *ah* of pleasure
at the day, wondering if
today . . . for eight years
until the trees grew thick
with colour, the lake
darkened and their bodies'
cool formation fixed
beside the admiring water.

Then Murray came

It was the morning for
selling the car, but
when I went out to start it,
it wouldn't go. Greg went
to get petrol on the bike. I
rang the AA. Then Ray
arrived. I said *I'm sorry*, he
said *don't worry* and looked at
the car and at the wheels and
in the boot and said *she's a lovely
old thing*. He tapped the coil
and the fuel pump to try to
make it go. Greg came back
with petrol, but that didn't help.
Then, because there was nothing else
to do, we went inside and had coffee
and Ray smoked and talked about
going to Outward Bound and sleeping
and losing a stone.

Then Murray came.
He drove up the hill in his yellow
AA car, shaking his head. Got out and said

I was sure you were having me on. Last time I was
here you said you were selling it
and the other day I saw you walking
through town and I thought 'thank god she's
sold that thing'. He cleaned the carburettor
and laughed. Put more petrol in, replaced a
filter. I said *I wasn't joking, there's*
someone here who wants to buy it. Murray
laughed and said *sure. No, no,* I said, *it's*
true. Ray. See, there he is, up at the
window. Murray looked up and Greg and Ray
waved. *How much is he paying for it?* asked
Murray. I started to say and he stopped
me. Said *no, on second thoughts, don't tell*
me. I don't want to hear about this.
Ray came down and took over
holding up the bonnet of the car.
What's your name? he asked Murray.
Murray, said Murray. *Well I'm*
Ray, this is Greg and this is
Jen. Hello Murray, we said.
And then the car started.

James Brown

James Brown took the Original Composition course in 1991, and presented his workshop folio as his Essay paper for English Honours. The first two poems here are from his book, *Go Round Power Please*, which won the 1996 Montana NZ Book Award for best first book of poetry. 'Cashpoint: A Pantoum' was written as an exercise piece during the Original Composition workshop. (See 'The Pantoum', p.288, and 'Found Poems', p.292, in 'The Exercise Chapter'.) 'Waterford II', a sestina, makes some reference to 'Waterford' in Bernadette Hall's collection, *Still Talking*.

Creation

He loves her for her atmosphere.
Which is why it is so important
to mention the clouds:
what they are like, how
they seem slyly not to touch, but stand
freightless together, slanting to let in
select tunnels of light.
          But then that old boy outside
(the one about to come into view)
doesn't look so happy.
Standing there dripping
he looks like he knows how it feels
to be described as having
'come down with the last shower'.
Now the light breaks

across his shoulders, like
pieces of some great glass elevator
he may have been waiting for
for years. Then the rain comes down
like glue. And on television
there is The Challenger, not quite
making it through
the hole in the ozone layer.
No wonder he turns away, that old boy,
the tunnel at the light's end
a mural on a brick wall.

     Though at the time it hardly mattered,
his sodden, leaden, darkened life:
because it seemed light-years away,
because it was hardly spoiling the view.
Because he was never supposed to be me.
Funny how you end up.

     But then every story has two sides
(at least), was how I worked it
all those years ago. And
for the time being, I think that we
could let that one hold true.
For there is always an argument
to which weight can be lent.
Like, Jesus wants me
for a sunbeam, while
this is still my poem,
where I am light in love.

Cashpoint: A Pantoum

Welcome to Cashpoint
Open 7 days
Please insert your card
To begin transaction.

Open 7 days
Please ensure no other person can see
To begin transaction
Please enter your personal identification number.

Please ensure no other person can see
Select service required
Please enter your personal identification number
Use a blue key.

Select service required
Select from account
Use a blue key
Use a green key.

Select from account
Please enter amount required
Use a green key
Cash withdrawals must be in multiples of $10.

Please enter amount required
$10.00 entered
Cash withdrawals must be in multiples of $10
If correct press O.K.

$10.00 entered
If incorrect press correction
If correct press O.K.
Your request is being processed.

If incorrect press correction
Then press O.K.
Your request is being processed
Please wait.

Then press O.K.
Transaction accepted
Please wait
For further transactions.

Transaction accepted
Please remove card if you have finished
For further transactions
Select a blue key.

Please remove card if you have finished
Please remove cash and transaction record
Select a blue key
Thank you for using Cashpoint.

Please remove cash and transaction record
Cashpoint is open every day
Thank you for using Cashpoint
7 AM to 11 PM.

Cashpoint is open every day
Please insert your card
7 AM to 11 PM
Welcome to Cashpoint.

Waterford II

Recently, Tony O'Reilly—the Irish businessman
and sporting hero who owns Heinz and half the world's
newspapers—took over Waterford
crystal. He'd already passed up a career in
politics, in favour of a wider market,
not wishing to be restricted to only the currency

of local taxpayers. Knowing the international currency
exchange (the exclusive realm of independent businessmen)
to be a truer site of power, Tony O'Reilly set about investigating
      the market
for Waterford crystal—which is sold the world
over, but primarily in the US. In
the survey, US consumers of Waterford

crystal were simply asked whether they knew that Waterford
is in Ireland? If they did, the Irish workers held some currency.
Since Waterford crystal had to come from Waterford; therein
lay their security against the strategies of global businessmen
and the ruthless mobility of capital around the world.
If, on the other hand, the US market

did not associate Waterford with Ireland, then market
forces could take over. Waterford
crystal could just as easily come from somewhere else in the world,
like Poland, with the workers paid in their own worthless currency.
It's not poetry, but it made sound economic sense to the businessman's
brain of Tony O'Reilly. The answers which came back in

showed that very few US consumers in fact knew that Waterford is in
Ireland. Good news for the global market!
It would now be possible for Tony O'Reilly's Business Man
-agement team to negate the physical locality of Waterford,
taking only the history and the myth. The town no longer held
     currency
as a geographic location in the world.

In economic terms, it had become no more than a world
renowned brand name—an aura of quality captured in
crystal, that could be owned by anyone with enough currency.
It seems Foucault was right about power as a market
place. But what of Chomsky's Human Rights? In Waterford's
future the workers wait in dole queues while politicians offer tax breaks
     to entice businessmen.

But don't world prices drop as a result of international business man
-oeuvrings? Aren't cheap third world labour costs passed on to eager
     first world consumers in places like, say, Waterford?
The faceless markets smile, as if to say, where does Chomsky think
     he's coming from, and, of what value today is a universal currency?

Adrienne Jansen

Adrienne Jansen was a member of the workshop in 1987; she went on to found the year-long, full-time writing course at Whitireia Community Polytechnic. In 1990 she published *I Have in My Arms Both Ways*, a collection of stories by and interviews with immigrant women.

Three Cambodian Women

Sophomea

You were born
to a shaded house,
tall trees, and a garden
of fruits, where the gardener
picked off the first, for you,
and the dripping juice
streaked the silk threads
of gold light in your skirt.

Now you sit
year by year
8 till 5
punching rivets
while the neon light
whitens the dust
caught in your hair.

Kem Sreng

The first time we met
you were raw from the war of Pol Pot,
caught in the cramping child-talk
of new English, locking
those years and those fears
in your eyes.

Now we meet, your words run
of capacitors, circuit boards,
electronic diagnostic tests.
But those years and those fears
are still in your eyes
unsaid.

Si Na

Then you said, Why are your
front doors always shut?
And your face was closed against
a storm of strange words
rattling like dead sticks,
a pressing crowd of bland white faces,
and a cold wind cutting in under the wall.

Now I say, Come in, Si Na
my door is open
just as you have shown me.
Your face is clear and laughing,
we sit and talk together
and have a cup of tea.

Dunedin: Playing Scrabble with My Aunt

She has fallen asleep
between words.
The white wave of her hair
(I always remember her
netting it in at night)
is tangling the line of her letters.

Outside, yellowed birches
fidget in thin grey rain.
In here, the late dark afternoon
sits still, and waits.

She jerks up. There's a small skitter
of letters onto the board.
She builds 'handle'
on to my 'flare'.

My turn.
Through the window
there are purple hydrangeas
and last brown dahlias.
Rain gathers
on the washing line
in grey glass drops.

I can put 'pause'
against her word,
or maybe 'span'.
No, 'pause' is better.

On the hill above,
a tall boarded house
juts its verandahs
out over the bush.

(Kinnersons', she'd said,
undertakers in town.
She remembers them all,
fathers, sons, grandsons.)
It stares down boldly
to see the next move.

It's hers.

But she's fallen asleep
again.

The Rain and the Spade

(a poem about clarity and ambiguity?)

I call a spade a spade, I say.
You look away, and shuffle the dirt
with your toe.

Come on, pick up the spade, I say.
You flex your thin webbed fingers
at it, not touching.

Now look, there's broad beans to plant, I say.
But you pull a thistledown out of your thumb
and blow it to tiny seeds all over the soil.

Why don't you hose them, I say,
why don't you work?
But you have curled up on a net of rain
asleep, with your head on the clouds.

✧

If you ask me to choose,
the spade or the rain,
I would choose the spade.
On the whole.

There's a risk, with the spade.
If you leave it lying around
you might put your foot on the handle
and the blade will swing up
and hit you.

But the rain—well, it skids
on your face, fingers your neck
and then it is gone,
and you're not even sure
it was there.

✧

You can use a spade
to cut a new spade
but rain
can only make rain.

✧

You laugh at me
because I lean on the spade.
I laugh at you
because you hide in the rain.

But the spade matters more
to me, than your laughing
and the rain matters more
to you, than mine.

✧

I usually work with spades.
I like to feel the grain
run into my skin
and the hard soil give way
under my heel.

But when others work with water
—a thin clear stream,
a mist that floats away
from your hands—
then I can use water too.

✧

A small shower of rain
has washed the spade clean.

✧

What happens when the spade
is left out in the rain?

First the spade turns dark,
defiantly defines itself
in bold wet metal.
Then water gathers
on the upper edge,
slips slowly down the blade
then faster, faster
through the metal
until the spade
is thin slivers, hung
from a silver strip.
Then a gust of rain
blows across, and all is gone.
Even the handle.

✧

Did you ask me to choose
the spade
or the rain?

Damien Wilkins

Damien Wilkins is a Victoria English graduate, though he never took the Original Composition course. He studied for his MFA with the novelist Stanley Elkin at Washington University in St Louis, Missouri, and there wrote his New Zealand Book Award-winning novel, *The Miserables*. He has published a second novel, *Little Masters*, a book of short stories, *The Veteran Perils*, and a poetry collection, *The Idles*. He received the prestigious Whiting Award in 1992, and in 1995 convened the Original Composition course at Victoria.

Opening the Bag

I was lucky enough to get Stanley Elkin in his last great puff. Three or four heart attacks, lungs that collapsed regularly and multiple sclerosis that made it painful for him to turn a page—we could have killed him by throwing a small book at his chest. Of course it was Elkin who killed us—every Tuesday and Thursday morning. The graduate fiction workshop met in his living-room; the four hundred metre wheelchair ride from his house to Washington University campus was too much for everyone. Whenever we asked him if he was going over to the Department to hear a visiting writer, he would point at his legs and grin. 'On a Thursday? They've got someone reading on a *Thursday* night—what are they, they don't get the *TV Guide*?' He didn't go to Derek Walcott and he didn't go to Toni Morrison. Joseph Brodsky didn't get Elkin either. He was a Nobel no-show.

Elkin's brilliant meanness was legendary. He was no good for a lot of people who came through the programme—and these were not necessarily sensitive souls or bad writers. Chemically they didn't mix in the Elkin solution. What the legend failed to communicate was that there was nothing gratuitous about Elkin. He was not awful on purpose or at least not just on purpose. He was awful with a purpose.

One time Mark wrote a story about a medical equipment salesman. The salesman goes door-to-door with his bag of demonstration models. He shows doctors and hospital staff the new tools and gadgets. But this is not quite what the story is about. The salesman's personal life is in bad shape—an unhappy wife, a difficult child, the landlord on his back. While he talks up his trade with the doctors, jollies them into their purchases, the domestic gloom settles like glue.

We each had our turn, called upon by Elkin. 'Mr Bumas?' 'Mr Hughes?' 'What about you, Mr Tysver?' Our comments fell on the carpet; Elkin looked at them. He was dangerously glum. We finished. Silence.

Now Elkin's father was a salesman. The salesman is everywhere in his own fiction. Work, the special languages of trades, the professions' prose—we all felt that Mark was about to learn a terrible lesson. Hadn't Elkin, once a tall, athletic fellow, given up his legs, almost his lungs, almost his *life* to be the best at shop-talk? The lesson, however, was a little different from the one we imagined.

'Turn to page six,' said Elkin finally. 'I want you to read that list, Mr Bautz. The things in his bag. Read that.' Mark read the list—there were stethoscopes and various gauges with medical names, other doctory stuff. 'What's wrong with that, Mr Bautz?' Mark didn't know, perhaps the grammar. 'Not the grammar,' said Elkin. 'I'm talking about the *list*. What this guy has in his bag. What he's supposedly showing these supposed doctors. What the hell has he got in there. Listen to this.' Elkin read the list. He looked at us. Peter tried his luck: perhaps the salesman had too many things in his bag, maybe he'd be carrying the stuff in his car. 'No!' shouted Elkin. Silence. All of us looking at our shoes or out the window or at Mark's ghastly flawed list.

'Mr Bautz,' said Elkin, 'it's your show.' Mark said again that he didn't know what was wrong. Elkin sighed. 'The things in this bag are not just of different weights and sizes,' he said. 'And some of these things the guy would need a goddamm truck to shift. These items are of different *orders*. They're not the same. They belong in different parts of the zoo, do you understand, Mr Bautz? It would be like a jeweller selling shoes, do you understand what I'm saying, Mr Bautz?' Mark nodded slowly. 'Now,' said Elkin, 'let's see what's in here.' Elkin started on the first item and worked from there, throwing nearly everything in that bag out on the floor and kicking it.

It's important to distinguish what Elkin was up to here. If he was simply making the objection that the real High Street runs north-south so how could the Town Hall's clock-face be drenched in morning sunshine, he would not be a great teacher. He would be a pedant, a pain. What I think he was demanding was total dedication on our part, a scout's two-fingered pledge that we meant everything we said and wrote. To be read was to be sworn in.

Under cross-examination—all of Elkin's workshops had the nausea, the odd moments of nervy boredom, the elongated orderliness of the courtroom—Mark admitted that he'd decided *at the last minute* to make his character a medical salesman. He could be something else, said Mark. This was a terrible confession for Father Elkin to hear. If the job was whim, everything was whim. The unreality that hung around the bag infected the life. If the selling was all hooey, what was really up with this guy? Suddenly the discussion took off. We all had something to say now. Our vague dissatisfactions assumed the necessary form of complaints.

The best creative writing workshops open the bag. They must forget the finish of something achieved, since the real work of the workshop reader depends on the half-formed, the false note, the promising, the wrong turn, the almost-there, the bluff, the under-imagined. In short, things must be unpacked and examined. Now because of my training and my temperament it took me a long time to figure out something very simple; the implements for doing this work are only partly discovered in the literary tool-box. As an English Honours student I was pretty good at images of strangulation in *Mansfield Park* but as a creative writing student it didn't seem to help me (though in fact strangulation itself is not a bad image for some creative writing classes).

Commenting on a piece of writing when the author is in the room involves massive and complex delicacies. Perhaps the author has come from a sick child, the dentist, a demeaning job. Maybe the author is a friend or at least friendly, bought you coffee, loaned you a pen, an umbrella, perhaps gave you and your fledgling work tentative hope the previous week. To mention the word 'psychology' as a means of describing what goes on at this moment of 'living critique' is to flatten all the nuances, all the nerve-endings of the transaction between reader and writer.

I've been in workshops, both as student and teacher, when people have wept at the mildest queries and laughed at the harshest rejections. This sort of unpredictability makes creative writing classes exhausting and exciting. It's common for students to speak of 'recovering' from a workshop. No one ever needs to recover from a *Moby-Dick* lecture. Certainly I've been in literature classes where people have argued passionately about Brecht and Beckett, spoken rapturously about Janet Frame. I've also been in writing classes where visiting writers have held everyone's attention. But Brecht and Beckett and Janet Frame and the visiting writer are all, in a crucial sense, finished. Whereas Mark and Peter and Ethan and James and Sarah and Linda are not. I've felt it myself when listening to the established and the famous talk about their work—deep impatience. What about *me*?

In the States, well-known writers get invited to join creative writing programmes for a few weeks at a time. They receive a nice honorarium in return for which they must live on campus, give a reading, a seminar, and hold office hours. The readings are attended dutifully by a hard core of graduate students and junior faculty. It's the office hours that draw the crowds. Angela Carter reading Angela Carter in a public place is okay, but Angela Carter reading *me* in her private room is something else entirely. Anyone on campus who has ever written a story, half a story, a haiku, knocks on that door. An audience with the Pope still puts you in a crowd; office hours give you one-on-one with another kind of holiness.

In a recent interview, film director and actor Sydney Pollack talked about the signals that a director is always unconsciously giving to actors on a set. The actor, Pollack says, is terribly disappointed if, during the filming of a scene, the director is staring at a monitor instead of watching the actor 'live'. Of course it would be fairly disastrous if the director/actor model was applied to the teacher/student relationship in a creative writing class. Yet there is something very touching about the film actor's need to be seen in the flesh—some basic human desire to be paid active attention—which has a counterpart in a writing class. Here the writer too, if he or she is serious about it and wishes for something more than just applause, hopes for a reading which catches him or her in the act of writing.

The truly valuable and invigorating moments for me have always been when a writing class has begun to turn back the clock on a piece of work, not to start some cock-eyed guess-work on the buried sources of the material (though cock-eyed guess-work has its place), but to uncover the choices that the writer has made at crucial points in the writing. The writer, and perhaps especially the student-writer, before he or she is a maker of things—stories, poems, novels—is a maker of choices. This seems such a basic point that it is sometimes ignored. Who is telling the story? How does this character sound? Why is this character's mother not present? Where did they get the money from? Should this sentence be three words longer? Do I write this with proper paragraph breaks? Keri Hulme gets away with it, why can't I? A revisionist reading takes us back—sometimes uncomfortably, even painfully, occasionally with marvellous accuracy—to the founding interrogatives on which we have set our certainties.

I am always surprised, though I shouldn't be, at how successful a workshopped story can become when the writer thinks hard about some large or small aspect, not of meaning or significance, but of method. When a piece is changed from, say, first person to third person or vice versa, or when a character's age is altered from thirteen to seventeen or vice versa, or when someone previously silent is given a speech or a loud person is quietened down. Our reluctance in this matter comes from an otherwise sound fear—that of accidents.

In 1995, when I was teaching English 252, I invited Maurice Gee along. At one stage, Maurice revealed himself, with a cleansing cheerfulness, to be a veteran producer of 'accidental works'. He said that he found himself a few years ago writing the following sentence of what became the first paragraph of *Going West*: 'He had two wives, two daughters and two sons . . .' When he read it back he was surprised—where had all this family come from? He decided those numbers sounded interesting after all and he would have to write them out. Maurice then used a phrase which despite its plainness had enormous resonance. Early on in his career he decided that he should have '*the freedom to invent*'. Nothing should be an impediment to a novel's progress as long as it could be intelligently imagined, vitally rendered. That was a nice thing for Maurice Gee to say. And perhaps I'm just being stuffy, but alongside that dictum I want to place an equally onerous gift—the freedom to revise.

We are back at Stanley Elkin kicking that medical salesman's bag. Now Elkin was frequently wrong about a story. He read our work lying in bed late at night, and he read it once only (this was a matter of pride to him—Faulkner was what you read twice). I imagine he had the TV on too; perhaps he was getting a foot rub at the same time. As he revealed in an essay the following year, he was shortly to become temporarily insane because of a change in his medication. In class he would occasionally mix up characters, miss pages, launch withering attacks based on some factual error in his own reading and remembering. Which introduces one final point in this business: self-protection.

The creative writing class is always in danger of sending the wrong signal when revision starts to look endless to the writer. Where ten readers' opinions, in all their differing emphases, seem to carry equal weight. Your fourteen pages of prose have been sliced fourteen ways and the worst thing is the butchers are people who want to *help* you. I've seen students attempt revisions in the immediate aftermath of such classes. They've written crazily for days and nights when they probably should have had their keys taken away from them. The lesson here is: read your readers, find your friends. Not because friends say nice things about us—often they don't—but because they share a tone. Or if not a tone, then some other talent for closeness—yes, they seem to meet us with a remarkable intimacy. As if they've been there too.

Alison Glenny

Alison Glenny took the Original Composition course in 1990. In 1992 she was awarded the Todd New Writers Bursary from the Arts Council of New Zealand. She currently lives in Melbourne.

Mutes and Earthquakes

There are many stories which could be told about this land.

There is 'The Magic Kumara', which tells of an old woman, a digging stick and a pair of magic gumboots. Of an enchanted flock of sheep, frozen on a hillside, and a kumara that sings and dances as it jumps from the old woman's frying pan:

> Peel me, slice me, pop me in the pan,
> Fry me, salt me, eat me if you can!

This story asks the questions we are always asking, the questions which haunt us: 'What has been lost? And what has been stolen?' But like most such tales, it hugs its answers to its chest.

Then there is the story of the girl whose mother drowned herself in a wash-bucket. The water from the wash-bucket spread out and covered the land, and saved it from drought. But the girl went out into the world in search of her mother and received strange gifts: a needle, sharp as a rapier with a smooth, oval eye to carry the thread, an inexhaustible skein of yarn . . .

It is said that my great-grandfather, who was a descendent of pirates, was also a collector of stories. 'Myths and Legends of the Tartan Isles', 'The Magic Kumara and other stories', 'The Trembling Isles: a personal record of the Seismological Crisis of 1907'; these are some of them. But mostly, he collected words. He collected them wherever he went. The lists grew longer and longer until, many years after he had first begun, they became a book, his *Dictionary of the New Shetland Vernacular.*

Once, I possessed copies of all my great-grandfather's books. But a few weeks ago, I noticed that some of them had disappeared. I searched for them all over the house, but I did not really expect to find them. You see, it is a familiar pattern in our history. First the earthquakes and then the thefts of language. Straightaway, I knew that it was happening again.

✧

Oh, they began well enough, those first white settlers! Their hopes were high, they had crossed the oceans on a raft of raised promises, loans and expectations.

Homesick and seasick, they clutched the deck rail of their ship. They saw the land dimly, through a mist of demanding memories. In their minds they named it 'The Tartan Isles'. The hills seemed to sing to them in familiar voices as they glided past. 'Oh, ye banks and braes!' And soon, they unrolled across the country the carpet they had brought with them, a plaid of lines and rectangles, fences, farms and paddocks. The plaid was strong and stubborn. It erased everything in its way. It had a familiar pattern.

✧

Here is another story about arriving.

My great-grandmother was little more than a girl when she arrived on the good ship *Pride of Erin*. She had been named for a flower, the iris. And yet in Ireland, where she was born, and where her local renown as a singer of popular, sentimental ballads had earned her the soubriquet 'The Nightingale of County Clare', she was also a bird. (In her new country she should, perhaps, have been a bellbird!)

This is how my great-grandmother tells of her arrival in the Tartan Isles, in a letter written home to her family in Ireland.

'You have asked me to describe our first sight of the land . . . I shall say then that it appeared to me like a shawl, spread across the ocean, fastened at both edges and billowing in between.

'A shawl, a token, a sign to shipping, the land of the long white tablecloth . . . Later there would be time to think of what might be spread before us when we came to land. For the moment it seemed enough merely to feast our eyes . . .'

But there is no record of the words she exchanged, on closer acquaintance, with her new land. I do not know what messages she addressed to the hills and valleys where my great-grandfather strode, his mind a collecting bottle, gathering the words which he took home and arranged in mute, alphabetical ranks in the back of the family Bible. Arranged, with either supreme confidence or an equivalent lack of imagination, on the blank pages which follow the Book of Revelations!

Was he handsome and stalwart, silent and strong?

Was she young, spirited and inwardly vulnerable?

Once, I saw their portraits: matching daguerreotypes in frames of polished wood, backed with velvet the colour of plums. From my great-grandfather's likeness I retain only a memory of whiskers; of a lichen-like growth concealing the lower part of his face, of hair which, though thinning, was bushy about the temples, and eyebrows that resembled wiry gorse. Probably he was a pink and white man, susceptible to freckles, wrinkling easily, with fair hairs sprouting along his fingers . . . The nightingale, in contrast, was dark, although her portrait was pale, faded almost to a silvery absence, its surface more that of mirror than of photograph. I recall the sinuous line of her back, curving from shoulder to bustle. Her eyes, which had been hand-coloured by the photographer; faded violets. The fall of lace from her throat, like the perfect bells of foxgloves.

Together they lived in the house that my great-grandfather, who made his living as a builder, raised on the edges of the tartan. Over time, they filled the house with children. The place was called 'Katote'. Once, it had been forest. Did they know, I wonder, that one of the meanings of its name is 'quake'?

✧

It seems as if earthquakes were always a feature of the land. The original inhabitants, a race of noble Polynesians, devised many strange and haunting legends concerning the tremors.

Many of these tales concern an earthquake god, Whaka-ruaumoko, whom they propitiated with gifts of kumara and intricately carved wooden boxes.

The legends and the gifts, although beautiful, do not seem to have stopped the earthquakes. However, most people agree that matters have become very much worse since the arrival of Europeans.

Sometimes I wonder what they must have thought, my ancestors, when they first felt the ground trembling beneath their feet. Perhaps they thought little of it, blinded by the richness of the land, the abundance of nature. So much rich, loud rain. The wind. Sunlight, abundantly bright. So, there were earthquakes as well . . . So, the country was young, it was enthusiastic!

Such a young land.

✧

My great-grandparents must have survived the first great seismological crisis with a sense of relief. And then it began, the thefts of language. All over the country, in small numbers at first that rapidly increased, men and women began to lose their voices. At the same time, books began, mysteriously, to disappear. Nobody knew why. It was as if they had simply dematerialised, melted into thin air. There were theories, of course. Some people said that there were thieves of language hiding in the hills, the mountains, the bush that had continued to lie just beyond the fringes of the tartan. Some said that it was a virus that had been lurking all the time in the swamps, with the sandflies and the moa bones. Whatever the reason, it was clear that something was being stolen. Or, perhaps, merely lost.

One morning, my great-grandmother woke up and discovered that she was mute. How upset great-grandfather must have been! He, a collector and defender of words, a self-appointed guardian and advocate of fragile and endangered meanings! To have the thieves of language strike at his heart, in the centre of his home. He raged, impotently. For how can you rage against an invisible enemy? The nightingale no longer sang about the house. Silently, her sorrowing family cut up sheets of wrapping paper and left them, with pencils, in strategic places throughout the homestead. Communication went on, although the difficulties were greater than before.

✧

Arriving back by plane, I find myself released into the golden light of late afternoon. How familiar it is, how well remembered! And yet, almost at once I am aware of a subtle change. Something is missing. Lost, perhaps, or merely forgotten . . . Then I realise what it is. The rich, buttery haze, the reflection no doubt of our perfect dairy products, our abundant produce, no longer hangs over the land, softening the harsher edges with its tender, translucent glow. Everything seems harder and brighter. At the same time I recall the anxiety in my father's voice, crackling, long distance down the line . . . 'We've had some trouble at home . . . it's your mother . . . we had to let you know . . . she's lost her voice . . .'

✧

Do you remember the last great seismological crisis, the earthquakes of '89? The year, unprecedented in the history of our occupation, when the earth buckled and gaped, when buildings shattered and fell? Those were dangerous and disturbing times! Bewilderment was general and extreme. The rivers rose and shrank accordingly. The mysterious comings and goings of the ocean swallowed chunks of land we'd been familiar with all our lives, or, even more strangely, threw up others where no land had been before, and this newborn land was still moistly pale, strewn with evidence of its former life as ocean floor: a litter of weed, small shells and slowly expiring sea creatures. The capital sustained some of the worst damage. I was there at the time; it seemed that every day brought a new tremor. The Quay and The Terrace were canyons, filled with shattered glass. The Houses of Parliament remained standing, but tilted dangerously to one side, so that they resembled a crazed, antipodean version of Pisa's more celebrated leaning tower.

At that time, sects sprang up amongst the homeless, who roamed what remained of the streets and made a living by begging; they claimed that responsibility for the quakes was ours, and that the earth, like an angry beast of burden, had finally risen up in protest against our mistreatment of it, the constant prodding and digging, burning and scarification.

At the same time, a strange exhilaration seemed to have sprung up amongst the ruins. The normal, numbing routines of work and travel had been disrupted. We were like pedestrians, released by a changing light from the weary confinement of the kerb, who seem suddenly to have woken from a dream and been propelled forward into the empty street. Those of us who had survived became accomplices in an almost festive elation, flip side to our coin of despair. Discernible emotions could be read on the face of every passer-by. Strangers grew chatty and intimate, liable to tell their life stories to anyone they met.

When I went home to visit my parents, they seemed, in comparison, tight-lipped and solemn. My father's face, bent over the food to bless it, seemed to have grown cadaverous, his prominent nose a bony ridge from which an imaginary explorer could have surveyed a landscape of plains and furrows. At first, excitement made me loquacious. But their silence reproved me. I remember thinking, with a kind of despair, that if I reached my hands down their throats, still I would never be able to find their hearts.

❖

On the train going north to my parents' house, I gaze out the windows. As we pass the bay there is a clear view out to the treble cones of the Trembling Isles. Today, the islands live up to their name, trembling and shaking beneath the long cloud of steam which hovers above them. I cannot shake from my mind the sound of my father's voice, distant on the line. Love and fear fill my heart in equal proportions.

I read the book I have brought with me. My great-grandfather's *Myths and Legends of the Tartan Isles*. The story I am reading tells of the great Polynesian hero, Maui-of-a-thousand-tricks, and of his attempt to challenge the earthquake god, Whakaruaumoko. The author claims that the story was told to him by a native farm-hand, a man of prodigious memory. He says that he copied it down exactly.

Although, recently, scholars have thrown doubt on my great-grandfather's stories. It seems that he was not a good listener. That he made his stories up. That they are more pakeha lies.

How Maui Challenged the Earthquake God

Everyone has heard of the adventures of the great hero, Maui. Of how he stole the fingernails of his grandmother, Mahuika, so that he might bring fire to the earth. Or how he wounded the sun with a magic jawbone, so that it was forced to move more slowly, thus giving us day as well as night. Here is another of the trickster god's adventures. It tells of how he travelled deep down beneath the surface of the earth to challenge the mighty earthquake god, Whakaruaumoko, so that the earth might be freed from earthquakes. For in those days Whakaruaumoko walked indiscriminately across the surface of the world and his passing caused great fear, for fire and earthquakes sprang up in his footsteps, and the earth trembled and shuddered at his approach.

It seems that the earthquake god lived in an enormous whare set on an island in the middle of one of the mighty rivers that flowed into the underworld. The river was swift and dangerous, its waters boiling hot and filled with sulphurous fumes. Nonetheless, Maui and the two brothers who had agreed to come with him succeeded in bringing their canoe unscathed through the water, until they came to the rapids in front of Whakaruaumoko's island, and there, standing up in the rapids, and towering over the tiny canoe, were three enormous gateposts, intricately carved. Fire flickered behind their flashing eyes, inside their grimacing mouths. They were the sentries of Whaka-ruaumoko, whom he had carved himself and set there to guard his house while he slept.

When Maui's brothers saw these terrifying figures they cried out in alarm and confusion, and would have paddled back the way they had come. But Maui instructed them to hold the canoe steady against a rock while he himself stood up and addressed himself to the gateposts, greeting them boldly. The gateposts did not answer. Instead, they reached down and seized hold of Maui and his two brothers and their canoe, and they held them tightly in their wooden arms, without saying a word. And this is how Maui and his brothers might have stayed until the earthquake god came out of his whare and killed them, if Maui had not seen the reason for their silence. The reason for the gateposts' silence was that they had been carved without tongues, for Whakaruaumoko believed that they would make better sentries if they could not speak. But when Maui saw that the gateposts had no tongues, a plan began to form in his mind, for he knew that above all else, all living things desire a voice.

Then Maui addressed himself to the gateposts. 'Gateposts,' he said, 'if you release my brothers and me and our canoe, I shall carve each of you a tongue.'

One by one, the gateposts released Maui and his two brothers and their canoe. Their huge wooden arms dropped back to their sides, and Maui climbed up on each of them in turn and carved tongues in their huge, horrible mouths.

When he had finished, and was back in his canoe, the gateposts began, one by one, to move their tongues in their mouths.

The first one said, 'Whakaruaumoko sleeps in the afternoon. That is a good time to approach him.'

The second said, 'Behind the whare of Whakaruaumoko is a small whare pataka. That is where Tuatara lives, in whose body the earthquake god keeps half his strength.'

The third said, 'Next to Tuatara in the whare pataka is the net which Whakaruaumoko uses to fish, and no other in the world is as large or as strong.'

Then Maui and his brothers passed through the rapids beneath the gateposts, but the gateposts did not notice them go, they were too busy trying out their new tongues.

Soon Maui and his brothers drew near to the island of Whaka-ruaumoko, and saw his whare which was as big as a forest. The floor was filled with ash and lava, fires slumbered uneasily behind the doors and windows, and dimly, in the glow of the embers, they could see the gourd containers in which Whakaruaumoko kept the floods and tidal waves.

Maui and his brothers paddled to the far side of the island where they would be out of sight, and they waited until the afternoon, when they could tell by the rumbling and shaking of the ground that Whakaruaumoko was asleep. Then they came on shore and crept across the island to the whare pataka, and Maui climbed up inside it and found Tuatara dozing there, just as the second gatepost had told him. Before Tuatara had time to wake, Maui bound his limbs with flax cords and popped him into his kete. Behind Tuatara, just as the third gatepost had told him, he found the fishing net and he brought it out with him. Then Maui and his brothers spread the net over the entire island, and when it was fastened, Maui began to pull on it.

The movement woke Whakaruaumoko from his sleep. He emerged from his whare in a fury, and when he saw that he was surrounded by his own net, he raged and fumed and tried to break out of it, but Whakaruaumoko had knotted the flax himself and strengthened it with powerful spells, and it could not easily be broken.

All the same he would have killed Maui and his brothers with his fiery breath if Maui had not stood up in the canoe and showed him Tuatara. 'Now you must obey me,' said Maui, 'or else lose half your strength.'

Then Whakaruaumoko raged and fumed some more, but he saw that he had been tricked, and he asked Maui what he wanted of him.

But Maui saw that Whakaruaumoko, even with only half his strength, was too strong for him ever to destroy. Then he racked his brains to think what good might come of the adventure, and he said to the angry god: 'You must come with me to a place below the regions of the earth, far away from the villages of men and women, and promise to remain there. Tuatara shall be my hostage. As long as you keep your promise Tuatara will live. But if you ever break it and walk across the earth, then Tuatara will die.'

Then Maui dragged Whakaruaumoko deep down beneath the earth, the lakes and the rivers, below even the ocean floor. Down, down, into the underworld, he dragged the weary god. And he tied him there beneath the roots of the mountains, to sleep for eternity.

Whakaruaumoko sleeps there still, and the children of the earth are able to continue with their lives; to build villages and prepare gardens for the cultivation of plants. But every time that Whaka-ruaumoko has a nightmare, he turns in his sleep and wakes to find himself trapped beneath the mountain; then he struggles and tries to break free and the force of his struggle sends tremors as far as the surface of the earth, before he feels the folds of his own net about him, and remembers his promise to Maui.

Whakaruaumoko has never broken his promise, and for that reason Tuatara is still alive, and is the oldest living creature in the world, and he is so old that he has almost turned into stone. And some people say that when Tuatara turns into stone, then his strength will return to Whakaruaumoko, and on that day the earthquake god will wake up, shake off his bonds, and return to the earth.

By the time I have finished reading this story the curve of the bay and the outlines of the Trembling Isles have dropped far behind us.

I put the book aside and gaze out the window again. Oh, but this is an attractive part of the line! Ferns brush the top of the carriage and purple foxgloves grow amongst the wild grass in the cuttings. I doze uneasily beneath the flickering shadows of the telegraph poles, and then I must fall asleep, because I dream.

In the dream I am walking up a hillside. The hillside is bare, except for some patches of gorse, dried and stunted by the wind. Wind scrapes the surface of the hillside, the side of my face. I must lean into it to make any progress. In my arms I am clutching a copy of the *Dictionary of the New Shetland Vernacular.* It weighs me down, its sharp edges bite into my arms. However, I clutch it more tightly and toil on. There is a voice in the wind. I listen hard, I strain to catch it, but I cannot understand what it is saying.

I wake beneath the flickering shadows of the telegraph poles, still struggling to understand.

❖

My mother is in hospital for tests. Although it is not expected that the tests will reveal anything useful. Later, I will be allowed to visit her.

I stand in the middle of the living room. It does not seem to have changed much. Although I notice that some of the books have gone;

there are bare patches on the shelves. My father, coming through from the kitchen, notices the direction of my gaze. 'They keep disappearing,' he says. 'We try to fill the empty spaces, but . . .' His voice trails into silence, as if gravity itself were standing in the room with us and draining his sentences of their words, swirling them, like water, down an invisible plughole. My father coughs nervously. Abruptly, he thrusts a cup of tea into my hands. I have taken the stairs to the very top of the house. Here, amongst the attic clutter of dust and broken furniture, I am delving into my grandparents' iron-bound chests, digging down through the layers of their history, the sedimentation of their lives.

One layer is a christening shawl of fine wool. I set it to one side. Here is a pair of linen sheets, still faintly scented with lavender; silent accomplices to intimacies of which their owners preferred not to speak. And here is the daguerreotype of the nightingale, my great-grandmother, still in its wooden frame. Yes, it is as I remember, she is standing with her hands resting on the back of a chair. Behind her, the photographer's backdrop of mountains and waterfalls is almost invisible. Indeed, her image is even fainter and more fugitive than I remember. Little remains besides the faded violet of her eyes, the froth of her lace jabot which falls from the high collar of her bodice in folds that resemble the perfect bells of foxgloves . . .

I cough. What is this contraction in my throat, the sudden thickness? My hand flies to my mouth, while my lungs, a useless bellows, pump frantic air.

All that emerges from my mouth is a soft sigh.

And yet, I am still holding my great-grandmother's portrait. As I put it down, I see that it has begun to fade.

Look: she is disappearing before my eyes. Soon there will be nothing left but a silvery rectangle of glass, a wooden frame, and a velvet backing, the colour of plums.

Paola Bilbrough

Paola Bilbrough was a member of the 1990 workshop, since when she has spent time in Japan and Australia. Her poems and prose poems have appeared in a number of places, including *Landfall* and *Sport*.

Ceilings

Hepatitis turned my father's skin and the whites of his eyes the colour of old butter. He journeyed out of the suburbs, away from his own father who wanted to put him in hospital, to the house of my mother and her German husband.

My mother and I inhabited a world of constant tea parties, where all the characters were feline. Down the long kauri hallway, tossing under flannelette sheets, my father did not know he was the Yellow Cat. He was grateful not to be in a sterile ward in the city. He often stared at the ceiling; the patches of damp were like the coat of a piebald horse he rode as a child.

For as long as I have known him, my father has camped out in his houses. He lived in one which filled with silt and river water every spring. There was little point in bringing things back down from the attic. Always, though, there would be outposts of civilisation at the corners and edges of rooms.

We have all talked of how to improve these houses. Once, my mother was laid up in my father's house with chickenpox. The ceiling was a landmark, a point of reference in the parched terrain of her illness. It was white and peeling, but still ornate with roses and leaves. My mother wanted to paint it. Lapis lazuli for the background, dusty pink with a touch of cadmium yellow for the roses. We could both see these colours quite clearly. Only when her temperature began to drop did the colours fade, disappearing in patches like the welts on her skin.

I lie under white lace, wool next to my skin. I drink coltsfoot tea and suck horehound toffee for my cough. I read about Vanessa Bell; murals she painted on the walls of her house, her mauve curtains with yellow lining. At the back of the book is a toothpick my mother must have marked a page with ten years ago. I think of her back then, in her kauri house before bedtime. She is picking her teeth and reading about Vanessa Bell while her bath heats. She doesn't stop reading until condensation begins to form on the low kitchen ceiling. A drop separates and slides down her face, settling in the hollow between neck and clavicle.

Just prior to sleep I shut *The Life of Vanessa Bell* and leave my mother about to hop into her bath. I lift slowly out of the blankets and am in the spare room at my father's house. My forehead touches a cold plaster rosebud. I run my hands over the ceiling's tightly ordered garden.

Kirsty Gunn

Kirsty Gunn did the Original Composition course in 1980; her work-shop folio was a volume of poetry. Since then she has lived mostly in the United Kingdom, where she has published two highly praised short novels, *Rain* and *The Keepsake*. 'Grass, Leaves' is published in Faber's *First Fictions: Introduction 11*.

Grass, Leaves

Nan reckons rain. Feels the big, sticky clouds, she says, pumpkin-yellow and mean as a man's eye, piling up over the far mountains. In her mind's eye she sees it, the storm. Brewing to pour and the air aching for it. The poor ground's dusty mouth gaping for water.

In the paddocks across the road, cows doze and the sheep pick at yellow grasses. The land behind them goes barren and lost all the way to the sky. It's our view, it's safe. I could dream all day up here with Nan, sitting on her front verandah. The things she says turn into pictures in my own mind, things happen there.

Peas in a pod.

Drops of water like flowers.

Nothing could be more lovely to me than sitting here with Nan, Little Si playing beside. The three of us alone and nobody else to worry for.

The hot wind shudders through the pines, stops. Makes me think what the rain will feel like after all these weeks of dry. Will it be a refreshment? Perhaps a sign? When Jesus died, the storm clouds opened and it rained for three days before Mary could gather up his ghost and fly with him to heaven. Rain can be important to a person who waits for signs. It could mean summer's ending and everything will change.

Little Si thinks about none of these things. He runs around with the hose, filling up his paddling pool. Backwards and forwards to the tap, a little cut-out boy, just his underpants on, a leaf.

'Look at me, Nan! Look!'

He swings the pipe so the water flicks a necklace against the blue sky. He dances through it and the plastic tube flicks and turns. The water an arch for him, a circle, a window.

'I'm magicking! I'm magicking!'

He waves his arms and leaps through the water again.

'I'm swimming around the world, Nanny-Nan! Look at me!'

Nan shakes her head, she smiles. She reaches for the bowl of peas to start shelling. She could eat that child on toast, that's what she says.

Little Pixie Darling.

Little Pea.

When she cuddles him, she kisses his face all over, she nibbles at his ear like an old fish. She could bite his head clean off.

Little Si is her own favourite boy, my own brother. Perhaps this will be the holiday that we'll be able to stay here for ever with Nan and be our own complete family, just the three of us like in the Bible. A sign may never come that says we have to go home and we could stay here instead, quite safely, with Nan. The bowl of peas there for us to shell and no storm for trouble.

Last night in bed, that's what she talked about, about keeping us with her. How we could go to a little country school, if we liked. Have a lunch packed, with sandwiches and a piece of fruit and a cake to finish off with.

'Would you like that, honey? Come home here for your tea every day?'

I couldn't speak at first, it was so like a miracle. I'd been praying to God: Why should our mother want us back when the bad sickness is over? Wouldn't she like it more if she could be on her own? And us not there to bother her and make her ill?

Nan said, 'Stay up here always, how would that be?'

And as I held her in bed, my arms tight around her body said *Yes*. I wanted that wish so bad I could have broken with it. And if Little Si was older I know he would have wished for it too. *Please, please.* Let us stay. Change our names and be Nan's children. *Please, please.* Make the wish come true in heaven.

In my mind's eye I saw all the white angels gathered with our bleeding Lord, but even then I couldn't stop the creeping spider thought: Does Nan mean it this time? Because why had she said it before, said we could live with her always, when it didn't come true? Why had she let us go home in the end?

I'm evil in that way, not believing hard enough for my prayers to come true. A person without sin knows that to truly believe, you must put yourself square in God's eye. Have Him see you and notice your wish. It's not enough just to pray for miracles, you must prove your love to have them come true. You must stretch the boy's throat back on the altar, your own son. Or perhaps it is an animal that must be killed . . . But always, in the Bible, it's the murders that make the wishes come true.

If you're stained and contain demons, it's not easy to try for miracles. When I clean up afterwards, I know it's my fault that our mother gets ill—she never wanted that baby. How can I pray when I spoiled her life? Her dances and balls and all her boyfriends? How can I pray now, torn out of her wedlock? When I'm the reason she's sick now, and frightening?

Nan says to give up on praying because it's all rot. She used to, she's stopped. She gave birth in a thunderstorm, a man she hated for a husband and a daughter man-sick . . . All these things come out in the songs she sings instead of hymns.

My roof's got a hole in it and I might drown.

There's whiskey in the jar.

Nobody knows the trouble I've seen.

All the songs have people hanging, wading in water, birds drowning. What do these signs mean? How much of these songs are true? Maybe there's a jump in the song, a joyful note. Nan might whistle the songs instead of sing them, but even then the pictures they contain are full of sadness. The earth crying, a baby born naked somewhere and left that way.

She sings these songs to us in bed at night, she never leaves us in the dark. Tonight, when the sky splits into rain and wind ghosts through the skinny old pines so their barks creak and moan, we'll be safe. We'll be inside the lemon bedroom with the roses on the wallpaper that look like little faces in the dark, with eyes and mouths, but kind. Nan will cuddle us up at her front and back, the blankets folded over and all the soft sheets. Little Si held in her lap like a cat or a plate of cakes or something else that you carry with gentleness . . .

Peas in a pod, sad babies.

Drops of water, grey goose-down but nowhere to sleep.

In bed, I pray hard to Heaven that we can stay here in the room with the lemon roses. Pray that everything Nan says will come true and that all the songs will have simple pictures with happy endings and no one killing the bird or causing that boy to hang. And we'd never go back, because from now on Nan would decide things, not our mother.

Pray, pray. Make her die, Jesus Christ. Snatch her to Heaven. Don't let her come for us, like when she came the last time and took us away.

'Darling. Look how *tall* you are. How you've *grown*. How I've *missed* you looking after me . . .'

She wore red lipstick gashed across her mouth, and high pointy shoes. The tips of them went click-click as she walked across the floor.

'And my little boy, let me kiss him . . .'

Little Si was on Nan's lap, tucked under her cardigan. His face was hidden in her shoulder.

'We don't have to go back with you,' his voice was muffled from hiding. 'Nan says we don't have to.'

My mother looked at Nan then, her eyes had a glint. 'What have you been saying to them?' She took a step forwards with her bent body, on her pointy high-heeled shoes. 'What lies?'

At first Nan didn't say anything, she was stroking the hairs at Little Si's neck, that tender part. She was stroking.

Then she made her reply.

She said, 'No lies.'

She said it was just a story.

She said it was nothing that was ever meant to come true.

How my mother's red lips parted then. She smiled, she was so glamorous. She took my hand in her cool hand.

'I have presents,' she said, 'for my own two darlings. For being so good and staying with their old grandmother while Mummy was sick.'

Her bracelets jangled as she searched in her bag amongst her cigarettes and the little bottle hiding there. She picked out two packets with papers that were bright and tinselly. Little Si peeped out of the cardigan, seeing the present that was to be his own. His hand reached out.

'But only if you kiss me first,' she said, she was walking towards him. 'Only presents when you kiss . . .'

Click, click. She was coming closer. Her hand containing the tinsel and bright paper, and Little Si still reaching. Later, his face would be smeared from chocolate and from crying, but for now he stretched out his hand towards her.

'My darling boy . . .'

She was using all her special loving words, all her jewellery was shining.

'My precious darling boy . . .'

There was nothing Nan could do to protect us.

But why am I thinking about these mean things now? When the blue sky's an apron? When Little Si is a boy carved out of a nut, running freely in the sunlight and his own paddling pool there for him?

'Watch me swim?'

He runs over to his pool, jumps in, thrashes there like a caught fish. His smile and shriek and the trinkets of water all little hooks to keep us, caught and safe on God's line.

Nan looks up from the dish of peas, plucking out the peas from their neat homes and letting them drop. 'I'm watching, honey . . .'

She splits a pea like a trick, pops the pod into her mouth and swallows it whole.

'Just think,' she says to me. 'All this will pass. Grass, leaves. Our little piles of twigs . . . How they will wither. Everything to dust . . .'

She looks around herself, at all the bright day.

'We can't change things, you and I. We sit up here all day, under a bad sun, but we can't stop the weather turning. We make our piles of earth and they become graves around us. Nothing's as important as it seems.'

Across the garden, the hosepipe spins crazy water on the green grass. The glitter from the little pool could hurt your eyes. The red flowers lining Nan's paths and borders could hurt your eyes. Little Si's voice, calling out, calling to her, that could hurt you.

'Watch me swim, Nanny-Nan! Watch *me*!'

Nan loves Little Si because he's easy, just a stick. He's always been her own little boy, she's kept him safe and he's never had to pray to an angel or cut for blood to say sorry to Jesus. The red petals are thick on the path from where I picked them—but they wither under God's eye.

The world turns to dust, dust in the paddocks rising. Even the wet little boy out swimming had better cuddle up quick, he's another fish caught, safe but dying. Nan says she'll keep Si little for ever but one day he'll realise thoughts poke in.

The shelled peas are filling the bowl. Nan whistles the song about the poor Irish boy hung; she huddles against the weather turning. But now she can't always decide things and have them come true. She may know the storm will come for us tonight, banging on the roof, the wind hungry, but she can't know it all, only God, and He won't come back again unless I cut. In the darkness tonight I will reach for them.

I love you.

I love you.

Nobody will ever see us in the lemon bedroom.

Nobody need ever learn who I am.

Hinemoana Baker

Hinemoana Baker was a member of the workshop in 1994. She lives in
Wellington, and is a poet, musical performer and storyteller, as well as
a short-story writer. (On the genesis of this story, see 'Five Things' in
'The Exercise Chapter', p.286.)

Hiruhārama

Have you ever taken the hand of someone not quite twice your age, a
girl, a girl with twisting black hair? At night, when the river is a wide
streak of shine swelling with sandflies. Did you lose your shoes in the
stinking mud and then cling to each other, pale blue and winceyette
in the wet grass, lips apart, daring to breathe? Did she tell you the
moon was a woman and so were all the saints, and did she show you
their pictures?

It was after she first saw the nuns that she decided to wear pale
blue. She only had two pale blue things: a long dress to her ankles and
a jersey from her cousin who was three years younger. She wore both
that night. And always the necklace, the tiny birdcage tinkling against
her chest. Did I take it between my fingers that night, hold it to my
ear, hold it there and sway so the chiming bell would ring for me?

Help me to remember. Trace it with your finger in the dark
in the woodshed. Wade into it up to your knees, bunching your
skirt between your thighs and skim stones across it. Brush it, smell it,
plait it.

On one wall in the lounge is a black-and-white photograph of the
river Jordan. On its bank stand three men with black skin, one with a
moustache, they are old and one stands with his foot on a boulder.
They wear flowing trousers and waist sashes, hats like cones with

flattened peaks. They stare so intently at the water, it's like they're waiting to glimpse a tuna, or saying how bloody poor the whitebait have been this season. The opposite wall is pinned with coloured postcards of the city of Jerusalem. Domes and sky and Sacred Mosques, The Church of the Nativity, The Manger at Bethlehem.

We trail in. In front of the postcards we stop, staring, and she drops my hand. Then she springs aside and meets my eyes.

'Kia haere ki te tiki i te pukapuka!' and we uplift the book, nod to it, walk sacrificially back from her uncle's bedroom to the sofa beneath the river Jordan. We sit, she reads aloud, '*The Children's Picture Dictionary of Saints*,' and places her palm on the cover. I trace the shape of her fingers in the red leather, we marvel at the gold leaf. Then it is opened: one side rests on her leg, one on mine.

Perhaps it was just that the female saints were the ones who always got their pictures painted. Some of them did have names like Andrew and Barnabas but their hair was so long and their faces so smooth, and we'd never seen any men who looked like that, so soft. One of them, called Saint Phillip, looked just like her Aunty Marama, even wearing a headband that looked like a tupare.

'All the saints are women,' she hums into my ear. 'They all live up the river, at Jerusalem. They wear blue dresses and blue veils, I've seen them. I'm going to be a saint one day.'

I drop onto the floor and put my chin on her knees.

'I've seen them.' She turns her head to the net-curtained daylight. 'And I know the real name of this river, e hoa. To us it's Whanganui, Te Wai-nui-a-Rua, that's what we've always said, that's how we've always known it. But that's not its real name. It's Jordan. It's the river Jordan.'

Her hair and her brown eyes gleam.

The man who lived with them, we called him Uncle Crim, he always felt angry to me, but with a smiling face covering it all up, like scalding milk with a skin on it. His eyes had a milky look too, but he could see out of them OK. His face looked sunburnt all year round, his hair was yellow next to it. Sometimes in the afternoon when he was in his bedroom he would be talking away, booming, like he was really telling someone what for. Aunty Marama told us he was talking to his tupuna,

Captain Cook. We giggled, but she didn't.

'Kei konei tēnei tangata, e noho rawa ana,' she said sideways, while she set the table. 'Go and have a look.'

So we snuck to Crim's bedroom door and saw the dummy dressed in a blue uniform with gold fringe and gold buttons and a sword on its belt, and a picture of Captain Cook sitting where the head should be.

When we asked Aunty Marama what Crim stood for she said Criminal and laughed. I thought it stood for Crimson. Aunty Marama said he was a bit strange, we had to make allowances. He had had a hard life. She said no one else would be kind to him except us so be patient, be loving.

But the thing was that it was never Aunty Marama that he played tricks with. It was us kids, me and her, but mainly her, and he was cruel.

The weta wasn't the worst, but it was still bad. He just walked up behind her one day while she was at the table and placed it on her head. I was on the other side of the table but I didn't see the weta until it fell in her plate and panicked and ran towards the edge of the table and then dropped into her lap. Then she started to scream. The weta clung to her blue dress and even when she stood up and stamped and backed into the wall and hit at it, still it clung there until I smashed it off with my shoe and stood on it. For ages she wouldn't stop flicking and rubbing her hair.

That night, was it so long ago? That night was the worst. When like balsa my bones floated to sleep in the warmth of her bed and her circling arm; but then waking, waking with the shaking bed, that red face right up to hers, her knees forced apart and one pressing into my side again, again, again.

Afterwards she said she wanted to wash herself in the river, to cleanse herself of sin.

She says this while she piggy-backs me over the stile, while my wet cheek rubs her hair with the rhythm of her steps, while the shining chime in the tiny birdcage around her neck sings. And when she has taken off her pale blue jersey and her pale blue dress; and when she has opened the book at St Phillip and placed it in my hands; and when she has clasped the chain and its birdcage around my neck and I have felt its delicate shiver against my skin—by then the river is wider and darker than ever. By then the woman she calls The Moon is already walking on the water.

Gabrielle Muir

Gabrielle Muir took the Original Composition course in 1991, when she lived in Tua Marina, and often flew across Cook Strait to workshop meetings. She is a poet as well as a fiction writer; her work has been anthologised in volume 3 of Witi Ihimaera's *Te Ao Marama* series.

The Gorse Thicket

for my sisters

On her first day back at her old school she was late. The gorse would not let her through. In the three years she had been away, the gorse had grown up and had spread right across the gully. Now it presented itself, a spiky barrier, green and vigorous, broader than a football field, higher than her head. Nearer its base, it had grown old, the bare branches all knuckled and sinewed, with here and there an isolated thorn jutting like a magnified bristle. The ground beneath the gorse stretched away, naked and dusty, until it became twilit, secret and dense. Her ear caught the dry rasping sound of branches scraping together in the wake of some small animal as it scuttered deeper into the thicket—a rabbit, or a possum perhaps, or a cat, or—much worse—a rat. Peering into the gorse she thought she saw, for one electrifying moment, rats seething over the roots, hundreds of them. She blinked in horror but when she looked again there was nothing, only the tangle of roots and branches regaining their stillness in the uncertain, rat-coloured light. Somewhere to her right, from a long way in, a bird shrilled, and seconds later a flock of starlings rose up out of the thicket and flew away above her head, their calls loud and alarmed. Craning her neck, she watched them fly off towards the state houses until they settled, a small black cloud on the roof of her own house, then she turned again to face the wall of green. The gorse nodded back at her. She would have to go around.

The footpath she hurried along was new but the gorse already hung over in many places where she had to step off the path and walk on the bitumen, which was also newly laid—so fresh, the smell of boiling pitch made her lungs contract. The tarred gravel attached itself to the soles of her shoes as she went and before she could get back on to the path she had to keep stopping to scrape the stones off on the edge of the guttering. Once, as she did this, she saw her brother's initials carved into the cement, and the corrugated imprint of the sole of his college shoe. He must have done that at the start of the school year, before she and her little sister had come home. Nana was too old to keep them any longer, so they were back with their mother and their big brother, this time for good. She remembered her first ever day in primary school—Primer One, her brother leading her up to the teacher because their mother was working and couldn't get the time off. The teacher was a lady with hard-looking hair and beads around her neck that disappeared down the front of her dress. She remembered her brother letting go of her hand, and the teacher saying, Now I'm going to show you something very interesting—but it turned out to be nothing, and when she looked around again, her brother had gone.

Now as she stood in the gutter scraping tar off her shoes her brother sped by on his bicycle, loose gravel pinging in the spokes. She shouted out for a dub, but he only pumped his legs faster, yelling back at her over his shoulder, Can't. Late. Before her mother sent her away to join her little sister at Nana's house across the harbour, the gorse had been only knee-high, but she had been afraid of its spikes even then. Her brother would have to coax her along the thin track that wound through to the roughly mown paddock on the other side. He used to say the quicker they went, the less it would hurt, and he would try and get her to run. He made a game of follow-the-leader out of it. He would jog ahead of her, calling, Swerve here. Go left. Go right. If she got muddled with left and right, which she often did, she would run straight into a gorse bush. Then all she could do was stand there, rigid with panic, while he gingerly plucked the young branches back to free her, swearing under his breath at her clumsiness and her fear, mindless of the fact that his own bare legs were covered in scratches and little spatterings of blood.

When she was sent to Nana's, no one told her she would be living there. She thought she was going for the weekend, to see her little sister who had nice toys, and tidy clothes, and pink lino on the floor in her bedroom, and a gap between her two front teeth, and long, long black hair that their nana brushed a-hundred-strokes every morning till it shone with blue and green and purply streaks, like coal. Her little sister owned ribbons, and cardigans, and socks that stayed up, and shoes that were not lace-ups like her own, but which fastened with a strap and a buckle. She had a doll's pram too, and in it lay a doll dressed up to look like a bride, with a mouth like a perfect pink rosebud.

She understood somehow that her sister had been given all this to make up for the fact that she didn't live at home in the dirty house with the unmade beds, and the piles of dirty washing , and the stacks of dirty dishes. But she also knew that she would never swap the house and her mother and her brother for her sister's life, not ever. Not even for the bride-doll which her sister would never let her play with.

But she was left at Nana's, and when she asked about going home, no one answered. Her nana clipped her nails right back because they were filthy, and cut her hair off because it too was unclean, and sent her to a new school dressed in hand-me-down clothes because Nana wasn't made of money and couldn't afford to buy them both new things every time they wanted them. Her nana made her hold hands with her little sister each morning when they set off for school, but as soon as they rounded the corner, out of the old lady's sight, they dropped hands quickly. They hated each other.

She knew how to pray, and every night she asked God to bless her family, even her little sister and her nana, even the father she had seen only once but whose image she polished and treasured till the memory of him shone like a bright medal. Her brother and her mother she saved till last, blessing them and telling God about them, and asking God to keep them safe until she fell asleep, sometimes even forgetting to say Amen.

At first, whenever her mother visited she expected to be taken home, but gradually she gave up asking, especially as the visits became shorter, and the time between them longer, and the look on her mother's face when she visited made the dull ache that lived in her heart swell—and with such a ferocious pain she thought her chest would burst open. The visits would all end the same way—in smacking and crying because she thought her mother came only to see her and refused to share the attention with her little sister.

Nana's house was near the sea, and once or twice over the summer her brother might turn up. Just turn up without warning, wearing shorts made from cut-off trousers, and a shirt without buttons. He would have one or two friends with him, and they would have spent all day at the beach, and be thirsty and sunburnt, and maybe have lost their bus fare home. Nana would pretend to be angry, but would give them each a tall glass of water with ice in, and their bus fare if they needed it, because Nana liked boys. Sometimes the boys would twist up their wet sandy towels into thick snakes and flick them at the girls, but mostly they laughed and shouted at each other, shadow-boxing and feint-kicking, their aggression only half concealed. At these times, if she caught her brother's eye, he would look quickly away.

Come sunset she and her little sister would trail along behind the boys and their flicking towels as they walked down to the bus-stop, and when the bus came, her brother would leap aboard without saying good-bye, and race his friends to the long seat across the back. But as it pulled away, he would turn, his face small and white in the bus window, despite the sunburn, and would raise his hand to wave. And she would stand there waving back till the bus turned the corner. Even when it was out of sight she waited, listening till the far-off noise of the engine blended with all the other sounds that make up a still evening in summer.

Then winter would come, and after three winters the visits had tailed off almost completely. Once she got sick, and she was left in a chair, wrapped in a blanket, for three days during which time she was spoken to by no one except ghosts. Doubt began to grow that she would ever get home. By the third winter, past hoping, she went on waiting. That last winter she willed them to come. She would stand in the freezing hallway of her nana's house and stare and stare at the frosted glass panels of the front door until she could see right through, and down the path, and down the road, and along the harbour, and then into her own street, and she could see her letterbox, and the path leading up to her house, and the door opening, and her brother running down the front steps, his breath steaming ahead of him. Sometimes too she could see her mother looming on the other side of the frosted glass, about to raise her hand to press the bell on Nana's front door, which throughout the winter remained locked, as if to keep out the cold.

Then Nana fell over one day, for no reason. The two girls helped her to bed and got her water, and the old lady went to sleep for a day and a night. When she woke up, she rose from her bed as if nothing had happened, but her speech and her step had slowed, and over the next few weeks, got slower and slower. So their mother took them back, and Nana went into hospital and stayed there. The big-armed woman, whose slap could knock you across a room, shrivelled up under the white hospital sheet until she became nothing more than a piece of leather stretched taut over tiny brittle bones, her hands like bird claws, clinging to the edge of the counterpane.

Home.

At first she and her sister made too much noise. They spoke to their mother and she would press her palms to her ears. It was because they had grown accustomed to shouting at Nana whose deafness they acknowledged, but never fully accepted, believing instead that she heard when and what she wanted. When they asked her for something, she was deaf, but if they whispered to each other, or conspired together in a rare moment of friendship, she heard them—even if they were way down the other end of the house, even if they were outside in the garden. At home there was no garden, just long grass at the front, and a packed clay yard out the back with an old forty-four-gallon drum for burning rubbish, and a pit dug into the ground for the stuff that couldn't be burnt.

That first day back at her old school, her mother had taken their little sister early, but the older two had been left to fend for themselves. Having dressed herself and made her own breakfast, she was sure she would make it to school in plenty of time. As it was she arrived late, and had to hide behind the milk shed while everyone else lined up at assembly and marched into class under the beady eye of the headmaster, Mr Brownlie, who had smacked her around the legs for having lollies at school in Primer Two.

Hiding behind the milk shed, she wondered if anyone would remember her, or whether they would treat her like a stranger. She couldn't decide which would be worse. All the first-day strategy, worked out so carefully the night before, had gone completely out of her head when she confronted the wall of gorse. Now she cowered behind the shed, her stomach churning to the smell of rancid school milk, and when someone whispered her name and touched her on the shoulder, she almost wet her pants in fright.

It was a boy whose name she couldn't remember—someone she'd never once thought of since she'd been away—but here he was, saying, I remember you. And he was in her class. They went in late together. The teacher wasn't angry, and the class regarded her with curiosity, not hostility. Coming in with the boy had saved her. She remembered his name; it was Lawrence someone, but at lunch-time everyone called him Larley. After school he offered to show her a short-cut through the gorse.

It was easy after that. She learnt there were many short-cuts through the gorse—as many as there were kids who passed that way going to and from school. She would be dawdling home from school, vaguely aware of a group of three or four kids straggling home ahead of her, when suddenly one of them would peel away, and appear to walk straight into the thicket. She learnt to look through the gorse, not at it, and in this way, eventually she found her own paths.

In the early summer, towards the end of her last year in primary school, the gorse bloomed, and she swam beneath its surface through a sea of yellow flowers. Sometimes she and her sister walked home through the gorse together, but she liked it better when she was on her own and she could take her time, examining the treasures and the mysteries gathered that day in the net that was her life—lines from poems and stories out of the *School Journal*, scraps of conversation that would replay themselves word for word in her head—the things she overheard, the things that were said to her, the things that she said to others. Much of it was jettisoned and forgotten immediately, but some of it she kept, believing it would stay lodged in her mind forever, ready for her to recall at a moment's notice whenever she wanted. And if there were other things trapped in her net that she would rather not have kept, but which stayed with her anyway, she only distantly admitted how deeply inside herself she buried them.

She repressed too the new awareness that a certain group of girls in her class were not children at all, and that their first-hand knowledge of sex united them in an exclusive secret circle. That these girls had hair between their legs, breasts and periods filled her with envy and disgust. While she was clever, and could answer all the questions the young male teacher put to the class, they lounged in their seats, the buttons of their summer blouses undone to the point where he could glimpse the line of bra against the swell of warm brown skin, if he cared to look. And he did. Or else, in the blue-bottle heat of the afternoon he would take the class out on to the field for a game of softball, and he would position himself behind the prettiest one, lean over her, and pretend he was teaching her how to swing the bat. This picture stayed in her mind: their four hands clasped around the bat, with the teacher breathing hard, red in the face and bent over the girl, who kept her eyes levelled on the pitcher, and blushed. It made her ache. She recognised her need to be loved and at the same time buried the certain knowledge that she wasn't.

Her mother was too busy, too tired, too sad, too preoccupied with her own dreams and nightmares. Her brother had long since become a stranger—allied to their mother—and the one who meted out punishment, where and when required, in her name. They fought. In the hours between after school and when their mother got home from work, the house resounded with their battles—she and her brother, she and her sister, her brother and herself against their sister, and the two sisters against their brother. Yet it never happened that her brother and little sister united against her, and though she noticed it, she never once let herself wonder why.

Because she thought she knew. Those two needed her. She was

their middle-man, the one who translated for them. They did not speak to each other often, except through her, and she believed she knew them better than they knew each other. She would sometimes come home after school to a silent house—her brother would be at his desk in his bedroom, drawing fighter planes, and her sister would be lying on her bed in the room the two girls shared, her bride-doll clutched to her chest. She would throw her schoolbag on the other bed, then amble through to the kitchen to do the dishes, the radio up as loud as it would go, till her brother came in and yelled at her to turn it down, and she in her turn shouted for her sister to come and help with the dishes—then the fighting would begin. She felt she could walk into the house and set it going like a motion picture.

Then it happened that, coming home from her last ever day in primary school, the bag slung across her shoulder weighted down with exercise books, and the sun bearing down from a stone-white, windless sky, she hesitated a moment before entering the thicket, and was, in that moment, lost. Even without a breeze, the gorse stirred softly and gave off thick waves of heat as she skirted along its edges, searching for a way in. She inhaled shallow draughts of lifeless air and loneliness. She would have been glad if someone—even her little sister—had come along, but not a soul was passing. And, with the stillness of the air and the shifting of the gorse, she had almost made up her mind to stick to the footpath and go the long way around, when out of the corner of her eye she saw something shining. It was her brother's bike, lying just inside the wall of green, its front wheel still turning, and clamped beneath the carrier, their little sister's schoolbag. She waited for the wheel to stop spinning, and then all she could hear was the gorse as it ticked, and popped, and whispered in her ear. The bike's front forks pointed out the way they had taken and, abandoning the path, she stepped forward into the thicket to follow them.

Her brother heard her before he saw her, and by the time he saw her, it was too late, though at the first snap of a rotten twig in the undergrowth he had jerked himself up from where he knelt, and now he stood with his hands dangling stupidly at his sides. And there they suddenly found themselves—facing each other over the body of their younger sister who lay as he had taught her—one arm across her eyes, and her chubby legs splayed stiff as a doll's. Otherwise she held herself perfectly still.

The little girl, obedient and only half aware, heard the dry rattle of gorse bushes springing apart and closing together, and when she dared to open her eyes again, found herself all alone in the clearing where she lay for a long time staring up at the tiny patch of white sky above her head.

That night, under a fat moon, the centre of the thicket began to steam like a head of damp woolly hair, except that the air was terribly dry. The rats were the first to notice, then, quickly, all the other creeping, crawling, scurrying things (not the sleeping birds, who never even woke) began to run. Anyone watching at the perimeter, where rampaging gorse met tidy footpath and newly sealed road, would have seen what happened next. Rats, hundreds, thousands of them came pouring out of the thicket, falling over each other, squealing and biting in their panic to get away. They swarmed over the footpath and filled the street, and in a broad stream they followed the road as it wound up towards the state houses. Anyone watching would have seen the gorse at their backs bursting into sudden bloom, and great clouds of orange flowers rising up to meet the moon. The rats spread across the front lawns and into the backyards of the darkened houses. People turned over in their sleep at the stink of singed hair as the rats ran past beneath their windows. They ran on until they reached the bush-covered hills that towered behind the estate, and even within the safety of the tall trees, the rats never stopped running.

In the morning the people woke to see the charred remains of the thicket—all black and silver ash, and as flat as the footpath and the road that encircled it. Many had dreamt they heard thunder in the night and believed the fire had been started by lightning. One girl believed nothing and said less. One boy, on the brink of manhood, believed he had somehow escaped punishment for the evil he had done, until he went out on a day just before Christmas to burn rubbish in the rusting forty-four-gallon drum that squatted in the backyard.

First he loaded the drum with armfuls of cartons and newspapers, and the discarded exercise books of his sister's last year in primary school. Then he went back inside and took an over-sized box of matches from the window-sill above the kitchen sink. Outside again, he stood for a few seconds beside the overflowing drum and watched the wind page lazily through his sister's books (the handwriting was so neat), before he thrust his fingers, without looking, into the matchbox. Then he screamed and threw the box away as if he had been bitten. Attached to his thumb was a finger-length snake of bright green gorse, and more than an inch of thorn had gone in under his nail, embedding itself beyond the quick. He broke off the piece of gorse and shook it free, but the thorn remained. The boy sank to his knees in the dusty yard and clenched his hand between his thighs, blood from his pierced thumb welling as he howled out for somebody's sympathy or forgiveness.

But his mother was doing overtime, wondering how she was going to pay for Christmas, and his sisters were in their bedroom with the door shut, and the radio up as loud as it would go. And the wind paid no attention, but went right on fluttering the leaves of one of his sister's exercise books, went right on reading her story.

Lauren Holder

Lauren Holder was a member of the 1990 workshop. 'We Have Lost a Woman' was first published in the 1991 edition of the annual Blooms-bury anthology, *Soho Square*.

We Have Lost a Woman

Around in this garden there are a lot of empty flowers. She must be here somewhere, she must have been here. She must have wanted to be. And that's it, she wouldn't be here, but if someone brought her here, she wouldn't want to go back. But she would say nothing if they brought her back.

I brought her here a few times. The first time, she could walk in tiny shuffling steps with just my motivation to help her. The second time, I had to push her in the wheelchair everyone said she didn't need until someone put her in it and then nobody could get her out. It seemed she had no need for walking any more, I wonder why.

And when she got out into this garden, the garden overwhelmed her and she wouldn't talk to me, it was hard work. I thought up one thing to say and then another but they all sounded strange and out of context. And then she started bird-calling. It seemed she had quite a lot to say to birds, but I don't speak bird so I don't think I knew what she was talking about.

If you don't know what someone's talking about, you don't know what they're thinking about, do you? Sitting in the cloudy sky with the green grass bright and swarming at our feet like the starving millions, and the trees pulsing with the conversation of invisible birds, I had some idea, but I couldn't translate it and the information was of no interest to anyone anyway. And then I took her back because she was hard work and she had filled up all the time in the day that I had for her, which was fifty times as much as anyone else had for her and this was an unfortunate thing. She thanked me a hundred times, and she meant each one twice.

The other time I took her out to the garden, I had to push her up the driveway and the tyres were flat on the wheelchair and she weighed as much as two moas. Wasn't there a team of horses for this job? Don't trust me to do it all by myself, I'm not Popeye (the sailor man), gravity will drive her back over me and we will both be dead. But I struggled up against gravity and reached the flat bit and she wasn't worried and soon we were flooded with the smells of a million eager flowers, and they all wanted us to see them and we saw all of them.

She sucked the scent right out of them, she was excessive with them. Her method is very greedy and straightforward, she sticks her nose right in like it's a bee. She is greedy with her food, her manners are indelicate in this area also. But not to condemn her, there is a joy in watching her utilise all her senses, she doesn't waste them. She doesn't ignore them. She loves a good cooked chicken, she doesn't wait for it to go cold (like a lot of the others), she likes to see so she stares, she turns around to have a better look in town and my mother gets embarrassed. She has low self-monitoring, it could be said. She has eyes and a nose for the things around but no ear for social customs.

Once we have emptied the flowers in the hospital's garden, we drive across the road in the wheelchair to use up the council's ones. We throw caution to the wind, we drive like a racing wheelchair, we have become loosened and reckless, powered by the scent of so many gaudy flowers. We make it up the hill of the road easily. She can't reach the roses from her wheelchair this time, there is a moat of earth seeming to guard them from the likes of her so I have to tear them off at the necks and feed them to her.

My brother comes and helps, his jeans reach almost to the top of her white head, his hand arrives out of the blue sky with a different-coloured rose each time and stops at her nose and hovers there like a hummingbird. She takes a lot of feeding. I think this is because she is herself a flower. She acts like a greedy bird but she is only a friendly flower.

This explains too why in her younger and juicier days she would take the kids uptown and we would all be walking around and slightly behind her and she would at some stage not be there. Instead she would be walking down a dark, carpeted tunnel with the colours of dusty burgundy gleaming from a million corners, and then into a large and dark and round room full of tables, at each but one of which would be sitting other people's dusty old aunts. At the table with no aunt at it, there would be a tiny fluted glass with a waist so slender and elongated it was like a neck (I would hesitate to call it a stem for this word belongs to flowers). The glass would be like a star on a stage because a lonely yellow shaft of light would hold it in thrall like a spotlight and it would sparkle with a rich red light, like a lead chorus girl who has a tight round belly full of sherry.

She who we had come with would sit at this table with her green coat still on while we would stand around her, small and many and like her chicks, and watch her hand with the papery skin and tapered fingers wrap itself around the glass and lift it out of the limelight just like King Kong and the girl who kicked. King Kong's hairy hand lifted the girl-glass up to a mouth that was not King Kong's, but was the mouth of a moa, and the beak of a moa would dip into the hand-wrapped crystal glass and all its contents would be sucked into her mouth as if it were going up an escalator in buckets very fast.

And then, and then, she would relax on the chair like a daisy that had opened its petals because at last daylight had broken, and we would take our seats at the table like the small children of a daisy, but our petals were closed because it was dark in there and the colour of old blood was lying on everything.

But now it is time to take her back again for she must be stashed under a roof that is discontinuous with her life. We leave the council's roses but the flowers have bony arms which hold us in thorny, sentimental reluctance until I have the idea to take some with us, so I cut them off at their grabbing hands and decorate her with their fists.

I tuck their knobbly wrists into her lapel and into the crevices in her coat and when she is a fully decorated Buddhist shrine and I, as an Indian, am finished with my arranging in church, I turn the wheelchair around and aim it down the hill.

Thank you, she says, with such vehemence that it stands apart from all other utterances, in a museum case alone, this is what sincerity sounds like, sounded like.

Released from the council flowers at the top of the driveway, there is nothing to keep us away, except the fact that she would rather stay in the garden, but she doesn't say anything so I don't know exactly and anyway the garden she really wants to stay in is another garden. One in her past.

I deposit her back into the chair she has in the hospital lounge, she offers no resistance. I feel like I have driven her in in a wheelbarrow, she seems like an uprooted polyanthus with a clod of dirt around her feet, what is a polyanthus doing on that chair? I have driven up in my wheelbarrow and tipped it up on its end and she has fallen out, her yellow petals are papery, she has fallen on her side. She smiles at me from among a community of withered leaves, her smile is like a watery winter sun, I bend down and straighten her up. I ask her if she would like her handbag and of course she would. This is one of the few things we know about her. So I hang the beige handbag, which has not been uptown since it was young, on a furry green leaf and lean into the pale yellow petals and kiss the face that I find in there goodbye.

And I don't see her again, ever.

Anthony McCarten

Anthony McCarten was a poet when he took the 1983 Original Composition course. Subsequently he has become best known as a playwright (*Weed*, *Filth* and others, as well as *Ladies' Night*, which he co-authored with Stephen Sinclair). He has also published a volume of stories, *A Modest Apocalypse* (1991).

The May Bride

Who has ever lost something in a May
    as cold
    as an egg is smooth as the head of a bald man
    contemplating lifting his 65 kilo bride over the threshold?

Or have you smelt your lover approaching
    and it's stronger
    than a muscle man is cold saying 'I do' in church,
    and he is very cold, and bald?

I tell you, I have smelt mine going and it's very heavy
    and cold
    as May is to all heads that resemble eggs
    but it is pointless to pursue this.

However, I might as well,
    sensing a clarity smoother than you know what
    or a lost lover's indentation on a white pillow
    which is cold as a church in any month
    and, 'You shouldn't carry all those indentations
    in the same basket,' advises the wife of the man
    with the muscles over the garden fence.

Simply,
    the lifting of the 65 kilos
    went smoothly as an egg,
    and since those newly-weds moved in next door,
    and you've gone like May on a cross-town bus
    to an unheated church, I get about as much sleep
    as an indentation is bald.

Twenty-Two Winters Not Quite

Twenty-two winters not quite but the change
Between cold and day or hot and night is more
Than enough to make twenty-two seem like
A three-quarter consumed cake of chocolate and
Quite recently I started stubbing my long
Toes, reaching out of jandals, as nature
Began pitting its strength against movement.
Familiarity is the process of association,
Therefore the more articles or instances
I associate with another individual, the more
Familiar we become, not quite: familiarity
Breeds its own kind of ignorance and
Disenchantment as new becomes commonplace
So that the whole thing is an animal
Eating itself irrevocably to death, it seems.
But still, the point to it: I have never
Associated more. I have never been more
Familiar. And twenty-two has never seemed more
Like a three-quarter consumed cake
Of chocolate. Doctor, why is that?

Fifteen Poets

A selection of poems follows. Rather than interrupt with frequent biographical notes, I have simply noted the year in which each writer did the Victoria workshop at the foot of his or (more frequently) her poem. It is worth saying that Saut Situmorang is an Indonesian writer, writing in English as his second language, and that Jane Gardner acknowledges the example of the Glasgow poet, Frank Kuppner, for her poem.

Laurel Stowell

Heather Spoke of Marahau

Marahau, Marahau
When she spoke of Marahau
Her voice took on a lonely sound
Lonely valley Marahau

The hills enclose that valley now
The water flows through Marahau
The other people settled there
She never came to Marahau

Marahau, Marahau
When she spoke of Marahau
Her voice took on a distant sound
Lonely distant Marahau

1981

Alison Wong

The river bears our name

As the sun eases red over Pauatahanui
You stand alone at the Huangpu River
Layers of dust catch in our throat
The water is brown with years of misuse

You stand alone at the Huangpu River
Your card lies still open on the table beside me
The water is brown with years of misuse
I write out your name stroke upon stroke

Your card lies still open on the table beside me
A white ocean breeze slaps at my face
I write out your name stroke upon stroke
My hand is deliberate like that of a child

A white ocean breeze slaps at my face
You are more fluent in a foreigner's tongue
My hand is deliberate like that of a child
I lick the sweet envelope, seal up my word

You are more fluent in a foreigner's tongue
The heat of exhaust swallows your breath
I lick the sweet envelope, seal up my word
I know you will tear it, one trace of your eyes

The heat of exhaust swallows your breath
Layers of dust catch in our throat
I know you will tear it, one trace of your eyes
As the sun eases red over Pauatahanui

1995

Saut Situmorang

sleep cicak

sleep cicak though the walls are burning
let the chickens have a party on your ivory tail
sleep cicak sleep

sleep cicak on your ivory tail
let the chickens and the walls burn
sleep cicak sleep

sleep cicak sleep sleep cicak sleep
cicak sleep sleep sleep sleep cicak

cicak cicak on the walls
come come the chickens
the walls are burning on your ivory tail
sleep cicak sleep
and dream
the chickens have a party
on your ivory tail on the burning walls

cicak cicak on the walls sleep sleep

1992

'Cicak' is a small lizard that can always be found on house walls in Indonesia. If attacked, the cicak usually drops its tail, which keeps moving, to take the attacker's attention away from it. The word 'ci cak' (chee-chak) is an onomatopoeia for the sound this lizard makes.

Annora Gollop

To Mrs Bold from Little Gollop

I held that silver lizard until I mislaid it
and was covered in grief.

I held that silver lizard until the filigree of its memory
no longer matched the flattening detail of the silver.

I held that silver lizard until the silver lizard tail
bent and broke off and could not be kept
because the lizard became complete without it.

I held it until it lost its tail
I held it until its memory wore thin
I held it until it held within it death

And still I held it,
the gift of my childhood in silver.

1996

Betty Bremner

Piano on Petone Beach

This is a strange place for you Kirchner,
leaning gaunt on the sea wall

like an old emigrant yearning
toward Europe again, at the last,

the north wind freeholding
among your estranged strings

all your handsome housing gone
scathed by saltspray and the mindless sun.

I too remember the days of dancing,
the singing, the touch of hands,

a time when music was all
about us like a good omen.

Here is no melody save
the cadence of little unimportant waves.

1981

Catriana Mulholland

The Pass

all day, it snowed

the slow sky slipped
past the children
with their open
mouths, their dancing
fists, to settle
at the place I
could not find you.

I could not find
you. 'Ah, it shifts

it shifts,' the old
man later said.
'It drifts like heaps
of petals, love.
Today its teeth
are razor sharp.'

1990

Julia Wall

The High Commissioner's Bookshelf

Vanuatu, August 1990

I have just opened
Ovid's 'Erotic Poems'
Homer
Rips someone's dress off
And someone else asks to be taken:
The usual stuff.

As usual, I have over-done
And fallen asleep in the sun
Which no one bothered to correct.

I'm missing you more than I thought,
Or ought to
In the sunshine
Our life-together history
Gets the scrutiny.

1990

Andrew Loughnan

Leavings

I

It is a passport photo
taken in, I guess, the thirties.
Somewhat brown. He's just
got his degrees, just got

this job, and he is leaving
his homeland. Here he is:
thick brows, expectant gaze,
high forehead, rough fringe,

the moustache he never shaved
once he could grow it, and
behind that, the ill-set teeth.
The collar of his gaberdine

turned up, and a slouch,
he hides himself, he is
looking out at a wider
world that opens itself,

feeling the mental lurch
on the edge of the voyage.
The rest of his life
holds itself to him.

2

He comes home once, when on leave,
sees the same green countryside
he put aside years ago,
but bound to him by a strand

of memory and dialect.
Walking across a field
with his then wife, they discover
three children kicking in the grass.

Where are your parents, he asks.
They reply in Gaelic, so that
the field is unbound, knit back
again, with him outside.

3

He's a student living in Dublin, eyes drawn to a young
woman, blonde and bobbed, and she's drawn to him.
Time brings them together, there's talk of settling down,
there's mail.

Relationship long-distance: stretched to a thread, it snaps.
Somewhere overseas, he meets a sensible girl, leaving
the other one and her dangerous bob behind. All three
agree things have worked out as well as they may.
Although there is mail.

4

Measure procedure and practice.
Once he tried to brain a man
with an empty jar of ink.
Unwritten words tracing a graceful
parabola over the room.

5

A favoured scrap-book clipping:
'The man who plays the Irishman
is hardly convincing. Such a poor
attempt to speak the accent.'

Yes, he laughs, he's not real,
not convincing at all. Damn his
white collar! Damn Dublin!
Damn the Church of Ireland!

But also, perhaps, damn years
away, damn his years roaming
through the Empire, where
the standard voice came from

somewhere else, like London;
and his window now looks out
from the top of a hill toward
Golden Bay.

Perhaps a lack of conviction:
has he been anywhere that fits
its own romance? Born in
suburbia, and always returning.

6

Is this anything to pin him down?
The photo is fading, aging,
warping in my hands, and his youth
is long gone, only what I can

see and as quickly put a name to
before the word fades again:
liquid language—you
cannot hold it in your hands,

it's nothing as yielding as
the chemical bath
that gives me this image.
What is he really looking at?

Anything really? Anything
other than the reflection of light
off the lens, or the absence
of light behind the lens?

1996

Caren Wilton

Grandfather, 1931

I see him as he falls,
a big man, he is caught in the act of falling
and when he finds the ground he will be dead.
A horse steps backward in alarm:
someone else will drive the carriage today.
The stable boy sees him
and turns, mouth open, to run for help.
This is the dead man. He will not
go home tonight expecting dinner, he will not
ask are the younger children clean and ready for bed,
he will not watch the angry mouth of
his eldest daughter who would rather have her job
in the hat factory. She hates housework. She is angry that
her mother is dead and she must
stay home, look after the young ones,
wash and cook. She is missing out and she knows it.

Here he lies. Pigeons watch him
from the tiled roof, but his eyes are blank.
I watch him, I see the fall,
I see how he lands among scattered straw
and pieces of horse dung. It is not a fit place for a death, really.

I have the certificate.
At $5.50 it was a snip.
Here is his mother's name,
here his birthplace, his home, his job, here
they have listed the living children.
It does not say what he died of.
Here it is winter.

When I look up he is still beside me,
his big face,
his hands wide,
and the way he is falling and falling.

1995

Ross Hattaway

My Cranberry Hero

At the start of that part of my life
in which these things mattered
I thought of you as the original
No-holds bard:
Treehuts tears and tabbies from when
Your years were a trio
Sheets of rain of cotton
Shrouding your
Crises your
Tender sad-eyed angels.
Fuck was a pretty cool word to use a lot.
We thought so too.
And you
Who by turn were
Comic cosmic orgasmic
While making I's at the single ladies
As in
I feel this
I suffer that
Oh God I'm so sensitive.
You garbled and gobbled
But we never noticed the feathering fattening
For Thanksgiving approaching quickly.
We thought you were terrific.

1985

Matthew Goldie

Chicken

Chicken

is not half as difficult
As it looks.
With one fell swoop
We can catch the

pizza

And look like the part
Which we most admire.
Do not apply too much salt
When using a

spoon

though.
The general idea is to use
Your discretion in everything
And not meddle with

Anything

which is not there.
I have tried to keep
The recipes at their
Easiest

to

allow the
Natural flavour
Of the vegetables
To come

through.

If you want to
Add anything to them
Depending on your taste
Then feel free.

1988

Virginia Fenton

Survival Strategies of the Young

Our last house guest was tidy
and hungry. Alice ate no bread
with her jam. Rent was paid in ten
cent pieces and stolen property.
She came in through a window
and left when we showed her how
to operate the door. Alice caught the bus
out of town, taking nothing of ours she
couldn't carry. Later, she will learn
the difference between right and wrong
and literature.

1994

Wanda Barker

On tracks to be with angels

the train approached in the crisp morning light
jackie johnson
told
her
sister
brother
cousin
she
wanted
'to be with the angels'

she was struck and killed
by the freight train

ronald wright ruled the death a suicide
today
the
youngest
ever
recorded

for the rest of the day jackie's family
friends
neighbours
struggled
to
understand
why one so young would ever end her life.

perhaps it was her mother's terminal illness

the kids
jackie 6
stephateria 7
valerius fox 8
were staying with gloria wright to finish school

she never talked about her problems

'i told her to get off the train tracks'
said lakita wimberly 7
she said
'no i don't want to i want to die'
with her back to the train she waited.

1993

Jane Gardner

Kitchen, Morning

Here is the kitchen of a house in Mount Victoria,
Forties cream and green with a big wooden table.
Two old people and their little daughter eat here.
A little dog sits on the stairs over there.

The stairs leave the kitchen like a shaft of darkness.
Up them is a living room no one uses much.
There are books, an empty sofa, a sewing machine,
A twangly piano that the child is exiled to.

She prefers to come back down to the kitchen
Where the colour of the lino suddenly reminds her
Of the scummy green colour of polluted Tiber water
In Rome, where she went in 1977.

She arrives back in the kitchen in 1956,
And has breakfast with her father before he goes to work.
He wears a dull suit, a boring tie, a moustache
Dark from smoking. They eat in friendly silence.

These are radio days. Dad listens to the News.
The BBC Home Service is the best news to get.
It has a strange echo sound, the man talks under water.
It goes on for a very, very, very long time.

The news says lots of things about the Suez Canal.
Dad came here in '29, but still claims he's English.
He starts to go on about the end of Britain's greatness.
His daughter doesn't want the news to upset him.

The announcer has a very nice British-sounding voice.
Dad sounds like a New Zealander except when he's angry.
Then you can tell he's a Londoner, really.
He says 'bloody' and 'Mondee', and 'fire injin red'.

The child is a New Zealander and wishes she were English.
This is because she loves her father best.
Her mother is the parent who hits her with a stick (a lot).
Her mother is the person who speaks the mother tongue.

Mum's proud she's a *third* generation Kiwi,
But she calls England 'Home' and is a snob about accents.
If the little girl says 'mulk', her mother corrects her,
'Milk!'   The child is allergic to milk.

Dad will be leaving for work in a minute.
Mum is crashing noisily, she does this every morning.
The child asks her father how the man on the radio
Knows to stop talking when someone turns it off.

Dad explains about radio waves. They can't get in
If the radio's off. The child has a thought of little lost birds.
Her father says 'Cheerio', and goes out of the house.
'Don't forget to pick up the meat,' says his wife.

Now it's time for the child to walk to school.
It seems to be a very, very, very long way.
Some radio waves flap about in the sky,
Crying bitterly. Many of them live near here.

1995

Miro Bilbrough

Nuclear Family Album:
Rongelap 1954–

After the documentary 'Half Life'

Your sons were fixed into photographs
still
breathing.

Here
your son removes his shoes,
decorous,
before he steps inside the iron room.

Here
five men,
—your sons—
step out in double-breasted suits
their skin like burnout
in the emulsion.

Here
your sons' eyes are dreaming in American.

Once a year their doctors tourist your innards.

You have a daughter
that tumid flower her head.
You remember the alien snow
—*National Geographic* fallout—
where your children played.
These are the photographs they never made.

1988

Joy Cowley

Joy Cowley is renowned as a writer of fiction for adults and children, and—especially in North America—as a teacher of creative writing. This informal talk is one she has recently used in workshops for writers for children.

Developing a Plot

I was with a group of seven- and eight-year-old authors who were comparing notes on writing. Questions and answers went back and forth, and someone mentioned 'plot'.

'What is plot?' I asked, not expecting a reply. They were, after all, very young.

Up shot a hand, and a small boy said, 'It's a kind of problem which gets solved.'

Well, I've seen some long and convoluted adult definitions of plot but that's about as clear as it comes. Plot is some kind of problem which gets solved. In a plot something happens and the resolution of that happening comes at the end of the story. It's so simple, and yet we can miss it. Sometimes we write stories with plots so slight they don't hold the weight of words we put on them. Or we write stories which have themes but virtually no plot at all.

And here is another definition for you. This time it came from a high-school writing class, students of fourteen and fifteen. I asked them, 'What is the difference between theme and plot?'

Back came the reply, 'The theme is what the story is about and the plot is what happens.'

Again, this is a very clear definition. I can write something for children on the theme of patriotism, loneliness, greed, kindness. I can write on the theme of celebration—Hanukkah or Christmas. But theme is not plot. Plot is what happens within this theme. And if there is no plot, I do not have a story, I have an essay or a vignette. Plot is essential to story. It gives the story its movement.

Now, stories have different lengths, according to the complexity of the plot and the number of characters. On one hand, we might have a 300-word text for a picture book for pre-school children. Another idea might lead to a 30,000-word novel for young adults.

Every idea dictates its format and its length. But whatever we are writing, the movement of the story will be carried by the plot.

Novels require more complex plotting but at the moment, let us imagine that we are writing a story for younger readers. We are looking at the traditional three-part story—beginning, middle, end. All of these are concerned with the unravelling of the plot but we use the arbitrary divisions to describe how we deal with the plot—the way we pace it.

The beginning of the story introduces characters and setting. It lifts the curtain on the stage and brings out the actors. It's in the beginning of the story that we set up all those props we are going to need for the story. For example, if your character is going to escape by picking the lock of a door with a safety pin, some mention of the safety pin needs to come early in the story. Generally, the reader feels cheated if we introduce these elements as coincidence near the end. So, in effect, the beginning of the story can be compared with a musical overture. It gives the reader a lot of information and the enticement to read on. But it is also introducing the main action of the story.

The pace of the beginning is sometimes slowed with description. When pacing our plot, we remember that adjectives and long sentences will slow the action down. Verbs and shorter sentences will increase the speed. As we move into the middle of the story, the part where it is all happening, we use language to match the pace. The easier style of the early sentences picks up speed. In the most dramatic part of our story, our language is terse, almost breathless. But this doesn't mean that the big dramatic moment in a story should be dealt with briefly. All too often this happens. As readers we spend a long time getting to the 'crunch' of the tale only to discover that it is dealt with in two sentences. If my character falls from a yacht into a rough sea, I cheat the reader if I state baldly that he fell in the sea and was nearly drowned. I can pad that action out, maybe over one or two pages, giving a terse and fast-moving account of my character's struggles. After all, this is the main action in the story. I must not dismiss it or trivialise it.

We come to the end of our story. The drama has been resolved. There has been a well-constructed solution to the problem. The pace of the language can be relaxed. This final wind-up is brief and it leaves the reader feeling satisfied.

At this point we might look at the beginnings and endings of our stories and see how they are affected by the writing process. No matter how well we construct our plots, we always have a tendency to begin before the beginning and end after the ending. I think that this is because writing takes place on several levels. Externally, we are tapping at the word processor or moving a pen on paper. In our heads, we are constructing sentences and running mental spelling checks. But there is also a deep inner movement which comes to the fore as the story takes over and we begin to live it in the telling. You all know what I mean. Once we get down to that deep inner journey, the story seems almost to write itself. But in the process of getting to that stage we can write material which will not be part of the final story. Rather, it is a part of the warming-up stage. When you are editing, check your first few paragraphs and see where your story really does begin. In the same way, it can take us a little while to wind down when the story is finished. We come to the end but tend to keep on writing. Find out where the true ending of your story is.

We've looked at the pacing of plot and at beginnings and endings. Let us now look at credibility. A plot must be credible. It must follow logical development even if the story is fantasy. Our plots should not rely heavily on coincidence. Coincidence marks a weak plot. There should be a sort of inevitability about the development of the story as it moves from one stage to another.

I once wrote a picture-book story about a city school that got washed away in a flood. It was swept down a flooded freeway and into a harbour and was eventually rescued and towed back by a helicopter. The illustrator did a picture of the helicopter pilot throwing a rope out of his window and at such an angle that it was going to tangle in the rotor. I pointed out that this was not the way helicopters lifted or towed objects. The illustrator said that since the book was fantasy anyway, he couldn't see a problem. Well, no matter how wild the fantasy, it must still be attached to credibility if it is going to work. The illustrator eventually saw this and the picture was changed.

Another example concerned an early reading book which came to my attention. It was a story about a robot who ate too much, got too fat and had to go to aerobics. That doesn't work. Children know that robots don't eat and don't put on weight as people do and some young readers have a lot of difficulty with this book.

Let us give our plots the credibility test. Are they believable? Inexorable? Do they work like well-oiled machines?

It's all very well to talk about ideals, but how do we develop a good plot?

We come back to our seven- and eight-year-old authors who have a problem which I, as an adult, used to share. I would hear something, see something and suddenly wheels would spin, bells would ring and I would have a great idea for a story. I'd rush for a pen or typewriter and make a start. But after a bold beginning, the bells would stop ringing and the wheels would seize up. A few sentences and I would be frozen. Most young authors have had this experience. They get a great idea, start writing and stop after two or three sentences.

So, what is the problem? Simply this—we confuse an idea with a plot. An idea is not a plot. It is the seed of a plot and it needs a lot of nurturing, a lot of growth, before it can be usefully employed.

My own technique for helping an idea to grow is to keep playing with it, examining possibilities, asking questions, looking for characters. Any character we use is bound to be an extension of ourself with disguises added. The only characters who come from outside ourselves are the ones who aren't real. If you have written a believable character, you can be sure he or she or it is autobiographical. Once you establish your characters, the plot will develop in leaps and bounds, quite naturally. If you find that your plot is not developing as it should, back up a little. You may have the wrong character or be asking the wrong questions. Consider options. Try some lateral thinking and a different approach. Or maybe you are just tired. Writing takes a lot of energy and the term 'writer's block' is often just a euphemism for flat batteries. Take a day off, have an early night and come back to offer your writing peak energy. See what a difference that makes.

For shorter works, I tend to do all the plot development in my head. It sits there, growing like some cerebral pregnancy until it gets to the stage where I can't hold it any longer. It must be born. That is the time for writing it down. But by then I know the characters so well that if they knocked on the door, I would invite them in for coffee, and the development of the story is complete to the ending.

Some authors prefer to develop their plots with notes and character description on paper. Others, like me, do short stories in their heads. Choose the method which suits you best.

So far, I have been talking mainly about shorter works—stories and picture books. Let's give some attention now to the longer work— non-fiction and novels. For both fact and fiction we have much the same concerns—effective arrangement of material, dramatic move- ment, the rise and fall of events.

With shorter works we are usually concerned with one plot. It is simple and linear to fit the disciplines of limited space. In the full- length work our major plot often has other dramatic happenings or plots weaving in and out, and these minor plots all affect each other and the main plot, and all help the story to progress. Needless to say, full-length books are not usually planned in one's head, but worked out in outline, on paper first.

I can't remember ever reading a novel which wasn't in chapter form. There is no reason, from the reader's point of view, why a full- length work should be broken down into chapters. Obviously the convention was invented by authors to help them plan a book, and I'm sure it's no coincidence that chapters are about the length of a short story—each a manageable size—and that chapters usually have short-story shape—beginning, middle and ending—within the larger context.

With a full-length work, it is essential to know the characters very well indeed, before making a start. To some extent these characters will dictate the action. Some of the events that we had intellectually planned for our plot get changed by our characters, who refuse to obey our commands. When we know our characters, how they talk, eat, sleep, think, then we put them into situations to see how they react. As always, the most important part of the writing takes place before we get near the word processor—in our head.

When I plan a novel, the main plot comes first. Then one, two or three sub-plots suggest themselves. As I continue to plan the work, I see how the overall action has a natural rise and fall of time and movement which can be divided into chapters. As all this develops, the work will suggest the best way of presenting itself. Will the viewpoint be through one person? If yes, will it be told in the first person? Or third person? Will I have the reader see through the eyes of several characters? Or will there be an eye-of-God view over everything? Each method has its advantages and its restrictions.

Finally, I would like to share with you the process I go through with each work, whether it be a short story, novel or a picture book.

1. I have an idea for a story. I test it. Is it a strong original idea? Worth keeping?

2. I seek solitude and time to develop the idea.

3. What will be the final form of this idea? Early reader? Picture book? Early chapter book? Middle-grade fiction? Adult short story? Novel? The idea itself will suggest the age of the reader and its final form.

4. I expand the idea by asking questions of it. I keep turning it in my mind. A neglected idea will go cold.

5. At each stage of development I test the idea against real life, especially against my childhood and the children I know, to see if it sounds authentic.

6. I build the backbone of the story first—the plot. Everything else in the story will hang from this spine.

7. When the story line is so real to me that it has a life of its own, I start writing. I write freely, totally absorbed in giving birth to the story within me.

8. I edit, trimming away material which does not further the plot and perhaps adding where impact is lacking.

9. No matter how eager I am to display my new creation, I put the work away for a week or even a month, before I do the final editing. I need that space to emotionally disconnect myself from the story. Once I have 'fallen out of love' with it, my critical sense is sharpened and I can evaluate the work objectively.

10. I send the story out to stand on its own feet in a world busy with stories, and I avoid eye contact with the mailbox by immersing myself in another work.

A number of workshop graduates—Helen Beaglehole, Eirlys Hunter, Anne Ingram, Julie Leibrich and Pat Quinn among them—have had considerable success as children's writers; and children's writing has been an element in the Original Composition course over a long period. Most years we have been visited by Brent Southgate, editor of Parts One and Two of the *School Journal*. Brent talks about the particular requirements of writing for younger children, and usually sets an exercise—often something he is short of for the *Journal*, a folktale adaptation, for example, or a classroom play. Johanna Mary (see also 'Translation', p.290 in 'The Exercise Chapter') wrote 'Noise Biscuits' during the 1991 workshop, and it subsequently appeared in the *School Journal*.

Johanna Mary

Noise Biscuits

People in the Play:	*Noises in the Play:*	
MUM	CAT'S MEOW	HANDS CLAPPING
ROSE	DOOR'S CREAK	SPARROW'S CHIRP
MARCUS	WIND'S WHISTLE	SANTA'S LAUGH
	GUINEA PIG'S SQUEAK	PLUGHOLE'S SLURP

SCENE: ROSE *and* MARCUS *are in the kitchen. On the bench in front of them is a bowl, a spoon, an oven tray—and eight jars.* MUM *comes in.*

MUM   Rose! Marcus! What are you doing?
ROSE   Baking.
MARCUS We're making noise biscuits.
MUM   What on earth are noise biscuits?
ROSE   They're delicious.
MARCUS They're made from noises.
MUM   I've never heard of them.

ROSE	Come and watch us.
MARCUS	We'll show you how to make them.
MUM	Don't make a mess.
ROSE	Of course not, Mum.
MARCUS	Noise biscuits don't make any mess.
ROSE	All you need is a bowl.
MARCUS	And a spoon.
ROSE	And an oven tray.
MARCUS	And some noises.
ROSE	We got these noises today.
MARCUS	We put them in these jars.
ROSE	In this jar, we put the cat's meow.
MARCUS	Listen. [*Opens lid.*
CAT'S MEOW	M–e–e–e–o–w.
MUM	That's incredible! How did you get the meow in the jar?
ROSE	Well, first you have to get the cat to meow into it.
MARCUS	But the hardest bit is getting the lid on again quickly enough, so the meow doesn't escape.
ROSE	In this jar, we put a door's creak. [*Opens lid.*
DOOR'S CREAK	Cr–ee–ee–aa–aak.
MARCUS	In this jar, we put the wind's whistle. [*Opens lid.*
WIND'S WHISTLE	Woo–oo–oo–ooo.
ROSE	In this jar, we put a guinea pig's squeak. [*Opens lid.*
GUINEA PIG'S SQUEAK	E–eek–eek–eek.
MARCUS	In this jar, we put some hands clapping. [*Opens lid.*
HANDS CLAPPING	[*Loud clapping.*
ROSE	In this jar, we put a sparrow's chirp. [*Opens lid.*
SPARROW'S CHIRP	Cheep–cheep–cheep.
MARCUS	In this jar, we put Santa's laugh. [*Opens lid.*
SANTA'S LAUGH	Ho–ho–ho.
ROSE	And in this jar, we put the plughole's slurp. [*Opens lid.*
PLUGHOLE'S SLURP	[*A long loud slurping sound.*
MUM	I'm impressed.
ROSE	Now we mix them together. Marcus, you put them in, while I hold the bowl.
MARCUS	Right-oh.

MARCUS *empties the jars into the bowl one by one.*

CAT'S MEOW M–e–e–e–e–o–w.

DOOR'S CREAK Cr–ee–ee–aa–aak.

WIND'S WHISTLE Woo–oo–oo–ooo.

GUINEA PIG'S SQUEAK E–eek–eek–eek.

HANDS CLAPPING [*Loud clapping.*

SPARROW'S CHIRP Cheep–cheep–cheep.

SANTA'S LAUGH Ho–ho–ho.

MARCUS And last but not least . . .

PLUGHOLE'S SLURP [*A long loud slurping sound.*

ROSE Now I mix them all together with the spoon.

MARCUS This is the noisiest bit.

ROSE Yeah. You might like to block your ears, Mum.

MARCUS Ready, set, GO!

All the noises sound together as ROSE *stirs for a while.*

ROSE OK! I think that's enough!

ROSE stops stirring and all the noises stop.

MUM Can I unblock my ears now?

ROSE *and* MARCUS Yes.

ROSE Now we just put little blobs of mixture on this oven tray.

MARCUS And flatten them with the back of the spoon.

ROSE And put them in the oven.

MARCUS They'll be cooked in about half an hour.

MUM Well, that's amazing. May I have the recipe?

Jo Randerson

Jo Randerson is best known as a playwright, and in particular for her work with the theatre group Trouble. She took the Original Composition course in 1996.

The Knot

On Thursday the large girl woke with a small knot in her hair.

Her mother slipped her a comb.

Her father said, 'Not in my house.' (And there was.)

At school the teacher said, 'Fight with the lawnmower, was it?' The large girl smiled but inside she thought, 'What an old, dumb joke.'

By Friday the knot was huge.

> 'Get out of my hair,' the girl said to the knot.
> 'Get out of mine,' the knot replied.

The teacher sent a note home.

> messy hair
> is
> the devil's work

Saturday passed.

By Sunday she had given the knot a name. It was Shirley. The brother of the large girl offered her $2.50 if she sold Shirley to him. The large girl laughed. It was a big laugh. She didn't feel stupid.

On Monday, in the morning, her father said, 'It's the comb or the belt.'

Mum said although she had nothing personal against the knot she had to side with Dad and the belt. The large girl used the back door.

At school the teacher, who secretly feared his conversation was becoming repetitive, sent her to the headmistress.

The headmistress said, 'Today a knot, tomorrow you'll be pregnant. I've seen it all before.'

Shirley started running. The large girl tangled in her hair came with her. By Thursday she was pregnant.

GIRLS: LISTEN TO YOUR TEACHERS.

Why Our Washing Machine Broke

On the first day of school, I missed my mother. I had home-made beef-roast sandwiches but I missed her. There she was at home-time and it was all OK, all of it.

On the second day of school, I missed my mother. I had home-made beef-roast sandwiches but I still missed her. At home-time she was five minutes late but it was all still OK, it was all pretty much OK.

On the third day of school, it was making me cry. There was no beef-roast today and the school lunches tasted yucky. My mother came at home-time but the luncheon taste was in my mouth, pinky smelly luncheon and it tasted yuck.

On the fourth day of school, they gave me poison. I am sure of it. I was sick all day and sick when I got home. My teacher said it was nothing. My mother said it would pass. The poison said eat me, eat me all up. Grandma said you should do what you were told.

The next day I got very confused. When I tried to draw a seagull, it just looked like a straight line and I didn't understand how that big wooden box could be called a horse. When I looked around everyone was bigger and taller than me, and I felt a little dribble of something come out of my ear. I felt sick and I couldn't eat my meatloaf. I got told off. I had to eat all the leftovers.

That night while I was sleeping my brains leaked all over the sheets. My mother was angry that she had to wash them but she said it wasn't my fault. It is no one's fault. Some of us are just dumber than others. Some of our needs are very special indeed.

Pat Quinn

Pat Quinn writes fiction for adults and radio drama, but is best known for her work for children. Her novel, *The Value of X*, won the 1994 AIM Senior Fiction Award, and her other fiction includes the *Shortland Street* spin-off, *Kirsty & Lionel*. 'There's More to a Dog's Life than Bones' was written during the Original Composition course in 1990.

There's More to a Dog's Life than Bones

I've got this thing about gaps. It struck me one day when I was walking round Oriental Bay with the dog. We crested on an invisible wave that pushed people to either side, out of Pedro's range. They reformed behind us, joggers to the left, pushchairs to the right and skateboards knitting purl, plain, purl and turn in the middle.

Pedro and I were enjoying this, swooping across the pavement and watching the seas shift, until someone stepped in our space.

—Fuck off, I said.

He was thin and acned, pitted with my past. He bared his teeth and growled at the dog. Pedro growled back and swished his tail.

—Go on, Pedro. Eat the bugger.

But the dog backed up to a caged tree and squatted out his feelings.

—Haven't seen you for ages, Acne said.

—No, I said. Used to be that a girl could walk unmolested, but here he was with his arm around my neck so far it dangled on my breast. I bit it.

—Ah, I knew a girl who could bite like that, he said, waving a hello with the limb at a passing pram. —She had legs up to her breasts and knockers to her knees. Whatta girl.

—She got pregnant.

—Yeah, I was going to talk to you about that.

We weren't going anywhere without Acne so I turned round and we walked back. The fountain heaved up with a wet ejaculation.

—So, what's new? Acne revived a piece of gum that had wedged somewhere in his splintered teeth and chewed noisily.

—I mean, he expanded, what goes down?

We'd reached the takeaway caravan and I stopped to let Pedro clear the footpath of squashed snow freezes and lost buns.

Norman leaned out of the stable door and said hi, Nancy, like he always does, but with Acne wrapped tight to tit I didn't feel free to talk.

—Gotta go, Norm, I said.

Norman nodded and let it pass, this time.

The flat had been cleaned up, which made a nice change, but whoever did it took most of my belongings with them. There was a note from Gracie stuck with a slab of honey to the gap where the fridge had been.

—Who's Gracie?

—Nobody you'd know.

Gracie was big with the bailiffs, but the note said she'd run out of favours. I let Pedro clean off the honey, the last food I could afford.

Acne wound his tongue into my ear and tested my elastic, but I was deafened by saliva, and in case he thought to ask, said no, anyway. He had things in the right places but nothing in a bank account. A man with no security.

They don't like returns down at the SPCA.

—We checked you out, they said.

—It wasn't Pedro's fault, I said, he did his best. Ate vegetarian for the last three weeks.

They put him in a kennel and said welcome home in a kind but unnecessary way and added that it was coming up Christmas. A knell of doom for large crossed dogs.

—Hitch them to a sleigh, I said, for the James Smith Christmas Parade.

Christ, recyclable reindeer and full dog employment right there on their doorstep, but they wouldn't file the patent. No sense of occasion when you're killing them with kindness and Pentothal.

It was a long journey. Too many gaps in the traffic, though middle-aged matrons drive north out of Johnsonville every five minutes.

It was a panel van that stopped. Regular trade, that's the best, but it falls off every time there's a story running against hitchhikers. I told the driver about the one I knew.

—There's this girl, see, hitches a ride north of Bulls on her way to Hamilton. I'll take you to Taupo, the driver says, that's as far as I'm going. So he drives her to Taupo and she says Keep going or I'll say you raped me.

—Ha! The panel van man banged his palms on the steering wheel. —Is that it?

—Not quite.

—Well go on then.

—Okay. So the driver says Like hell I will and drives straight to the police station.

The panel van man grinned. He wiped his mouth on the back of his hand. He steered for a while with one hand and rubbed the other on the thigh of his jeans, where the denim was thin and pale like his hands.

—Yeah? he said.

—The police say Take her to Hamilton.

—They say what? He brought his hand back up to the steering wheel and wrestled the van into a corner where the camber curved the other way. —They say what?

—Take her to Hamilton. If she holds the charge against you we'll have to bring you in, investigate you, get a court case going, and waste everyone's time. So he took her to Hamilton.

The van man thought about that for a while. He changed down and passed a Mitsubishi and a Honda. The drivers were middle-aged women with their eyes on the road.

—Is that a true story?

—Yeah, happened to a friend of mine.

He nodded and swallowed and his Adam's apple escalated up and down. First floor lingerie and cosmetics. —I'm going as far as Palmie, he said.

He let me out in the Square and stood soup and toast at the Cake Kitchen.

—Good luck, he said.

—Watch your back, I told him.

Then it was short hops with businessmen and a stretch in a ute where the dogs eyed me suspiciously and grinned their teeth.

Acne picked me up at Manui. He said he'd borrowed a car from a friend but I recognised the sports job that used to park at the end of my street. He'd taken a chance, he said, on the Hawk-infested Foxton Straight and they were out to get him now, but he'd done it all for love.

I told him I didn't care, which was only partly true. My mother said never put your trust in a man because look where it got her and she was right.

A robust woman, my father used to say, give me a hand with the freezer. The truck. Carry me to bed, you're as steady as a rock. Dependable, my mother was, until she changed the locks and Mavis Briggs moved in.

—I'm not having a bloody lesbian in my home! my father shouted through the cracks in the floor.

—You've had one for years, my mother said and struck him between the eyes with a broom handle. She said she'd hunted her psyche all the way back to childhood, where she'd worked day and night to please her dad, but all he would say was that nothing beats the love of a good woman. Once she met Mavis, she knew it was true.

There were twenty dollars in the glovebox and coins rattling in the doors so we left the car in Taihape, behind the bank where it didn't look too out of place, and caught the bus.

I hummed a tune as the pastel shacks slipped by and the wheels beat the rhythm, but the old tart in the seat behind hit me on the head and the treble cut out.

—Hey! I said. Don't hit me! But she pretended to be asleep. She didn't fool me. I could see the spittle getting sucked back in every time she blew it out, and now and then the tongue came out to help.

Acne lifted my legs off the bench seat and draped them across his knee. His fingers ran absent-mindedly into my crotch and the old tart rose up.

—Driver! These two are having it off!

I was shocked. She was a good sixty years old and daft with it.

The driver waved at her in the mirror and said How's it going? She rested her elbows on the back of the seat and hung over us all the way there. A trip down Memory Lane.

It was getting dark when we got off, and cold. I'd changed my mind about it several times but Acne was adamant.

—I haven't seen her for years, he said.

In fact he hadn't seen her at all, an oversight he seemed to have forgotten. We walked across the main road and into the gloomy lights of the shopping mall.

It hadn't changed; Pepsi posters were starters in the slow crawl off the walls and the optimistic flowering tubs were spiked with bare-branched skeletons. At the back of the supermarket, Ranfurly Road slithered into the darkness of smashed and burned-out street lighting. Closer up, the footpath budded with pregnant green rubbish bags and the dogs played piddle and sniff.

Mavis opened the door.

—Oh god, she said. It's you. She squinted against the porch light, —and who else?

—Me, said Acne. I'm the father.

The door closed, breathing onions and warm air into our faces.

—What did I do? Acne asked. We waited while spiders clambered up towards snow-blind moths.

The door opened with a bang that unseated the insects. It opened so wide that it bounced shut again and my mother had to begin the movement a second time.

—So, she said when she'd wrestled the door to a decent position, this is he?

She'd once had a part in a medieval play at college level and the language had gone to her head.

Acne played for the crowds.

—It is I, he responded.

My mother reached out and hooked a finger into the front of his shirt. She tugged. Acne leaned dangerously far forward, but not far enough and two buttons resigned.

—Enter, she said.

She hoisted him up the front step and into the hallway. I followed into the back bedroom.

—See here, she said, which she amended to: Behold the babe.

We beheld.

Tracy was asleep. She lay outstretched on her back, arms wide, head turned in to the pink rabbits that pyjama-danced down her shoulder and disappeared under the moons and stars on the bedspread.

—Ah. Acne hovered over the small round face, searching maybe for inheritance.

—Go, said my mother, grounding him with a yank on his waistband.

—You're a hard woman, Acne said.

—You got what you came for.

—Not exactly. Acne looked at me in a way that I remembered. Hope and expectation and pig-headed optimism were all there. I was in the starting blocks, but my mother jumped the gun.

—She's mine, she said. Legally adopted to me and Mavis. Mavis, subpoenaed, materialised in the room and smiled.

My mother's heart softened to a spreading consistency.

—You, my child, may stay. Help out with the housework.

They relented enough to let Acne have the toolshed, where I joined him in a rug. It wasn't what I'd intended, but then nothing ever is.

I worked things out after that, crawling round the old cracked lino with a hot bucket of Handy Andy and rubber gloves. My childhood was wedged into that floor. Sunday roasts and school sandwiches when the going was good, and crayons after school. They called me Aunty Win in front of the baby because although a child needs a mother she had a surfeit if you counted Mavis, and she wouldn't be called Dad.

I lasted there a week. Then I phoned Gracie and said I'm coming back.

—Where is the stamina of youth? my mother asked. She knew it wouldn't last, but I was full of holes and being home slowed down the seepage.

—Where is last month's rent? said Gracie. She was still in the flat. Empty and barren as it was, she was calling it home.

My mother pressed a twenty-dollar note into my palm as she shook hands with me.

Mavis enfolded me in a bosomy hug.

—I think of you as a son, she said.

When I got back I called in at the SPCA, just in case. The place was full of puppies, seasonal mistakes with feet like Christmas stockings.

Acne was there, hosing out the kennels. The water swept the shit and piss out of the door where I was standing. It rose up over my shoes and climbed into my socks.

—A man's gotta live, he said, and flashed ten dollars at me. I showed him mine, a queen to his ten.

—Screw you, I said.

—I've got a place, he said, and he had, over the hardware shop on the main road. —The SPCA pays the rent but the bed's got lumps.

—Sleep in the gaps, Acne says, but I can't.

Pedro's coat was smooth, rippled over his ribs like corrugations on a road.

I'd rather sleep alone.

Catherine Chidgey

Catherine Chidgey took the Original Composition course in 1995. 'An Impression of Flowers' is a self-contained excerpt from her novel, *In a Fishbone Church*, which will be published in 1998.

An Impression of Flowers

Etta is running through a field. To the left and right of her are flowers. Tulips, irises, daphne, beds of lavender, all blooming at once. She does not find this odd. Her feet vibrate the ground. Pollen falls.

There are drawers and drawers in Etta's room. They are crammed with white pillowcases, made by her mother, Maggie, before she became engaged to Etta's father. Maggie never went to school; she was raised to be a lady. At home she was taught needlepoint, and crochet, and the art of conversation. She began making her trousseau at age thirteen, and by the time she met Owen she had a dozen hem-stitched supper cloths with matching napkins (linen), twenty-six embroidered tray cloths, eighteen nightdresses (smocked, pure cotton), four dozen fine lace handkerchiefs, twelve pairs of double sheets (lace-edged, linen), ten crocheted milk-jug and sugar-bowl covers (beaded), two dozen pairs of cotton bloomers trimmed with lace, and forty embroidered pillowcases (crewelled).

Fortunately, Owen's house had a lot of space where things could be tucked away.

Etta does not know how many pillowcases there are in her room, exactly. She knows there are enough for her to use a different one every day for a month, and still not have used them all. She has tried this.

They are all embroidered with flowers. A discreet bunch in a corner, usually, or slim garlands, or a ring around a butterfly. More occasionally, an initial. They smell of mothballs.

Etta thinks they are very beautiful. She can't imagine how her mother had the patience; Maggie is not a patient woman, on the whole. Etta sleeps with her cheek on the stitching, and when she wakes there is an impression of flowers on her skin. In the mirror the patterns are the right way around, the same as on the pillowcases. This is all as it should be.

They fade in the bath, and by the time the steam has cleared from the mirror they have gone. Etta can go down to breakfast then, and nobody will say a thing.

She would not call herself a secretive person, but there are some things one simply does not discuss. This is not lying, exactly, but it can lead to a certain awkwardness. She creeps out at night, sometimes, and goes for a walk.

She walks down the sharp drive in bare feet. The house grows smaller behind her. It is a relief to reach the road. She avoids the edges, with their dark macrocarpas, choosing instead to walk right down the middle. It is the safest place.

Mr Blumenfeld, their German neighbour, sits at the piano in his front room. Sometimes Etta thinks she can hear him playing, but she's not sure. Sometimes he just sits there staring at it, his hands folded in his lap.

She strolls past the swings, which are always deserted after about five o'clock. She supposes it is the sort of place odd people might go, but she has never seen any. At the other side of the field is the stream. It is the same one that flows through their farm, but it is wider and deeper here. Sometimes it floods. A few years ago a boy was swept away, and all his mother could do was watch, but Etta does not remember this very well. She crosses the field. It belongs to nobody. A couple of years ago there was talk of planting it with potatoes for the War Effort, but nothing was done about it.

Etta is not afraid of the stream (she should be). She paddles in it during her walks. There are no sharp stones. Then she goes back through the field, and past the swings, and home. She creeps in the back door, which is never locked, and up the back stairs. She knows to start with her left foot, otherwise the ninth stair creaks. Then she sleeps.

It is almost spring. Already some lambs have been born, and there have been the usual tragedies. Up until now, Etta's father, Owen, has always given her one of the motherless lambs to look after, and it has always been called Topsy. Nobody has mentioned that there is a new Topsy every year, and that she never gets any older. This year, Owen tells Etta that she can choose her own lamb.

She goes to the sweet-smelling shed and offers a finger to a moist bundle. It stands up, sucking, fluttering its tail.

'I'll call her Dandelion,' says Etta. She inserts the teat of a bottle into the pink hole. One of the farm cats curls around her legs, then springs off to a corner, where it has spotted a mouse.

'Not Topsy?' says Owen.

'Dandelion.'

Owen lights his pipe. 'Well, don't go getting too attached, love, will you. She'll have to go out with the rest of them next year, when she's bigger.'

Etta is aware of her clothes tightening. The stitches in her jersey are pulling sideways, opening almond-shaped slits. Behind them is her skin. She will have to mention this soon. They let the air through, especially at night, when she goes walking.

Owen puffs a cloud into the rafters. 'Your mother thinks it would be better if you didn't spend so much time outside.'

Etta stiffens. She must have been seen.

'She could do with your help inside, now that Bernadette and Theresa are out so often with their young men. I've got men out here to help me. They're around here most of the time. We both think it would be for the best.'

Etta breathes. 'All right.'

'There's a good girl,' says Owen, but he doesn't touch her.

Etta tucks Dandelion into a blanket and takes the empty bottle.

'Nip in to the meat safe on your way back, would you Eileen?'

says Owen as Etta is going out the door. When Maggie isn't around, he sometimes calls her Eileen, which is her middle name. 'Your mother wants that roast for tonight.'

Etta passes rows of hanging ducks and rabbits, their necks at strange angles. Their eyes are open. There are a few chickens, a turkey. One wild swan. A string of fat white sausages, untouched. Weißwurst, from their German neighbours.

'I doubt even the cat would eat those,' said Maggie after Mrs Blumenfeld brought them over.

Mrs Blumenfeld spoke with a strong accent. She wore her hair in fat white plaits crossed over the top of her head.

'She means well,' said Owen.

Etta's jersey brushes hanging carcasses, ribs splayed like wings. She prefers these to the smaller ones which are still feathered or furred. There are no eyes. She unhooks the beef for her mother.

'How now, brown cow,' she says. Sister Michael has told her to practise her elocution regularly. Maggie doesn't want her ending up with an accent from hearing so much Irish. Maggie was born in New Zealand, but she ended up with one.

'The leaves on the trees leaped in the breeze,' says Etta. 'Father started for the dark park.'

'Good Lord, girl, you're filthy. Into the bath with you,' says Maggie. She sips her sherry, and does not get up from her chair.

'I brought the roast for tonight.'

'Just leave it on the bench.'

The McClinchies have a deep, deep bath made of Royal Doulton china. It is dark green on the outside, and paler on the inside. A person could drown in there, says Maggie. Owen's Uncle Henry brought it out with him from Ireland. Owen says when they got off the boat they couldn't walk properly for a fortnight. Three months on water will do that to a man, he says. So will three months on whisky, says Maggie, but Owen just smiles at this. He doesn't drink. When Uncle Henry died, Owen got the bath, and the house around it.

While the water runs, Etta undresses in front of the mirror. The glass clouds, until all she can see is a luminous after-image of herself, a ghost. The mirror came out on the boat too.

The bathroom smells of Three Flowers face powder, and Lily of the Valley. Bernadette and Theresa, Etta's sisters, have been getting ready for a dance. Bernadette must be feeling better; she's had the flu for the past couple of days, and has stayed in bed. She often gets the flu; it seems like every month to Etta. There is a smudge of lipstick on the mirror, as if someone has tried to kiss it. The hand basin is streaked brown. Bernadette and Theresa have been painting their legs; stockings are still scarce.

Just as Etta is stepping into the bath, Maggie shoves the door open.

'You brought the wrong one,' she says. 'I wanted the mutton.'

Etta has one foot in the water and one on the floor. 'I'm sorry,' she says.

'The cat was in there. You let it in, didn't you?'

'I don't know.'

'Idiot. All that meat, ruined.'

'I'm sorry.'

Maggie is raw in the face. Her breath is stale, acidic, the way Bernadette's and Theresa's floating dresses smell the day after a dance.

'I'll teach you sorry.' Maggie's hands are raised. She has beautiful hands, white as linen. Flowers have spilled from them, pastel petals, the initials of someone cherished. Etta concentrates on these. She thinks: satin stitch, loveknots, lazy-daisy, chain stitch, crewelling. Her mother's hands, her needle fingers. Idiot. Wicked. I'll teach you.

Etta is giddy. She feels as if the bath is moving away from her, like a ship leaving dock, with only half of her in it. She will be pulled in two, starting at her thighs, straight down the middle. She is giddy. She is falling.

'Be good,' says Bernadette, stroking a gloved finger over Etta's cheek. Then she and Theresa float out the door in their butterfly dresses, leaving the scent of flowers behind them.

Etta is good. She has been good all afternoon. She cleaned up the mess in the meat safe; the cat was nowhere to be seen. The cool air was soothing on her bruises. She picked up the feathers from the ducks and the swan. They shone. Precious things, kept in a safe, kept safe. She waited for Maggie to come and let her out. There was no sign of the cat for the rest of the day.

'A bit of face powder would cover those for church tomorrow,' said Theresa when she saw the purple marks on Etta's face.

'She is thirteen years old,' said Maggie. 'I will not have my daughter looking like a hussy.'

Etta slipped over when she was getting out of her bath. She's at a clumsy age. She'll be all right.

It is night. Etta has tiptoed over the cold cattle stop. She has wondered how it would feel for a foot, a leg to slip through those bars, to have to wait there all night. The air is cool on her bruises. The flag on the mailbox is up, and she can hear the stream. She pauses at the Blumenfelds' house. Mr Blumenfeld is sitting at the piano; the lid is down. She passes the swings, which are still. She is in the field. A button pops off her blouse and is lost in the grass; she does not stop to find it. She goes to the stream. She stands on the bank and dips one foot into the water. The stream has swollen, she thinks. Under the water her foot is luminous. She steps from the bank, pulls off her skirt. She stands thigh-deep in water. Her legs are made of moon. The water flows between them. She smiles. Another button pops from her blouse, and another. They sink and become stones. She has no need for stones. Her blouse crumbles from her shoulders and dissolves. She inches down into the water, into the bed of the stream. Until she is kneeling. The water creeps up her body, parting to let her in. She glows. She is silver from the neck down.

Maggie cannot sleep. She throws back the hot eiderdown and places a foot on the cool floor. It is a high bed. She can just reach. Her hand hurts. She hit her knuckles too hard. She didn't mean to hit so hard. She wonders how these things happen so quickly. She thinks, I am unravelling. She will try to be more understanding, less irritable, more generous, less impatient. More gracious. More serene. More Christian.

She will have a little brandy and fall asleep.

Owen is sailing in the green bath. It is the colour of leaves. It turns the water the colour of leaves. The mirror is foggy. Owen looks through the fog and thinks he can see land. A misty green island. His Uncle Henry plays the violin. One of his feet is placed level on land. He ripples. Owen's other foot is removed from the water and placed on land. He shivers like a view through old glass. People think he is drunk. He is not. For two weeks he cannot walk without falling over. His Uncle Henry plays the violin, and gives him a job cleaning the silver, so Owen can sit down.

Maggie's glass—finest Waterford—drops from her fingers. Her face sinks into white linen.

'Violin,' says Owen.

Mrs Blumenfeld is back in Dresden. Buildings are cracking like bone china. She must run to avoid the falling shards. A library smashes to the ground; pages flutter around her, shuffling themselves to form stories nobody would ever believe. She looks again, and people are cracking. Life-size, bone china people. A man on a bicycle shatters. A girl with a dog smashes to dust. A woman in a floral dress explodes, showering Mrs Blumenfeld with sharp flowers.

Mr Blumenfeld watches the shut piano. He thinks, ivory, ivory. Such a strange new language.

At the dance, Theresa knocks back another vodka.

'That's the end of Bernadette's,' she says. 'Time for mine.' She produces a hip flask from the folds of her dress, and leans back against George Morton's best suit.

'It's lucky you girls have such long frocks,' says George, slipping his hand under a layer of voile. 'What else have you got under here?'

'Dirty bugger,' says Theresa, laughing.

'Where did a good Catholic girl like you learn that sort of language?'

'Some of the men on the farm will teach you anything you want to know. Isn't that right, Bernadette?'

George snorts.

Bernadette arranges the powder blue layers of her dress around her, smoothing them over her knees, folding them along her body like wings.

'She's a quiet one, your sister,' says George. 'You girls still thirsty?'

Theresa drains her glass. 'I am now.'

George reaches inside his coat and slides a bottle out.

'Gin!'

'Nothing like a drop of mother's ruin.'

'Shame we haven't got any proper glasses.'

'The first champagne glass,' says Bernadette, 'was formed around Marie Antoinette's bosom.'

'Pity it wasn't round Theresa's,' says George. 'Lean in front of me while I open it, would you love?'

Etta stays in the water until she cannot feel her bruises. She does not think she is cold. She can smell flowers. Under the water she gleams bone-clean. She stands up, slowly. Being careful not to slip. She is so clumsy. She curves her feet over round rocks, gripping with her toes. There is a shadow in the water where she was kneeling. It washed out of her; it spreads in the water. It is possibly red. It is possibly the colour of wine. It is dark.

It is dark. Etta can't find her clothes. Something brushes her thigh, and when she looks down she sees that her skin is still glowing. As if she has become a ghost of herself. A velvety moth has landed on her thigh and is beating its wings, slowly as a heart. Another one is on her foot, fanning her toes with cool breaths. She can feel them settling on her back, her arms. They are clouding around her, making the air whisper. They are covering her shoulders, her chest, her small breasts.

Her mother hates moths, especially the fat ones that beat against the windows at night. When they get inside, she hits them with the back of her shoe.

'They're just night-time butterflies,' says Owen. 'They're a hundred times smaller than yourself.'

'Dirty creatures,' says Maggie.

Etta holds up her fingers. They are covered with moths. She is not afraid (she should be). She feels warm. They do not fly away when she walks.

She crosses the field, passes the swings. She comes to her road. She wonders if anyone will see her. Macrocarpas arch across her. The light is still on in the Blumenfelds' front window, and a few moths are drumming on the glass. Etta stops and looks in from the road. Mr Blumenfeld is still sitting at the piano; the lid is down. The moths on his window come and sit in Etta's hair. Mr Blumenfeld looks up, and frowns. He walks to the window and cups his hands round his eyes. Etta stands in the middle of the road (it is the safest place) and stares back. Mr Blumenfeld pushes up the sash and leans out.

'You are Etta.'

'Yes. Henrietta.'

'Hello.'

'Hello.'

'I have daughter called Ete. Margarete.'

'Oh, I haven't met her yet.'

'She is in Germany. She is died.'

'I'm sorry.'

'In bomb.'

'I'm so sorry.'

'Yes.'

'Thank you for the sausages.'

'Ah, please, please.'

'They were lovely.'

'You enjoy Weißwurst.'

'Yes.'

'We give you more. You come tomorrow.'

'Thank you.'

'Please.'

'Goodnight.'

'Goodnight.'

When she places her foot on the cattle stop, Etta hears a sigh. Or rather, hundreds of tiny sighs. The air around her is moving; the moths are leaving. They arc away from the house, growing smaller. Etta looks at her body. It is not glowing any more.

She creeps up the stairs, starting with her left foot so the ninth stair won't creak. She is very tired, and she buries her face in her pillow. The pillowcase smells of mothballs.

Maggie bursts into Etta's room at seven in the morning.

'Up you get! I want to get the washing done before church. And you have to feed that lamb of yours, it's driving me mad with its noise.' She pulls back the blankets. 'Your face is all marked. Looks awful.'

Etta gets up to look in the mirror. 'Oh, that,' she says. 'That's just from the pillowcase.'

Maggie is looking at her sheets. There is a stain on them. Etta doesn't know where it's come from. She didn't think she'd been cut when she fell over in the bathroom, just bruised. She's hardly ever been actually cut. She hopes she won't slip over in surprise. She's so clumsy.

But Maggie just strips the sheets off the bed and bundles them up. Then she sets her jaw, pulls off the pillowcase and tears it down the seams. She folds the pieces into squares and hands them to Etta.

'Here. You'll need these.' She sighs, picks up the sheets, and leaves.

In the bathroom, Bernadette's and Theresa's dresses are hanging to air. They look like shrivelled skins, and are stained under the arms. Etta looks in the mirror. There is an impression of flowers on her cheek, circling a butterfly. At least, she thinks it's a butterfly. She turns the pieces of pillowcase over and over. They are still warm. She wonders what on earth she is supposed to do with them.

Vivienne Plumb

Vivienne Plumb did Original Composition in 1990. 'The Wife who Spoke Japanese in Her Sleep' is the title story of her prize-winning 1993 short-story collection. She is also a widely published poet (see the very last page of this book), and a playwright (she held the *Sunday Star-Times* / Bruce Mason Award in 1993).

The Wife who Spoke Japanese in Her Sleep

In the winter the nights become long and cold. In Honey Tarbox's house, all is hushed on a frosty midwinter night. Then slowly, slowly, Honey rolls over in her bed and starts to wake. She is speaking Japanese.

'Kyoo wa samui desu ne.'

'What . . . ?' she thinks.

'Ohayo gozaimasu,' she says out loud. The words echo around the cold, still bedroom. Her husband groans. 'Huh, wozzat?'

She stops speaking but her mind keeps turning, rolling around. What did I say? she thinks. She doesn't know it was Japanese. She's the wife who spoke Japanese in her sleep.

✧

At first Honey didn't speak much Japanese.

Howard, her husband, stayed awake one night and described what he saw happen. He watched her go to bed. Gradually she fell asleep, then after an hour she started speaking in another language. She spoke for a little time.

When she woke in the morning, Honey was amazed to hear

Howard's description.

She never felt tired. She was always rested, relaxed. But Howard often looked exhausted.

'The talking keeps me awake,' he said.

At first they couldn't understand which language it was. Neither of them had ever spoken any language other than English. Honey had once gone on a holiday to Fiji, but Howard had never travelled.

So one night Howard said he would tape Honey talking in her sleep. The next day they took the tape to the School of Languages and asked to see a teacher. While they sat waiting, they watched six goldfish swimming in a large tank.

'Mr and Mrs Tarbox?' said the teacher. She wore spectacles and a maroon cardigan. Her hair was pulled back into a bun. To Honey and Howard she looked very educated.

'I'm Miss Florica. How can I help? What would you like to learn? Arabic? Spanish? Lithuanian? Mandarin? We offer them all.'

'Please listen to our tape,' said Howard, his face slightly flushed. He switched on his pocket machine.

'Nan desu ka,' said the voice on the tape. It didn't sound like Honey at all.

'What language is that?' asked Howard. The teacher listened.

'Why it's Japanese,' she said. She listened some more, then laughed. 'Good grief,' she said.

'What is it?' asked Honey.

'Well it's rather rude,' said the teacher. 'I don't think I could give you a direct translation. Where did you get this from?' Howard and Honey looked at each other.

'Umm . . .' they both said. Honey looked at her shoes, and Howard looked at the ceiling.

'Wait a minute,' said the teacher. 'Now what's she saying?' She leant forward, concentrating on the tape recording.

'Wow, incredible. Who is this woman? I'd love to meet her. What a wonderful woman she is, she seems to know so much.'

'Why, what did she say?' said Howard. He wriggled on his chair. Honey watched the fish flipping around the tank and waited to hear what the teacher would say next.

'Well, it's a kind of speech, about mankind,' said the teacher. 'Sort of prophecies . . . it's hard to describe.'

They stood staring at each other. The voice on the tape had stopped.

'She says things. She's like a kind of . . . oracle,' said the teacher. 'I'd really like to meet her. Is she a friend of yours?'

Howard giggled. Honey looked at the fish. One really big goldfish swam right up to the glass, its mouth opening and shutting at Honey. 'Oh! Oh! Oh!' it seemed to be saying.

'It's me,' said Honey in a flat voice. 'That tape recording is me.' 'You?' said the teacher. She was obviously surprised. She took her spectacles off and polished them and put them back on again.

'I don't understand,' said the teacher. 'If you speak Japanese, why don't you know what you're saying? Also, excuse me if I appear rude, but that voice doesn't sound like you at all. Hajimema-shite. Watashi wa Florica desu. Doozo yoroshiku.' She bowed low towards Honey.

'No, no!' whispered Honey. She backed away. 'I don't understand you! . . . Tell her, Howard. Tell her what happens.'

Howard moved closer to Miss Florica and lowered his voice.

'When Honey goes to sleep at night, she speaks like that.' He nodded his head towards the tape recorder. Miss Florica gasped.

'She speaks in her sleep?'

Howard nodded.

'And in a language she doesn't understand?'

'Yes,' said Howard. 'We don't know what to do.'

'But do you realise what she's saying?' asked Miss Florica. 'This voice on the tape is making prophecies. On the tape she made some predictions about the government of our country.'

'No!' said Howard. Honey looked away. She was feeling so embarrassed. She wished they'd never come.

'You must have a very special power,' said Miss Florica, 'to be able to perceive things that we cannot. A clairvoyant power.'

She smiled at Honey. But Honey said to Howard, 'Howard, let's leave, I just remembered I left the heater on at home.'

Howard came straight away. He'd never encouraged large

electricity bills. In fact, he was quite a penny-pincher when it came down to it.

'Which heater?' he kept asking all the way back. 'The big one or the little?'

'Oh Howard, shut up,' said Honey. She withdrew to the bathroom where she ran a long hot bath. She didn't come out until she heard Howard leave for his afternoon class at the Community Institute.

(He was learning patchwork. Now he was retired he had nothing else to do with his time. As for herself, the children had all grown up long ago. She had no hobbies, no pastimes, no job, but now she had this.)

She looked at herself in the bedroom mirror. She saw a short, stout woman, with blonde hair. A fleshy, plump body. She pinched the flesh on her face. When she pulled her fingers away, a white mark was left on the sagging pink skin.

She thought she knew what a clairvoyant was.

It was a woman, dressed with a scarf on her head, and wearing rings and jewellery. She had a rich plummy voice, and she waved her hands around in an artistic manner. She'd seen them in old Sherlock Holmes movies. The lights would be dimmed, and then the spirits would come. They would fill the room, knocking over lamps and tables in an effort to make their presence known.

Was she a clairvoyant?

She laughed. She shook her head and her blonde hair fluffed around her head like a halo. What a preposterous idea!

Or in the newspaper. Sometimes she'd seen them in the newspaper. A woman would be called in to assist the police in finding a dead body. 'CLAIRVOYANT HELPS POLICE,' it would shout across the front page. And there'd be a photo of her, hand outstretched, eyes shut. Could that be Honey?

Or at school, many years ago. She remembered they had learnt about the Oracle at Delphi. A woman had sat on a sacred tripod over a deep fissure in the earth. The mists of the inner earth would rise and send her into a trance. Then she'd speak, tell everyone all manner of things. She might talk for hours, then collapse exhausted. A priest interpreted her messages. People would come from everywhere to ask her questions. And often her answers were correct.

Honey considers herself. Looks at her hands, not artistic, but capable.

She glances at her bed, smoothly made, her fuchsia-pink nightdress rolled up and slipped under the pillow. And she wonders what the night will bring.

✧

At nine o'clock that night there is a knock at the door. Howard answers it. Miss Florica is standing on the step, her eyes shining.

'Good evening, Mr Tarbox,' she says. She has someone else with her, a friend, another woman. She introduces her as Mrs Brunt.

'Mrs Brunt knows a little of these matters,' says Miss Florica. 'She once had a psychic experience herself.'

Mrs Brunt wears short, black rubber boots, and a thick woollen coat. A black beret is balanced on her large square head.

Honey enters the lighted hall. Howard is excited. He is gabbling to the two ladies. It is apparent to Honey that Howard skipped his patchwork class and went instead to ask Miss Florica here tonight. Honey's shadow falls across the rose-patterned carpet. All three stop talking and turn quietly towards her. Howard clears his throat.

'Honey, I know you won't mind if Miss Florica and Mrs Brunt stay to listen to you. It's in the interest of Science, I'm sure you'd agree.'

The two women smile and nod their heads. Their heads look strangely loose on top of their wooden necks. Honey stays quiet, she doesn't smile back.

Please themselves, she thinks. She feels in control. All her life she's had nothing. But now, she has this. And this is becoming important, making her important.

'Have they brought me anything?' she asks.

'Brought you anything?' says Howard.

'Yes, a gift, a present. They must have something.'

The hall light hangs behind her, lighting up her body in silhouette, but they cannot see her face.

'I did bring something,' says Mrs Brunt. She pulls a rectangular object out of her crocheted shopping bag.

'A box of chocs.' She beams.

'That's good,' says Honey. 'If any more people come, Howard, you must ask them for their gift.' She turns away. 'I'll go and make a pot of tea.'

Howard is embarrassed.

'Really, she's never acted like this before . . . Come in. Come in.' He leads the two visitors into the lounge.

The fringed lamp shines a soft glow over the room. The television is on with the sound turned down and Honey's knitting lies on the sofa.

It isn't long before Honey brings the tea.

'I'll get ready while you all have a drink,' she says. She goes into the bedroom and changes into her nightdress. She sits waiting on the edge of the bed.

Howard comes in. He says, 'You go to bed Honey. I won't ask anyone in until you're asleep.'

'Howard,' says Honey, 'what do they want?'

'I think they want to ask you some questions,' he says.

Howard, Miss Florica and Mrs Brunt stay waiting in the lounge. The clock ticks on. They make small talk. Mrs Brunt examines Honey's knitting.

'She's dropped a stitch ten rows back,' she says.

Suddenly they hear a voice talking in the bedroom. Miss Florica is on her feet straight away.

'That's Japanese!' she says.

Howard leads them at a trot down the passage. He turns on a bedside lamp. Honey is lying on her back in the bed. Her arms are folded across her chest. Her face is smooth, wiped of all expression. She is apparently fast asleep.

'Komban wa,' says Miss Florica. She bows towards the bed.

'Komban wa,' replies Honey. And a torrent of Japanese follows. She still looks like Honey, but she doesn't sound like Honey. The voice is higher, more penetrating.

Miss Florica introduces Mrs Brunt. She presents the box of chocolates and says, 'Tsumaranai mono desu ga, doozo.'

Mrs Brunt smiles.

'Now she'll explain my problem,' she whispers to Howard.

Howard pulls over another chair and they both sit down. There is a pause, then Honey says, 'Doomo arigatoo gozaimasu. Watashi wa ureshii desu.' Miss Florica smiles. She talks to Honey for about five minutes, explaining Mrs Brunt's problem.

Honey replies, she talks on and on, hardly stopping for breath. The Japanese syllables sound strange to Howard. He crosses and recrosses his legs.

Finally Miss Florica turns back to them both.

'It's wonderful,' she says. 'It's all so clear. Her answer is simple.'

'What did you ask?' says Howard. Miss Florica and Mrs Brunt exchange looks.

'I don't mind if you tell,' says Mrs Brunt. 'I think we can trust Mr Tarbox.' Miss Florica explains.

'Mrs Brunt has a lovely miniature poodle, only three years old. His name is Schnookie. Schnookie is suffering terribly from arthritis and he may have to have plastic ligaments inserted in his front legs. Mrs Brunt was worried about the pain this operation may cause Schnookie, but now I have the answer.'

'And what is that?' asks Howard.

'It has been suggested Mrs Brunt finds a hypnotherapist.' Mrs Brunt grins. 'What a terrific idea!'

'I'm so glad Honey helped you find the answer to your problem,' Howard says. Miss Florica and Mrs Brunt prepare to leave.

'Do you think Honey could help other people this way?' asks Howard. Miss Florica's face shines. She comes forward and places her hand on Howard's arm in a warm, caring way.

'Without doubt,' she says. 'Without doubt, I think I could say that Honey's advice and predictions could be the light at the end of the tunnel for many people. And I would make myself available any night to translate . . . for a small donation. Think about it, Mr Tarbox, and let us keep in touch.' She squeezes his arm. He opens the front door for them and says goodbye.

The sound of their footsteps fades away into the still, deep night. The stars hang, glittering fiercely in the cold midnight sky. Howard hears a noise and swings around. It's Honey. She's wearing her fluffy lilac dressing-gown.

'Did I do it?' she asks.

'Yes,' says Howard. His voice is low. 'They were very pleased. You were very successful. Miss Florica thinks you could help even more people.'

'I see,' says Honey. 'Tell her she can have thirty per cent.'

She turns and goes back to the bedroom. Howard comes inside. He's surprised. Honey seems so different, so business-minded, it's not like her. He frowns at the lock, pulls the chain across and slips it into its tiny slot. Tomorrow he'll ring Miss Florica and make her an offer.

✧

During the next few months the Tarbox home becomes famous. Word gets around, and every night many people arrive at Honey's with a little hope in their hearts. Some have simple questions written on a tiny scrap of paper. Others come escorted by note-taking secretaries who read their questions out for them. They ask so many things. How to become rich, how to look more beautiful, how to become loved, and how to love. How to be good, to be received into heaven, to die happy. Honey answers them all.

Now Honey wears a beautiful peach-pink nightie. She has her hair styled during the day so she will look her best every night. Reporters come and go. Honey is a popular personality to interview. They adore her combination of mystery and modesty. They ask her opinion on everything, her favourite colour (peach), and her favourite food (watermelon). She's even been on daytime chat shows, and has been photographed with many of the famous and well-known people who pass through the portals of her house.

Her predictions are often correct. Her advice, politely and kindly offered, is always well accepted.

The Japanese ambassador has visited several times. The last time he came they talked at length about the future of Japan.

'Are wa sakura desu ka,' he'd said, peering out of Honey's window into the dark night.

'Hai,' Honey had answered. 'Haru desu.'

Waiting outside the door in the shadows, Howard had thought to himself how much Honey had changed.

To Howard, Honey now appears controlled, never flustered. She's always well dressed, her make-up well applied. She offers her opinions even when they've not been asked for. And she expects Howard to keep accounts that add up.

Howard thinks he liked the old Honey better. She pottered around the house in her fluffy dressing-gown. She always looked to Howard for advice about how to dress, and everything else besides. She was warm, caring, and she looked after me, thinks Howard. Now he thinks she's a Dragon Woman.

The business of the accounts upsets him the most. Maths was never his forte and he often makes mistakes. Sometimes, when it all gets too much for him, he seeks Miss Florica's help. In her old cardie and smudgy pink lipstick, and her dishevelled bun and glasses, she reminds Howard of the old Honey.

She is pleased to help Howard. She pats his hand and sometimes makes him a pot of tea. She calls him Howard now, not Mr Tarbox.

During the day Honey often likes to sit in the garden. Howard used to look after it. He would mow a flat square in the middle and clip back the rest.

But it's all different now. A young Japanese man, Kenta Yamashita, has offered to build a real Japanese garden for Honey. Honey's advice to Kenta about his problems with his mother has so touched him that he comes back all the time just to visit. Now he has offered to build the Japanese garden.

He has planted a cherry tree and wants to pull up all the grass and replace it with raked gravel.

He is setting three large stones in their geomantic positions. The large stones are covered with lichen. They are the mountains, says Kenta. The gravel will be the water. All the elements of life. Honey loves watching the transformation of the garden. She sees it as somewhat representative of what has happened to herself. She's looking forward to the complete removal of Howard's dusty geraniums and proteas and the installation of the raked sand. Smooth, flowing, meditative.

◆

One Monday morning Honey wakes earlier than usual. She walks up the hall and into the kitchen.

Howard and Miss Florica are pushed against the sink bench grappling each other's bodies. Howard's hands are up Miss Florica's blouse. Miss Florica's hands are down Howard's trousers. Their mouths are squashed against each other's. It makes Honey remember the goldfish.

She coughs gently and they spring apart. Miss Florica blushes.

'I don't know what came over me,' she says.

Howard looks smug. He says nothing. Instead, he leans across Miss Florica and takes two pieces of toast out of the toaster. He butters them evenly and eats them straight away. Miss Florica excuses herself and hurries out of the kitchen.

'Would you like some toast?' asks Howard.

'No,' says Honey. She prefers to eat fish for breakfast these days.

'You're so different now,' says Howard. It's the first time he's ever talked to Honey about the changes in their lives. 'You're not the same Honey I married.'

'We all change,' says Honey. 'From decay grows new life. From the old is born the new.'

'How poetic,' says Howard.

Honey pauses, and then replies, 'I must now take this opportunity to thank you for starting me on this path.'

'No worries,' mutters Howard.

That night Honey dons a white sateen nightie. She pins her hair up, adding a flower or two to the arrangement. She applies a little lipstick to her mouth and climbs into bed. She lies still, waiting for Miss

Florica to arrive. This is the way they always do it. When Miss Florica comes, she sits over near the window and Honey slowly falls asleep.

Tonight Honey is more voluble than ever. She is funny and witty, and very likeable in this mood. Her joie de vivre breaks the language barrier. When her visitors leave they are smiling and laughing. Miss Florica is kept busy. Honey talks at such a rate, she can hardly keep up.

Then suddenly Honey sits up in her sleep. She has never done this before, everyone stops what they're doing.

'Howardsan wa doko desu ka,' she says.

'Quick! Howard!' shouts Miss Florica. 'This is for him!'

'Watashi wa megami desu. Me ga mienai. Kiri ga mieru. Howardsan ga kiete iku!'

'I can't see. I see a mist,' translates Miss Florica quickly. Her face flushes. 'A disappearance!'

Honey falls exhausted onto her pillows and goes into a deep sleep.

The next week Howard disappears.

No one sees him leave, nor can anyone remember for sure what happened. One day he was there, the next day—zilch! No one had ever taken much notice of him anyway, except Miss Florica.

She is allowed to move into his old room. She touches the razor on his dresser and carefully runs her finger along the blade. The terylene curtains wave in the breeze coming through the open window. Miss Florica opens the drawers and wonders why Howard didn't take any spare underwear with him when he left.

Kenta Yamashita has finished Honey's Japanese garden. Ten tons of white gravel and sand was delivered and raked into uniform patterns. Only Miss Florica can remember the particular day that the gravel arrived.

Yes, she can remember the day, the month, and the year (in case she's ever asked). It was the day Howard disappeared.

Samara McDowell

Samara McDowell took the Original Composition course in 1991. Her course folio included poetry as well as prose, but its chief glory was 'Holloway Road', which was subsequently published in *Sport 8*.

Holloway Road

It was toward the raggedy end of winter that we all began to long for a death.

'I'm going crazy,' Kate told me. It was one of those impossible and dreary evenings that seem to happen a lot in August. I was curled in the ancient red armchair Christian and Boy brought back from the tip that time. It is very forlorn and rather misshapen. I sit in it with my legs over one arm, my back supported by the other. It was raining. I studied my nails, the phone crooked between my shoulder and my left ear. No one else was home.

'I know,' I told Kate.

'This winter,' said Kate, bitterly, 'is *never* going to end.'

'I know,' I said. Christian had spent the entire morning in a queue on the first floor of DSW. He had come home in a very bad mood.

'Fucking Social Welfare,' Kate said, intuitively. 'They've cut me off three times and now they've arranged this interview to reassess my *job* potential. I got the letter this morning.'

'I wouldn't worry about it,' I said, and yawned at the Mona Lisa on the wall. We got her out of the library. We've had her nine months already. They keep sending us these fines. 'There *are* no jobs.'

'I didn't,' Kate told me, very aggressive, 'study for three years to be fucked around by Social Welfare.'

'I know you didn't,' I said.

Mary Wollstonecraft came in silently through the gap where the door to the kitchen used to be and curled up on my lap.

'Stu's on the Sickness Benefit,' I told them both.

'Really?' Kate said. The air was suddenly thick with envy; Mary Wollstonecraft stirred in its draught and abruptly began to purr. Her evil green eyes regarded me intently. It's very difficult to get thrown off the Sickness Benefit, once you've manoeuvred the tricky matter of getting on.

'God. This whole year. I just don't feel—I haven't—Ohh, God, what a year. What a long, boring, terrible year,' said Kate.

'There was Waitangi,' I reminded her.

'Oh yeah,' she said; her voice lifted slightly and then dropped again—'But that was summer.'

'I know,' I said.

There fell another of those August evening pauses, late and dreary with nothing to do and no one home and the TV taken back because of the unpaid rentals.

It could be worse. Jeff and Stu have had their phone cut off. Telecon, as Boy would say.

I have a job. It is not, of course, a very good job; I temp, which is not exactly what a degree in Philosophy had intended for me, but with me working at least three or four days a week and Christian at De Luxe three mornings—they pay under the table—we do get to keep our phone. They won't let Boy work at Drama School, but he keeps seven plants in the hot-water cupboard. They're all called Audrey III.

I thought of the morning, curled up there in the red armchair, listening to Kate complain. We live in a tiny crooked-sixpence house in the mist and damp of Holloway Road, Boy and Christian and me, and it is never warm enough. Our landlady is a middle-aged Kiwi Chinese—her phrase, not mine. She adores Boy and Christian. She doesn't like me, I'm female. I don't like her, she's old.

Even with Mary Wollstonecraft a heavy weight on my stomach I was cold. It is not shivery cold in Holloway Road. It's more the sort where you get clogged and stilled where you sit; it is too cold to stretch, every muscle rebels against it, and with your body clogged and stilled your mind becomes sluggish too. To get up, to go into the freezing kitchen to make a cup of tea, requires a major exertion of will. Sometimes I go and sit and read in the kitchen with all four elements and the grill of the oven on, flickering blue and purple like a bruise, but the heat won't stay in because Lexa took the door to the living-room to make a workbench out of, and I can't do this very often because we can't afford the gas.

So I just sat there, too cold to move, listening to Kate complain, on and on, and thought of the morning.

An eight-thirty start. I have to be out of bed by seven-fifteen, when it isn't hardly light. The alarm goes off with its cheap tinny thrill and Christian knocks it off the orange-box, but it won't stop and Christian groans and rolls over and says *Fuck* at me. We are both bad in the mornings, but Christian's the worst. Unemployed people hate to wake up, I've noticed. I was the same, doing the obligatory six months after finishing up at varsity.

The alarm is whining to a stop, winding down. One last defeated-sounding chirrup and it's still, and I'm all rolled up in the army blanket and my grandmother's patchwork quilt on the sheets I found at the op shop on Majoribanks and I'm warm and I don't want to get up and put on my horrible work clothes and go out into the rain and file all day and I'm drifting back to sleep, and then the door flies open and there's Boy, and he grins at me and chucks Mary Wollstonecraft into the room and says, 'Time for all good Drake girlies to be out of bed.'

'Sod off, Boy,' I say, but sleepy, not vicious like Christian, and Boy grins again and stomps off into the kitchen and Mary Wollstone-craft leaps, purring, onto the bed.

'Jesus Christ,' says Christian.

'Hey, baby,' I say to Mary Wollstonecraft, ignoring him, and she steps delicately over him and settles on the pillow, and Christian rolls over and rears half-upright and stares into my face, all three inches of his hair on end—he's growing it out—and says, deadly, 'Get the fuck *out* of here, I am *asleep*,' and there's the good mood for the day, killed stone dead, and I throw Mary Wollstonecraft onto the floor and she stalks away and I drag myself out of the room with my feet flinching from the cold of the lino and into the shower.

Now, the shower in Holloway Road.

It's a trickle and you have to fiddle with the taps every ten seconds and it's either bitterly cold or scalding. When I had long hair I couldn't ever get the shampoo out of it because the water pressure doesn't exist. You know when you're little and you forget your coat and your mother tells you to dodge between the raindrops to stay dry?

You can *do* that, in our shower.

I lean my head against the mouldy wall, and I'm one sour bundle of anger and hate, and it's the same every morning, the slimy curtain that never gets time to dry, and I probe the shutters open to look out into the street and guess what, it's raining, and Boy is standing outside hopping from one foot to another, saying, 'Hurry up, hurry up, I'm going to be *late*, woman, c'mon, c'mon,' and I scraunch off the taps and wrap myself in a towel and I think how I hate the winter.

I thought of all this, half-listening to Kate, studying my nails. I looked around our living room; we keep forgetting to buy new bulbs for the lamps and it looked dreary and dingy under the one overhead light. Christian had scattered tubes of paint and the *Sunday Times* (days old) all over the sofa, and for once even the Mona Lisa didn't make it seem prettier, or all the things we have collected, from the market and op shops and friends.

I thought about Kate and Christian and Stu and Lexa and even Boy, who's usually so irrepressible, and how we've been passing our bad mood from one to another like a virus, a social disease indeed, the lethargy that goes with it, the sores. Winter, I thought.

There are the winter things, of course: the after-work, after-dark world we live in until late October, early November: the cold bright Wellington you can find after eleven, in the cafés and clubs all along Cuba Street. Kate and I do a lot of movies in winter—two o'clocks, when it's cheaper, and then there is the film festival, which is when Christian and Boy and Lexa deign to join us.

'The arty ones,' Kate says, with that particularly Kate blend of scorn and envy.

I usually make no response to this, although actually I consider myself as one of the arty ones, with good reason I think. There's more to art than Drama School and Christian in holey T-shirts hurling oils on enormous canvases in Lexa's garage. Art is refraction, reflection, manipulation of substance, and at this—I forbear to mention to Kate—I am rather excessively good. As she of all people should be aware.

Yes, but the thing about movies is that you have to leave from them, some time.

I thought of summer, with the windows open and the sun shining and the coloured lights they put on the trees on Oriental Parade, but it was too far away. I couldn't believe it would ever happen again. It was going to be winter and we were all going to be unemployed or in shit jobs forever.

It was at that moment that I came to a decision.

'Kate,' I said.

The drone stopped. The silence buzzed faintly over the telephone wire. I could half-hear a crossed connection.

'Yes?' she said.

'You know what we need, Kate?' I said, and all of a sudden my body unclogged and I stretched, slowly and luxuriously, daring the cold. It stayed at a safe distance. My fingertips were tingling with evil; even Mary Wollstonecraft was still, watching me.

'We need a death,' I said, and Mary Wollstonecraft sat upright with her tail twitching. I felt as well as heard Kate's quick intake of breath. Winter damages the telepathy between us, but it was suddenly working perfectly; I could feel her mind tumbling the idea over and over, examining it from kaleidoscope angles, and then it rolled into a niche and stopped.

'Yes,' she said slowly. 'A death.'

I was too excited to stay still; I jumped up and began to pace round the room with the body of the telephone in my hand. When Christian and Boy broke the phone, drop-kicking it, Telecom replaced it with this hideous new flat grey model, with a mute button, three different rings and a lot of other features we didn't need, but I made them give us a thirty-foot cord.

The room looked different, charged; the edges of it vibrated slightly as the evil in my fingertips began to pulse outward, banishing the cold.

'Can you do it?' Kate asked me cautiously.

'I don't know so. I think so. Not alone,' I said. I stopped in front of the mantelpiece. The silver pepper and salt shakers we stole from the Park Royal the night the theatre burned down trembled; I willed them still.

'I'm not very strong at the moment,' Kate said hesitantly.

'I know. It's okay. I've got Mary Wollstonecraft. I'll need you as back up, though, Katie, please.'

'When? Now?'

I raised my eyes very slowly until they met their reflection in the black-framed circular mirror; I looked into myself, then at the Mona Lisa, and met her smile for slow smile.

'The beginning now,' I said.

'Oh God. I'm really *not* very strong, you know, hon.'

I looked down; Mary Wollstonecraft was twining herself sinuously about my ankles.

'Have a shower, get into bed. Then if you pass out you pass out, it'll be okay. You won't, though. I don't need you to do anything, just be there,' I told her. 'You might need to hold me, it's been a while.'

'Okay,' said Kate, and hung up.

My hands were trembling. I picked up Mary Wollstonecraft; she pressed herself into the hollow of my neck.

'All right, baby,' I said to her. 'Time to go.'

The table was clear except for the vase of dried Botanical Gardens roses. I had turned on the gas, all four elements, but for their blue light rather than heat; I was no longer cold at all. I lit a candle and put it carefully in the centre of the floor, then sat down at the table and pressed my hands firmly together. I was shaking all over. Mary Wollstonecraft was already patting at the roses; she looked at me now and miaowed, and we settled in to wait for Kate.

But Kate was already there.

'A death,' I said firmly to the surrounding darkness.

The flame of the candle burned high and clear.

I let myself sink into Kate. It is always a strange sensation, something like what sex is for a straight man I imagine but far more intimate; I felt simultaneously her mind close around me, shift slightly and be still, and her body in her bed in Brougham Street turn as she moved to accommodate the weight of mine, which was not there. These physical twitches are involuntary, like the ghostly itch of the toes of amputees.

A death.

It would need to be a tragic death, which not all deaths are. No one wept at the death of the man who raped Lexa, especially not me. I had to do that one without Kate—all her energy was with Lexa. I was able to because my rage was already so great (kneeling on the concrete vomiting into the open mouth of the toilet, screaming at Boy and Christian to Get out, get out, get out). They haven't found him yet.

That was my first death. This would be my second.

A tragic death. The death of someone young, then: not a child, because children are not yet fully formed, and the grief is at least partly for a lost promise, for all the things the child might have grown into, for the roads and forks never trodden, and that wasn't right for us at this time. Not an adolescent, either—adolescents are too crazy, they're hard because they're so unreliable chemically. Someone just come into adulthood. Not a woman: enough happens to women. A young man, then. A man to die just as his life was opening up, just as the line had been found. And someone precious—someone brilliant, someone charismatic, someone to whom others clustered. This death had to have meaning.

Kate, I said without speaking.

I'm here, said Kate.

When I came to, the candle was a guttering stump and I was on the floor beside it.

I sat up slowly. I was so cold my feet were numb. Mary Wollstone-craft had gone. The house felt inhabited, though; it's funny how you can tell, even when there's absolute silence.

Someone—Boy, or Christian—had come in and put the grey

army blanket over me. That was why everything was so still, then. They hate seeing me like this—Christian in particular. I know, though we've never discussed it. I don't know what they think it means. They've never discussed it with each other, either. I do know that.

'Oh, God,' I said aloud. I felt incredibly depressed; it works that way, sometimes, after. I tend to be dehydrated; the best thing to do is to go to bed and sleep it off. Kate was already falling into a dream when I disentangled.

The light from the hall fell across Christian's bare shoulder. I climbed in beside him. He didn't move.

'Christian?' I whispered. Sometimes the after-effects, before things get realigned, are quite lonely. He didn't answer; I turned to cuddle into his back, and quite distinctly felt him shudder.

'What,' I said flatly. I'd known he was awake.

There was a long pause.

'You were lying,' said Christian, very cold, still with his face turned to the wall, 'in the middle of the floor.'

'Well, I fell, I suppose,' I said.

'You've been lying there for *hours*,' Christian said. 'It's three o'clock in the *morning*.'

'Well,' I said. I rolled flat onto my back and sent the ceiling a dirty look. I really am not in the mood for this, I told the dusty lightshade; but after a minor struggle I managed to say, sounding close enough to sincere, 'I'm sorry, Christian.'

Christian snorted. He thumped the wall, twice, and then struggled over in a great heaving of blankets and rearranging of pillows to lie facing me; he made a grunting noise which could have been read as either dismissal or acceptance.

Poor Christian, I thought, relenting, it really isn't easy, he doesn't get it, and I stroked his wheaty hair and listened to his breathing settle until he began to snore, when I took the opportunity to poke him rather spitefully in the ribs.

Just as I was falling asleep myself, Kate's dream, as I had caught it, disentangling, floated very clear into my head.

Christian and Kate, wound round each other on her bed in Mount Victoria; it was a fantasy, not a memory, I could tell by the lack of distinction in the picture. That's funny, I thought drowsily, I didn't know that. How about that.

When I woke up the dead man's clock (Lexa's grandfather's; she had not liked him) was tumbling its shutters over eleven-thirty and Mary Wollstonecraft was lying neatly across a shaft of sunlight that speared the fullblown roses of the carpet. There was a cold cup of coffee sitting on a note on the floor in orange crayon: 'Jessie—Drake called, you looked extreemly asleep, told them to buger off but very politely, so hey good morning girl, I'm cooking filo things tonight, so will you be around, love Boy.'

Love Boy, I thought, stretching, snapping my fingers at Mary Wollstonecraft, catching sight of myself in the mirror on the door of Christian's enormous mahogany wardrobe pilfered from his great-aunt's after the funeral—and retreating hastily back under the covers, why does witching always make me so pale, Love Boy, love Boy, we all love Boy, Boy is so lovable, I love Boy: 'Do *you* love Boy, Mary Wollstonecraft?' I asked her, and she let out a little chirruping miaow and pranced over the bed to settle purring on my chest.

'He's practically uneducated, mind you,' I reminded her sternly. Mary Wollstonecraft narrowed her eyes into slits.

Although so is Christian, if you don't count two terms of engineering which personally I don't.

Which is where they met, by the way, Christchurch. Not too many Maori boys down there (and not too many Boys anywhere). Christian had dropped out of the seventh form and wasn't doing much except mushrooms, I gather. Lots of druggies in Christchurch. Subcultures flourish in that kind of environment. Nice beaches but.

Anyway, so they were at the same party ('Our eyes met across a crowded room,' Boy informed me once, to which Christian responded, 'Fuck *off*—!' but nicely; they probably did, actually, the eyes, murder and mayhem being present in different quantities in both pairs. 'Christian looks like a fallen choirboy, and Boy like a good-tempered gargoyle,' Stu observed once, four o'clock in the morning: it's true). It was a party at one of those flats, you know those flats: in old houses with the huge brown sofas with broken springs and generations of sticky coffee stains on the arms, peeling walls with a few ugly posters, the flight of incredibly steep and narrow wooden stairs, the mannequin whipped from God knows where leaning very debonair against the mantelpiece. Boy was painting houses and Christian had not yet learned he wanted to paint anything at all. Neither of them are very clear about how it happened, but it seems the street outside was being facelifted and at four o'clock that morning Boy and Christian got done for stealing a front-end loader.

'We only got it fifty metres down the road,' Boy will say, exploding. The idea, I gather, was to drive it to the Square and leave it there.

'Well, it's *boring* in Christchurch,' Christian will explain.

They were, of course, taken to court, and were, of course, let off with a warning, being disarmingly eighteen and charming with it, but by that time they were, appropriately, as thick as thieves and the following year, after Christian had dropped out of engineering, they went to Dunedin and dropped out of a few more things there for the next couple of years—you could live on the dole then, especially in Dunedin. Christian bonked an art student and became seriously interested in his oil-throwing for the first time; Boy discovered drama and how good he was at it, and after a Speights-sodden conversation in the Gardens one February afternoon they decided they were bored with Dunedin and hitched to Wellington to visit Stu. Stu had been at high school with Christian and was then living in Boulcott Street; Stu had a new flatmate, a shaved-headed dyke called Lexa, who worked in stained glass and knew Kate from bartending; and here, three years later, we all are.

Mary Wollstonecraft turned up on our doorstep about a year ago, the smallest and most self-possessed kitten you ever saw.

Kate and I, of course, go back beyond back. Our mothers knew each other. We have the complicated, comfortable and irritated relationship of the long-married. We are usually tired of one another, in the way that one is tired of people who have known you so long they see you both less and more clearly than anybody else: we have, in short, the mildly resentful intimacy of women who were present and observing at each other's first school socials, 'Ginger crunch and orange cordial in plastic cups,' as Kate says. We cheer and secretly cavil at each other's successes, fancy each other's men, get jealous of each other's women, bitch about each other to Lexa, put each other down in company, bear each other up in private, get hysterical over cups of tea and what we did to poor frail Madame Rochelle in the fourth form: we hate each other quite a lot of the time but there is all that female stuff Christian finds so incestuous—Christian, with his straightforward male friendships, based on whisky drunk, drugs taken, front-end loaders: things *done*—all those years' worth, that sediment layer upon layer of knowledge, first periods, first boyfriends, first exams, braces off, homework not done, smoking Lexa's father's cigarettes watching ourselves in the bathroom mirror, the virginity fumbled and painfully lost, with guilt and exhilaration and regret: all those terrible family arguments we knew about, the times you run from the house sobbing with fury and call hiccupping from a phonebox, the times we crept out of our parents' houses and met in the Reserve, the times we stole my mother's car at two in the morning, just to drive, just to go round the bays, listening to music and not talking, the first flats, the first varsity papers failed, the times holding each other's heads when somebody had kept handing us tequila-and-orange at first-year Orientation parties and assuring us it was practically non-alcoholic; the terrible waitressing jobs, the one truly dreadful break-up with the boy you actually never forget, since he was the first to hurt you that badly and no one else will ever get the chance; the ridiculous painful arguments, weathered but not forgotten, the phases we go through still of ringing each other up on the phone and talking for six hours at a time.

The phone rang, making me jump. Mary Wollstonecraft had fallen asleep; I rolled her up in the army blanket and she miaowed, faintly. The carpet was cold to my bare feet. I was wearing a large ripped T-shirt of Christian's with The Pogues on the front, dating from his Christchurch days: a frigid breeze issuing from the back door, which had never closed properly, blew through the kitchen and around my thighs.

'Hello,' I said, insinuatingly, into the mouthpiece. I'd known who it would be. I curled up on the sagging couch and watched the Mona Lisa.

'Were you awake?' Kate said. 'Why aren't you at work? Are you tired? God I'm so uptight, are you uptight? I fell straight asleep but I had the wildest dreams, did you dream? I feel like I've got the world's worst hangover, yuk, the taste in my mouth, I'm seriously out of practice at this you know, do you feel like that?'

'It's the winter,' I said, and after a slight pause, 'Hush.'

The phone wire hummed between us, a rhythm like the sea, like someone breathing.

'Breathe,' I said to Kate. I closed my own eyes and leaned my head back against the wall; I felt Mary Wollstonecraft pad into the room, look at me and pad away. And then it came, when we were breathing together: two sets of ghost sensations at once, riding on the real. I felt the warmth of the pink lino beneath my paws, the stroke of the winter sunlight on the fur on my back; the smell of last night's mince congealing on the stove was suddenly sharp, divided into many layers of sensation. Simultaneously an image of the tree outside Kate's window and the little neon sculpture of a pear-shaped woman Lexa had bent for her superimposed itself over the red and black behind my eyes; I could taste jasmine tea and Kate's red phone slid in my/her dry little palm.

The cone of power: after a shared spell it lingers electric between the three of us, able to be tapped into for a couple of days.

After a while I opened my eyes.

'I hate that herbal shit,' I told Kate. She is currently affecting vegetarianism.

Kate let out a shuddering sigh.

'Sometimes I feel like that after I've made love,' she said. All the levels of intimacy had opened up into one: I scarcely knew whether we were talking aloud. This is the best part of the years of ginger crunch and orange cordial, our reward, and what Christian and even Boy don't understand. Even when they're present for these conversations they don't hear what we hear. What is articulated is only the smallest part of it.

'Like I can't tell whose skin is mine any more,' said Kate.

'Lucky you,' I said; the fuzzy image of Christian and Kate floated into my mind and I sealed quickly before she caught it.

'What?' she said, meaning, What just happened?

'Nothing. I should get moving on this, Katie mine.' I crooked up both knees and pulled Christian's T-shirt over them.

'Okay.' Her voice dropped. 'That's why I called. To see if you were all right. And if you need anything.'

'Just be around,' I said. 'Finding the plot's the hard bit. I can do the rest on my own. Just be there-ish.'

'Okay,' said Kate. 'Jessica, who—'

I dropped the phone back on its cradle. My reflection met me in the round black-framed mirror over the mantelpiece, eyes gleaming and hair attractively tousled; I pulled up the T-shirt and admired my breasts from several angles, played 'Greensleeves' on the piano (great-aunt) with one finger, stumped into the kitchen, switched on the radio on the fridge which is a Boy find from an op shop in Palmie of the vintage when they were known as wirelesses and only gets the National programme, drank half a carton of orange juice straight from the box, dropped it on the floor and cooked up—flashing stabs of spite at Kate, whose presence still turned around me like a draught from a suddenly closed door and who would be receiving ghost-imprints of everything I ate, drank and emoted for the rest of the day—four rashers of bacon and two large eggs, which I ate standing up from the pan with the last crust of Molenberg. Then I peeled an only slightly soggy kiwifruit, made a fresh cup of coffee and went back to bed. Everywhere else was freezing.

In my sleep—the guilty and luxurious sleep one sleeps during the day when one should be at work—I had a dream of a strangely shaped flower.

It was very small and beautifully shaped: each petal—in the impossible manner of dreams—was made up of a thousand iridescent fractures of light; it hung and glowed in my mind, deep violet and white and framed by tiny vivid leaves. Purple and green and white, I thought, asleep; the suffragette colours. A part of me registered Mary Wollstonecraft, back in Holloway Road, picking her way delicately under the covers and curling up against my breast.

I am the sun, I thought; I am the son; I am the sun, and my flower opened under the warmth of my gaze and dropped minuscule seeds, white and violet, on the pinky-brown plain on which it grew, and they began to blossom, a beautiful carpet all leaning their heads toward me.

And I saw through their translucent stems the blood flowing, up from the plain to the roots to the petals. The green of the stems turned its rich red dull, but when the flow reached each furled bud the bud burst silently open and scattered light all over the skin from which it drew its sustenance.

In my dream we all came toward this carpet of violets, Christian and Kate and Stu and Jeff and Lexa and all of us. In fancy dress, in carnival. Christian was carrying a sword; his ruffled white shirt was slashed to where it tucked into his grey trousers and the light gleamed from his boots. Jeff carried a cutlass between his teeth and a red bandanna on his head. Lexa was almost lost in black draperies; her small fierce face looked out from under a starched wimple. Stu was a court jester, Kate (trust Kate) a milkmaid; my brilliantly coloured skirt brushed my bare feet and—simultaneously with watching us all advance—I felt the heavy hoops dance in my ears, felt the weight of the crystal ball in my hands.

And this brilliant dream-company bore down on my flowers and began to gather them. With every snap of every stem someone cried out sharply against us, but we didn't seem to hear; we held the petals to our faces, tucked them into our bodices, twined them into each other's hair, and drifted away together, not speaking, and the flowers were all gone and, as I watched, the man's body from which they had grown twisted and shrank and melted away into nothing.

I woke up to the heavy early dusk of winter and Mary Wollstone-craft snoring snufflingly. Our window looks out on the blank wall of the house next door, perhaps six feet away; I lay and watched it disappear.

When I was properly awake I plucked the memory of the first flower from the fabric of my dream and placed it in the centre of my mind.

Grow, I told my flower: and then, rather theatrically, Go forth and multiply.

'Look at Mary Wollstonecraft,' Kate said admiringly. 'God.'

Mary Wollstonecraft lay in a sinuous silken heap before the two-bar heater. It was four o'clock Sunday morning, just for a change. I often thought then—looking around the circle of the beautiful, restless, dissatisfied faces of my friends, four o'clock Sunday morning—that it was always this time, this place, these people; that the rest of my life was a dream, or at the most a prelude to this.

'Where three or more are gathered together,' Boy had said to me once, in the kitchen, four o'clock Sunday morning; and I had turned to look at him. I was making coffee over the blue-purple of the gas; it takes concentration to do this without scalding it, in a saucepan. I'll buy a plunger, one day—but I was making coffee, leaning into the warmth of the oven, and I had not known Boy was listening to me think at all. I was a little stoned and had been overwhelmed, abruptly, with love, out there in the living-room. They were playing an obscene version of racing Scrabble Stu (it would be Stu) had invented, carrying on very noisy, very silly, very funny, beneath the remote chill smile of the Mona Lisa. My eyes had pricked abruptly and I had had to make a quick getaway from my love so I went and made coffee and Boy had followed.

'I have to be in control,' I told him now, sternly, of my love.

Boy leaned against the fridge, his hands in his bum pockets and his eyes on me, steady and whimsical.

'I *do*,' I said.

'Maybe,' Boy said. 'And maybe not.'

'Love's messy,' I told Boy.

'I know,' Boy told me.

'Who else will run things, if I get sloppy?' I demanded.

'Things run themselves, Jessie Kane,' said Boy. 'All those brains and you don't know that yet?'

'No they don't,' I said with certainty. 'Oh no they don't, Boy. *I* run things.'

'With a little help from Kate and Mary Wollstonecraft,' Boy had said then, very soft and only slightly questioning.

I froze over the saucepan. Dope betrays you; this was the closest we had ever come to—

And yet, I thought then, stoned, Boy *would* know. It isn't so surprising, when you think about it, I told myself.

Boy's always loved me the best, I thought; and I looked at him, challengingly, in the eyes.

'I can't imagine,' I said, with dignity, '*what* you mean.'

Boy laughed; there came a sudden swell of noise from the living-room: Stu had whipped one of Christian's counters and Christian was chasing him all over the furniture while Kate stood on a speaker and screamed.

'They're all so innocent,' I said to Boy abruptly. I wanted to cry; this dope-inspired sadness had come up so suddenly, so foolishly, a thick hard pain in my throat.

Boy didn't move; he shook his head at me kindly.

'And you,' I said to Boy, 'you're the most innocent of all. It's terrible, innocence,' I said, and began to weep into the coffee, 'it's unfair,' I explained, and I put my nose in the hollow of Boy's brown throat and bawled. I was astounded at myself.

'Poor Jessie,' Boy said. He stroked my hair, impersonally and kindly. 'Poor Jessica.'

'I was never innocent, Boy,' I wailed absurdly. I can't tell you how sorry I felt for me at that moment. Poor Jessica, always the powerful one.

'No, well,' said Boy. He put both arms around me, standing against the fridge, and hugged me, hard, and Christian exploded through the door with his hair on end and his green eyes crazily alight: he looked very handsome and not a little mad.

'Oy,' he said cheerfully, taking me and Boy in, and jumped in between us and kissed me on the mouth: 'Oy, what's going on in here then, ay?'

Then he kissed Boy on the mouth, and then me again, and then Boy and I kissed each other and Stu came in and lifted Christian off the ground by the belt-loops on his jeans and then kissed me and I kissed Jeff and Boy kissed Kate and then Kate and I kissed each other, amid much cheering, and it was all very silly and very nice and that was another Sunday morning, four o'clock, and the only reason I remember it, separate from all the others, is that intimacy with Boy, that intimation of Boy's particular wisdom.

'I'm going to make us a bath,' Boy announced.

'You don't *make* baths, Boy, you great berk,' I said irritably. 'Anyway, where would you put it, in the hall?'

'In the yard,' Boy said.

We have a smallish concrete square outside the back door, bordered in summer by orange nasturtiums which froth around the carcass of an ancient blue moped which Christian brought up from Christchurch once and never rode again. The distinguishing features of this yard are the gnome Stu and Lexa stole from a garden in Karori for my Honours finals and a couple of deckchairs you have to sit in very judiciously indeed.

'Why?' I said. I was grumpy; I had gone back to work that day. It had been horrible.

'So we can look at the stars,' Boy answered reasonably.

'How would you fill it, with buckets?' I demanded. Sometimes Boy and Christian are so impractical.

'Feed a hose through the shutters from the taps in the shower,' Christian said from the depths of *The Face*.

'Could put gas burners underneath it, to keep the water warm,' Boy said, perking up. Our hot water supply is not very plentiful even in summer.

'Where would you get the bath from?' I asked, as patiently as I could, which wasn't very; and they both raised their faces to look at me, wide-eyed and innocent.

'The tip,' they said in chorus, and since clearly the day wasn't going to go my way I put on my bear coat (wool-lined, was once my father's) and stomped out of the house.

I love Oriental Parade: it is unfailingly beautiful in any weather and at any time of the year (trees sea hills fountain). By the time I came back I was in a much better mood. Christian was sitting on the sofa playing guitar.

'Where's Boy?' I said as I unmuffled myself.

'Had a headache, gone to bed,' Christian muttered into the complexities of his fingering.

'Oh,' I said. I paused at the doorway of the kitchen.

'Want to go and get a drink?' Christian asked. 'Stu and them are at the Brunswick.'

'Okay,' I said. I didn't know what I felt like, all of a sudden.

'Want to have sex first?' Christian suggested.

'No thanks,' I said. 'Can we take the Morrie?'

'What're you asking me for?' Christian said, but when I peeked in at Boy he was just a hump under the covers, breathing stertorously, so we took it anyway.

'Oh Jesus *God* this rain,' said Stu. He stood at the window before Holloway Road, his arms wrapped around his own torso; he jiggled from foot to foot; he walked around the kitchen, picking up and dropping things, beating a nervous rhythm on the table.

'I'd almost rather have a job,' he added.

'Stu, king of the subculture, wants a job,' I told Mary Wollstonecraft. 'Honestly, Stu, you'd last five minutes before you punched out the foreman, the mood you're in lately.'

'That at least,' said Stu heavily, 'would make a change.'

'Bags me first,' Boy piped up from the windowseat where he had been playing patience (and cheating) for the last hour and a half. But Stu was not about to be charmed tonight, not even by Boy.

'Don't you have a play to rehearse or something?' he asked him rudely. Boy did not answer, casting me his best wry look over Stu's shoulder.

'I'm going to get a tattoo,' Jeff announced. He was, for some reason, lying under the kitchen table.

'Like Jessica. Jessica,' Boy declared, 'has a tattoo of a rose on her left buttock. Of the woman's symbol. In green.'

'How do *you* know?' Christian demanded.

'Saw it when she got out of the bath,' Boy answered succinctly.

Stu put his hand on the back of my neck. 'Now *that'd* liven things up,' he said. 'Want to have an affair with me, Jessica, and really piss Christian off?'

'Just fucking try it,' Christian muttered, but without, actually, a great deal of annoyance. I saw Kate glance at him and then, involuntarily, at me; I averted my eyes hastily and they collided immediately with Boy's. Stu had to be the only one who was finding the night so unfraught as to be tedious, I thought.

'Ohhh—I want to *go* somewhere, I want to *do* something,' Stu groaned; he hurled himself around the kitchen a bit longer, tripping on Jeff's legs. 'Let's go to a movie,' he suggested suddenly.

'No money,' Christian, Boy and Kate all said automatically and together.

'Let's go to a pub, then. Or a club. Let's go and have a boogie!' Stu looked almost excited for a moment.

'No money,' the others droned. Being poor in winter really isn't a good time. Some weeks I could've shouted, being as I was the only one present gainfully employed, but even the temp work was slackening off, these days, and there was the power bill to consider.

'Okay, then. Why don't we go and drive through Victoria Tunnel and honk and see how many people honk back?'

'Now *that* sounds like a good time,' Christian said sarcastically.

'The bath! How *is* the bath?' Kate interceded hurriedly; Stu was going into slow burn, and Christian can be incendiary to the most patient of people when he chooses.

'Bloody freezing,' I said. It was. Christian and Boy had brought home, in triumph, an ancient cast-iron thing on the top of the buckling and complaining Morrie, and it had been duly installed on bricks in our concrete square; in spite of, or perhaps because of, all my bitching about it I had been honoured with the baptismal bathe. Even though Boy had ripped out the door between the loo and the shower—which had been hanging around not doing any good to anybody, he explained—and balanced it across the bath to keep as much heat in as possible I only lasted five minutes: the water chilled as soon as it hit the cast-iron, which was so cold it burned my bum. Anyway, once you were in someone else had to slide the door up the length of the bath so only your head poked out and it reminded me uncomfortably of being in a coffin.

'Yes. It might be a summer thing, that bath,' Boy conceded. 'Be great though. We can have bathing parties—smoke a bit of hash—'

'Yes!' Stu cried. '*I* know! Late-night shopping! Let's drive through the Victoria Tunnel, honk, see how many people honk back, then keep driving till we get to Kilbirnie, get stoned in the carpark and go and look at the vegetables!'

'What?' said Kate blankly; the men were actually looking mildly interested.

'New thing,' I explained. 'It's the colours, you know how they have all the fruit and vegetables piled up in ranks all along one wall in the supermarket? All the colours? And mirrors above them? They go and stare at them and say "Wow" a lot and scare old ladies till they get thrown out. Very grown up, very discreet.'

'Everyone's old in Kilbirnie, I wonder why?' said Boy. 'Anyway, you can talk, Jessica. You should have seen Jessica,' he told Kate, 'discovering eternity in a handful of sunflower seeds.' He demonstrated; I scowled at him. Kate laughed.

'Sounds great,' she said. 'We are the people our grandparents warned us about. Can I come? I've always had a hankering to frighten old ladies.'

'Who's going to drive back?' I asked carefully.

'Driving stoned isn't dangerous, you go too slow,' Christian said. 'It's not like being drunk.' I looked at Kate; she rolled her eyes.

'I'll drive,' Boy said, patting my knee. 'Don't feel like getting wasted anyway.'

'You all right, mate?' Christian said to him; Boy had been awfully quiet lately, for Boy that is. But it wasn't a question that needed an answer. They were all suddenly galvanised into action; Jeff sat up so fast he cracked his head on the table.

'Serves you right,' Stu said, in a terrifically good humour, 'lurking about on the floor shamelessly looking up Mary Wollstonecraft's skirts.'

'Hyena in petticoats,' Boy said. I looked at him in genuine astonishment. The things Boy knows amaze me as much as the things he doesn't, sometimes. He smiled at me shyly.

'Didn't know why you called her such a stupid name,' he said, 'when it could have been Pawsy or Ginger or anything. So I looked it up. At the library. When she has kittens,' he added, showing off slightly, this was the Boy we all knew and loved, 'you can call them Mary Shelley.'

'And *her* kittens can be called Frankenstein,' Kate added.

'We all create our own monsters,' I said, not to be outdone.

Christian looked puzzled.

'Mary Wollstonecraft's not ginger, she's tortoiseshell,' he said, and lost interest in the hunt for the keys now ensuing amongst the sofa cushions.

'Katie,' I said, under the hubbub. 'Can you stay with me?'

'Aren't you coming?' she said. The pause hung. 'Is there something up?'

'Just want to stay home,' I said. 'With you and Mary Wollstone-craft. Drink whisky. Hid some in the laundry basket.'

'Okay,' Kate said slowly.

And so they all left, clattering rowdily down the hall and spilling out into the street. 'Something's going to *happen!*' we heard Stu yell, and then the Morrie starting up with its usual amount of wheezing and clanking.

'Famous last words,' said Kate lightly. 'They worry me sometimes, those guys.'

'They're great,' I said. I was feeling sicker and sicker. I got up, bent almost double, shuffled across the room to the sofa and curled up and closed my eyes. 'God, are you all right?' said Kate. 'I'm sorry, I didn't notice, Jess. Is it your period?'

I shook my head.

'Blanket,' I said. I was bitterly cold. 'Can you get me some whisky?' through clenched teeth: even talking was becoming difficult. 'Eggcups're on the bench.'

Kate disappeared; and so did I; I swung bodiless in a grey haze; I felt, very faintly, Kate lifting my head, putting it on her lap, tucking the quilt around my shoulders; then she and I and Holloway Road vanished and

The roaring of the Morrie cut in, very gradually, and then the bump and swing of the road, the low-slung springs creaking under me as we cornered, the smell of marijuana raw and familiar in my nostrils.

'Don't smoke it in here, are you crazy?' I said. 'What if we get pulled over? Car's full of it, man. And guess who'll get done? Me. Dumb hori boy.'

'You can't be serious,' Stu bellowed. 'This car,' clamoured Stu, rattling one of the back doors, 'this car has more ventilation than your average cheese grater. This car,' declared Stu, thumping on one of the taped windows, 'this car has more ventilation than your average prairie. This car—'

'Yeah, yeah, all right, all right, we get the picture,' I said. I hadn't been serious, really, anyway. I was perfectly happy, boys together, it's nice sometimes, even though Kate and Jessica are so neat, those two in the back making all that noise, Wellington sliding, wheeling, red and green lights and bush-covered hills past the windows, sea out there somewhere, wheel sliding through my fingers, Christian beside me, grinning and quiet, like he'd been for years. Christian, yeah, Jeff and Stu singing, doing a harmony, 'Summertime', and here comes the tunnel, opening up like a mouth, black mouth to swallow us up, hit the orange light and the petrol fumes, just a few cars, a couple ahead and one going the other way, and hit the horn with the flat of my hand and

With the blaring it comes up / it explodes / hits me at the same time as the noise

'Boy? Jesus—Boy—'

Christian's voice coming from out in the ether somewhere I can't see properly / catch this crazy glimpse of him, arcing / he looks ludicrous / it's almost funny how frightened / cos I'm falling forward I can't see Christian yelling and the car sliding

Everything went black.

The sound of a woman screaming, high pitched and horrible, snapped me back sharply and painfully into my body in Holloway Road.

I was on my feet in the middle of the living-room, Kate staring at me, white-faced.

'Jessica? Jesus—Jessica—'

'We have to go, we have to go, we have to go,' I was gibbering at her.

'What? What? Go *where*? Jessica—'

'Hospital. Have to go,' I said; I tried to turn around too quickly and fell over. I couldn't remember where the door was.

'Jessie. Calm down. Sit down,' said Kate. The soothing note in her voice contrasted oddly with how scared her eyes were.

'Mary Wollstonecraft,' I said.

'She's here. I'm here. Sit down,' said Kate firmly.

'No!' I screamed at her. 'We have to go! Jesus, Kate, Boy was *driving*! OhmyGod I'm so stupid, I'm so stupid, I'm so stupid!'

'I'll call a taxi, I'll call a taxi,' Kate was saying, even then not getting it, and I shoved her back into the sofa and ran past her down the hall, hitting the walls, bouncing off from one to the other all the way to the front door, and I fell against it and down the steps and landed on my hands and knees and picked myself up and jumped the gate and fell again.

We were already there when they brought them in. The Morrie had hit the wall of the tunnel, side-on. Christian had pulled on the handbrake and they had gone into a spin, into the path of oncoming traffic. Fortunately there was only one car coming and it had managed to swerve; it had bashed in a door on its way past and thrown Christian into the windshield. They hit the opposite side then and stopped. The Morrie's top speed had only ever been thirty miles an hour. They had been, in fact, incredibly lucky.

I found Jeff and Stu first. Christian had gone in the ambulance with Boy and was still refusing to leave him. Jeff and Stu were being treated for shock and minor bruises; the nurse said Christian had mild concussion. Jeff was crying. Stu, the most stoned, couldn't figure out anything that was going on; he just kept staring around him, crunched up in a little ball.

'Hello, Jessica,' he said formally when I touched him. 'Where are Boy and Christian?'

'Hey, Stu,' I said. 'Are you all right?'

'Oh I'm fine, thank you. And you?' said Stuart. 'Are you well?'

'Jesus,' said Kate under her breath.

'Take them back to Holloway Road,' I said to her. 'Put them to bed and make sure they're asleep before you come back.' She had caught up with me near the Mount Cook in Lexa's purple Volkswagen. Lexa was still in her pyjamas. She was wearing gumboots and a splash of green oil paint on her cheek.

'Hello, Alexandra,' said Stu, focusing on her, 'and how have you been?'

'Let me stay with you,' Lexa said to me urgently; she hadn't let go of my hand since I got in the car, little tough Lexa.

'No, honestly. I have to find Christian,' I said. 'Go and help Kate.'

'Dead on arrival,' said Stu brightly. 'What do you think that means, Jessica?'

And I felt as well as heard Kate's indrawn breath. The shock of knowledge crashing leaden-footed into her mind was like the ground tilting beneath my own feet. I turned around, slowly, to face her.

'Get them out of here,' I told Lexa.

Christian was sitting on a bench in A and E, leaning against the wall. His head was bandaged. He did not begin to turn toward me until I was almost upon him, though I had spoken his name, and when he did, it was very slowly, as if moving underwater. His face was quite white: a deep bruise showed up lovely against it on his temple. There was blood still in the process of congealing from a gash on his lip; his eyes were wide with shock, shockingly green. He looked beautiful.

'Christian,' I said, and took his face in my hands and leaned my forehead against his, very carefully because of the bandages. He looked up at me, bewildered. His hands remained still on his own thighs.

'Boy,' he said. His voice was quite dead.

'I know,' I whispered to him; I bent, I kissed the gash on his mouth. It felt strange, not Christian's mouth at all; as if he had forgotten how to hold it in the right shape. I ran my tongue along the cut; Christian suddenly took a rough shuddering breath in and said, anguished, 'Boy,' against my teeth and grasped my wrists and kissed me back, urgently and ungently. The blood ran between us, salty and invigorating, like whisky.

Christian was shuddering all over, from some deep cold. He leant his head against my hip, his arms around my thighs. I stroked his forehead, watching my fingers run through the wheat of his hair. I felt like an earth mother; I felt like a goddess. Christian's blood warmed my stomach like spirit. I stood in the dingy hospital corridor, huge and powerful, fiery all the way through.

'Boy,' muttered Christian.

He did not weep.

I did not speak.

There was nothing left to say.

But when we went back to the Volkswagen, walking separately, holding an invisible wire taut a foot between us, Kate was not there.

I found her at Scorching Bay. Dawn was already breaking. Christian had refused to stay in the hospital; he had been given a sleeping tablet and was now lying utterly still, curled in the grey army blanket on the sofa under the impenetrable smile of the Mona Lisa. He had refused to lie in our bed either. I had not pushed the point.

The sands were wide and empty. I parked the car across two spaces and got out slowly; the pine-covered cliff reared against my back. There were the faint beginnings of a wind and my feet in the holey black Commandos cut dark swathes through the silver of the grass.

The first ferry was cutting their mirrored images, white against the deadness of the sea, heading out into the Strait.

'Dire straits,' I said to the rocks, and felt the first jolt of grief, shocking in its intensity. I closed my throat and eyes against it and when I opened them I saw Kate, standing groin-deep in the waves with her back to me.

'Kate,' I said, 'Katie,' but she did not turn. The Commandos crunched through the sand; I stood on the edge of the sea and said, '*Kate*,' and fear came washing into all the empty spaces of the shore.

The winter sea was freezing. I touched her shoulder and she turned. Her face was utterly ruined by tears.

'Oh God,' I said, 'oh Katie,' and she said expressionlessly, 'Keep your fucking hands off me.'

We stood facing each other, breathing harsh and fast. Then (fifteen years of ginger crunch and orange cordial) her mind opened to me, as I'm sure mine did to her, and I saw what she saw.

'They'll tear you apart,' she said. 'They will, Jess. All of them. Even Lexa. When I tell them. They'll tear you apart.'

I stood staring into her eyes.

'Christian already half-knows,' Kate said. A wave broke against our hips and left salt water glittering on her face. She didn't bother to wipe it off. 'You know he does. All those times he's found you. He'll believe me, Jess. And I tell you. I don't care how long you've been lovers. Boy means more to him than you ever will, Jessica. I'm telling you. He'll kill you. He will.'

The wind blew off the Strait, whipping our hair around our faces.

'Oh Jessica, how could you? How *could* you?' Kate wailed suddenly; the sound made a hole in the blank wall of terror big enough for me to see through, and I saw that what I was afraid of was not anything the others might do to me but of Kate, of losing Kate.

'I didn't choose him. You know I didn't, Katie. It chose him Itself; he was the one; you know this, you know this!' I shouted at her; I gripped her arm and she twisted it free.

'You could have blocked it!' she yelled. 'You could have! You *knew*! You could have told me!'

'It was too late, it was already too late, it was always too late,' I said. 'Jesus, Kate, do you think it was what I wanted? Do you think it didn't hurt me? I did it for you, for all of you: don't you know what tragedy is for? Don't you remember why we started it in the first place?'

'He'll kill you,' Kate said, but her eyes were already filling with tears.

'I didn't do it on my own,' I said, very soft, and her head snapped back and she made a move for my face; I caught her hand and held it. 'There's precedents,' I said rapidly, 'you know that's all It needs. Precedent and due process, and we did all that. You can't do anything to me, Kate; you can't touch me. I'm protected. You can't,' and I sent flooding through her mind all the ones before, all the sacrifices I could remember, the harvest sacrifices and the spring sacrifices and the ones before battle: the Cretan tax and the Nazarene and the men they found in the peat.

She looked at me, open-mouthed and helpless.

'Anyway,' I said, 'it wasn't only witches they burned at the stake, Kate. You won't be able to stop at me. There's Lexa. And Jeff. That's why "faggot", don't you remember? And wise women. Healers. All your herbal shit, Kate. You'd have to go too. And Stu. Dissidents, heretics. Stu doesn't believe in any of the gods.'

Kate began to sob.

'There'd only be Christian left,' I told her, and she wailed at me, despairingly, as Christian had, 'Boy,' and I said, 'I know,' as I had to Christian, only unlike with Christian my voice cracked and then I had to speak Boy aloud too, because speaking him was the only way we'd ever have him, any more, and I said, 'Boy,' to Kate and the tears came up and fountained and waterfalled into the waiting sea. We stood facing each other and not touching, waist-deep in water. The seagulls that whirled above our heads were sobbing and screaming and howling into the empty Strait. They were crying for Boy, for the guilt that is knowledge, for love and loss and the twenty-four years none of us would ever have again.

'At the going down of the sun, and in the morning,' I told Kate. She leaned against my shoulder. We were both shivering and our bare feet looked like corpses', white and wet and dead. I put my arm around her and with the other hand took a swig of the brandy the Volkswagen had yielded up from the glovebox. It burned as deep as blood. Boy had got an ad last autumn; he had planted brandy, cigarettes and chocolate in all of our cars, with strict instructions that we were not to touch them unless in case of emergency.

'God bless Boy,' Kate had said, finding it, and we had laughed and the laughter had made us cry again, so we got the blanket he had whipped from the Youth Hostel as a present for Lexa because she liked the weave out of the back, and we sat on the bonnet and drank Boy's brandy and smoked Boy's rollies and blessed Boy's ghost, and the sun came up, eventually, as it always would.

There is nothing so enervating as grief, nothing so cathartic as a death. Kate and I were both still hiccupping slightly from sobbing.

Tears still slid out of our eyes and barely noticed down our cheeks from time to time; they would continue to do so for the next fortnight, and we would all continue like this, wrung out and hollowed out, exhausted and exhilarated, filled with our terrible sorrow that came bearing the gift of our aliveness in its hands.

'Did you always know?' Kate asked me once, four o'clock Sunday morning.

'That it would be Boy?' I asked Kate, although I already knew what she meant. Christian and Stu and Jeff were all out, dancing the steps of some male grieving ritual I knew nothing about. They would be back. We were all bound in those weeks following Boy's death by the absence at our centre that had been him. We did not go far from each other for long. Stu and Jeff and Lexa had practically moved in; often we all slept together, on the living-room floor, in my bed, in Boy's bed, limbs thrown over limbs, heads resting on breastbones, hands clasping over torsos, breathing into each other's hair, backs, underarms.

'Yes,' Kate said.

I sighed; I looked into the eyes of the Mona Lisa. They argue she's a self-portrait, now. But even artists cannot, finally, escape gender. It is destiny.

'We should take you back, I think,' I told the feminine of Leonardo, 'you're way late,' and she gazed at me with her intimate and knowing stare. For a moment I wanted, suddenly and quite irrationally, to scramble up and turn her face to the wall; but it passed. I love the Mona Lisa.

'Yes,' I said to Kate, eventually.

'Poor Jessie,' Kate said, sorrowing.

I accepted this: it was true.

'He always loved you the best,' Kate said. I glanced at her but her eyes were dry, her deceptively sweet face still and thoughtful. Her hands stroked rhythmically along Mary Wollstonecraft's back.

'He always thought you'd end up together, you know,' she added.

I turned around bodily to stare at her.

'What?' I said.

'Mmm. He told me, once, when we were really drunk. And,' Kate smiled at me rather shamefacedly, 'me with Christian.'

'*Boy* set you off on that!' I said incredulously.

'Oh. You did pick up on it, then. I wondered if you had. Sorry,' she said. 'Just a thought.'

'That's all right,' I said. I couldn't believe it.

But, I thought, as Mary Wollstonecraft rolled over onto her back and began patting at my fingers, it made a kind of diabolical sense. They would have suited each other, finally, Kate and Christian. They have similar limitations.

And Boy and I, I thought then. We had had similarities too. But it wouldn't have worked, not for me. Love's messy. I have to be in control.

'Never mind,' said Kate, astoundingly. 'Never mind, Jessie. You did what you had to do, you know,' and we smiled at each other the way women do when they are alone. I put my head in her lap then and cried very hard.

And of course we all went up for the tangi, crammed into the Volkswagen and Stu's Falcon, driving behind and in front of each other all the way. The sun shone that day and we sang a lot. The coast had never looked so beautiful.

And soon the summer will come. It was almost warm, today. We'll take baths outside, all of us, in the bath you built us; Stu and Christian will play and we'll drink to you, Boy, in red wine and passing. The summer will come and the jasmine will flower along Holloway Road and the stars will swing over the fires we light at Breaker Bay and we'll think of you, often.

But it won't last, you know. At the going down of the sun and in the morning we will not always remember you. I saw them today, stringing up the lights on the trees at Oriental Parade, and I went home and cried for you, Boy, for how you won't see them, but the thing is, I know this won't last. It doesn't make your death any less or any less meaningful, it's just the way it is, once carnival's over. I don't, of course, have anyone to talk to any more, but then none of us ever do, really, do we, Boy? Christian and I understand each other, that is I understand Christian, which amounts to the same thing. Our lives will go on. Rather successfully, actually, in spite of ourselves, being as we all are intelligent, well educated, inescapably middle class. Our lives are going to keep unfolding just fine without you. You'll come to mean something quite different to us from what you meant to yourself. I'll stumble across pictures of you, unexpectedly, every five years or so, tidying drawers, and every time I'll cry and I'll imagine I'm crying for you, but I won't be, you know. No one ever cries except for themself. You'll be our lost youth, or something, frozen forever at twenty-four, and we won't remember you before we reduced you to a symbol, after a while. It'll be, one day, as if you had never lived at all.

I'm telling you, Boy. I never asked to be a witch. I'm sorrier than you could ever have imagined for the things I know. But it's already later than you think.

Nikhat Shameem

Nikhat Shameem is an Indo-Fijian immigrant to New Zealand. She took the Original Composition course in 1994. 'The Lake', which was first published in *Sport 14*, was prompted by a John Gardner exercise (see p.299). She now lives and teaches in Auckland. Her first book, *Arrival and Other Stories*, was for adult learners of English.

The Lake

Her eyes dance at me out of their kohl-ringed sockets. Her hair, thickly braided, lies carefully, carelessly flung over her left shoulder. She had copied Juhi Chawla's hairstyle from the Hindi film she watched last weekend. I had watched it with her when she insisted, not because I wanted to but because I was biding my time. I wasn't ready to talk to her.

She smiles at me now, her teeth are white and even, as perfect as in a toothpaste advertisement. Her bright green and pink shalwar kameez clashes with the colours of the dam, the lake, the pines, even the gorse. I had tried to get her into jeans once—it had merely drawn a fit of giggles. I look away from her towards the lake. Jenny looks great in jeans.

The water is very still today. Hard to imagine that less than three metres below, enormous turbines are churning out gallons of water into the Waikato. From where I stand I can almost hear the machines, loud, intense, so much power under my feet.

She runs from side to side along the dam walkway, she gazes in awe at the ravine on the left, then runs back to look at the lake lapping close to her feet on the right. She calls out to me. I pretend I haven't heard. When she gets to the chute, she stops and looks back at me. I know the chute well.

When we passed through here last year on our first (and only) skiing trip Jenny teased me. She said that if I married the chosen Riaqat, she would kill us both and throw the bodies down the chute. No one would ever find us down there. Who would care about two missing immigrants anyway? We had both laughed out loud then.

She reaches the chute now, it clearly fascinates her as it did us that day. I remember the length of that solid concrete tunnel, slimy with the green kai that forms after each overflow. She climbs onto the fence that surrounds it to take a closer look. She's curious about everything. She found my letters once in my old suitcase. I had to almost wrest them from her hand. Then she made a silly joke about me not telling her about my gori girlfriends. We were married now, she didn't care, she said. But what can I tell her that she will understand? She with her sheltered existence waiting for the eligible match. What can she know about this ache? I walk towards her slowly. She is still peering into the chute, her face completely absorbed. Just as I reach her, she turns around excitedly, she is saying something.

A bird rises over the damp slopes, gaining speed with every flap of its wings. The glassy peace of the lake is shattering. Yellow flowering gorse lines both sides of the lake. The Tokoroa pines tower over the gorse and are starkly reflected in the lake, stretching to meet across the depths in the middle. The lake shifts against the concrete of the dam, laps, soothes. The dam itself is grey, cold, empty. There is power here and peace.

Emily Perkins

In 1996 Emily Perkins won the Montana NZ Book Award for best first book of fiction for her bestselling story collection, *Not Her Real Name*. She did the Original Composition course in 1993, and her end-of-course folio became the title story of *Not Her Real Name*. 'Dark Room' was written during the workshop in response to an exercise idea (see p.286 in 'The Exercise Chapter') and was eventually developed into the story 'Local Girl Goes Missing', also collected in *Not Her Real Name*. The poem 'July' was printed in *Sport 14*.

Dark Room

Mum was an amateur photographer. Dad gave her a camera when they got married. It lasted for years. None of us were allowed to touch it. We all chipped in and bought her a new one for her fortieth birthday but she loved the old one best. Most of the photographs in this album are taken by her.

Here's Bernadette at Piha. Sand all round her mouth. She must have been eating it. I'm not sure what she's pointing at—maybe Lion Rock. She first climbed it when she was about two or something. I never did of course. But Bern and Therese loved it, they were always on at Mum to take them up there. I'd stay on the beach watching my shadow make pictures on the sand. That black iron sand that would get so hot under your feet. And the blowholes, and the huge waves. That's what a beach was to me, burning hot sand and caves with water crashing through them and waves as high as the sky. I had a recurring dream for years, standing ankle deep in water watching a wave rise up before me getting bigger and bigger until it was all I could see and I couldn't run away and I knew it was going to swamp me. Well I know it's symbolic and I don't need a shrink to tell me what it means but it always makes me think of Piha. Look at Bern.

She was the happiest child you can imagine.

The three of us in our communion dresses. Mum never believed in God—I think she was brought up Anglican and when she left home she stopped going to church. But she always had this obsession with Catholicism. She was fascinated by the rituals. She didn't know very much about them and there were only a few we regularly followed, like fish on Friday, but the house always smelled of candle wax and incense. And when Therese was thirteen Mum made us all communion dresses. I was eleven and Bern was far too young, she was eight or something, but Mum wanted us all to dress up together. None of us had any idea what communion was supposed to be so we just put on our white dresses and Mum gave us each a glass of red wine. Therese was very grown up, she wore her hair all piled on top of her head and borrowed a necklace of Mum's. The worst part was, Dad rang and Bern answered the phone and said, Sorry Dad I can't talk now I have to go and finish my wine. He rang back furious but Mum pulled the phone out of the wall and put Janis Joplin on and we all danced to 'Me & Bobby McGee' till I threw up from spinning round too much. That's why we've all got Catholic names, Mum named us from the *Oxford Dictionary of Saints*. Dad hated it but he couldn't stop her— the deal was she'd pick the girls' names and he could name the boys. He'd had enough of her after three girls and went off to have boys with Angela.

John's painting the house. We haven't been here very long and it needs a lot of work. John likes that. Something to do on the weekends. It's not that he hasn't got other interests. He likes the physical side of it. He's more comfortable not thinking. I shouldn't have said that.

This is a really old one. It's Mum when she was about sixteen and the girl with her is supposedly Margaret Mahy. The only other photos I've seen of Margaret Mahy, she's been wearing a multicoloured fright wig so I can't tell if there's any resemblance. Mum swears it's her, reckoned they were at high school together, got up to all kinds of things when they were teenagers. Mum's a chronic liar. She dug this photo up when she was reading Margaret Mahy stories to Bern that time she had the chickenpox and claimed it was the two of them together. Bern fell for it completely. Therese thinks the other woman is Mum's sister Helen who died in the car crash. I don't know. I just know Mum likes to tell stories. And they're mostly about people who are either dead so they can't answer back, or so famous no one but Bern would believe her anyway. It's a funny photo though, Mum with a beehive, smoking, and Margaret Mahy laughing so much you can almost see her tonsils.

It's just about falling apart, this book. The spine's broken. I used to be scared of tearing the sheets of tissue that cover the photographs. I'd get it out when everyone was out of the house and look at the pictures for hours. Half my memories, I don't know if they're from what actually happened or from looking in this album. When I remember my childhood up to the age of about ten, it's always in black and white. But the sun was always shining. That's what everybody says, isn't it? We all had bare feet and the sun shone night and day.

I don't know where John is. I went to take him a cup of tea just before but he's disappeared. His brushes are still there, and his stepladder. It looks strange, as if he'd stepped off the ladder and vanished into the air. Last month I was in town and I saw a pushchair lying on its side on a street corner, empty. I came home and told John about it but he didn't think it was unusual.

Here's the one I was looking for. When Therese was in the paper. She ran away for two weeks and they printed the photo Mum took of her on her birthday. She had so much makeup on she looked about nineteen, not fourteen. Mum said the photo would probably start perverts hunting her down, not help anyone find her. She cried at the breakfast table every morning Therese was away. I never saw her so angry as she was the day Therese came back. Therese didn't talk for two days. She looked a wreck. When I asked her about it later, she said she'd wanted to give Mum a fright, see what she'd do. It can be hard growing up with a lot of freedom. You start to wonder if anyone knows you're alive. Mum was so proud of getting one of her photos printed in the paper she threw the original away and kept the clipping in the album. When John and I were clearing out her house the other day I found the piece of newspaper the photo was from lining one of Mum's kitchen drawers, a big square ripped out of the top left corner. Luckily, Dad was too busy with Angela and the boys to find out Therese had run away before she came back. She does look beautiful in this photo.

She was self-conscious about the gap between her teeth so she'd never smile. In most of these pictures Bern and I are grinning away like idiots while Therese looks mysterious and intense.

I should put this album away I suppose. No one's taken any photographs for ages, they sort of peter out after Bern's graduation. It even smells a bit musty. John'll think I'm weird if he comes in now and sees me holding it to my cheek, breathing in its dust. He said in bed last night did I think it was a good time to have a baby because he's really keen. I don't know. Maybe I'm not ready yet. I think I'd like to travel.

July

He's arrived, and the three of us
lie on the bed.

I open my eyes to see the sky
over the balcony wall. A water tank
on someone else's building.
The red geraniums I haven't watered.
Everything still.

You're on the other side of him,
breathing, and he's breathing too.

It's Independence Day. Firecrackers
bang under cars.
Alarms go off. Shouts, etcetera.
We don't know
what we're doing next week.

Does it matter, you ask,
if we miss all the fireworks?

And this is the way it is for a while,
with interruptions.

David Geary

David Geary is one of several survivors of the 1983 workshop. He wrote poems then went on to become an acclaimed playwright (especially for *Lovelock's Dream Run*), and has recently been writing poems again.

Original Composition: Class of '83

SCENE: *University lecture theatre. The sweet smell of decaying fruit and damp raincoats. A tweed-jacket professor makes his end-of-year address.*

You are the talented. What does that mean? It means you are survivors. It means you survived fifteen years of formal education out there, which aimed at smothering that talent. Killing it in its cot. Which aimed year after relentless year at severing your intelligence from your guts. Well, by some miracle, you bastards escaped the knife. Some by good fortune, some by cunning, and some with the help of that rare creature—a teacher unafraid of his pupils' talent. You arrived at my class with that tenuous thread between brain and heart intact, 'Mensa corpus fragilica intacta.' My job over the past year has been to nourish and toughen that thread, to weave a rope, a cable between your head and your gut. That way you'll have something to hang on to when things get tough. Because they will. It's a battlefield out there and, as on any battlefield, there are only two choices. You can surrender. You can join the ranks of those who queue for death, the carcasses of human potential, the flotsam and jetsam, the withered souls, who wait . . . wait . . . wait for death. Or you can fight. You can grab life by the balls and squeeze. 'Carpe Scrotus!' You can squeeze until you've wrung the last gasp, the last mandrake's shriek, from between life's crumbling teeth. I think you all know which path I would like to see you take. But my job is over now. I look before me and where once I saw apprentices I now see wordsmiths. Wordsmiths, who have the courage and the skill to hammer truth and meaning out of the raw iron of life. You are undoubtedly the best year I've ever had. I am very proud of you all. And now I hope you'll all join me in retiring to that traditional haven of the writer . . . the pub. [*Laughs.*]

Bill Manhire? No, Amos Huske, a character Mick Rose and I created for the play, *The Rabbiter's Daughter*. A burnt-out, cliché-riddled windbag, he ends up plagiarising a student's work and forcing the poor unfortunate into the madhouse. Amos visits with a typewriter and encourages his victim to write his way to sanity. I include this only as an example of everything Bill isn't. In fact, we invited Bill to the show, which he took with great humour. He remarked that he particularly liked the omelette jokes. The sort of left-of-field remark only he could make.

To say what Bill and Original Composition are is a trickier proposition. I must say I was somewhat taken aback to be asked for an autopsy of the course. I was there dabbling in poetry and ended up a dramatist. A B2 student. Quite a blow at the time. My close friends have dubbed me a crap archivist. And true to form, after an archaeological dig in my parents' back shed, I found my assessors' comments.

Indigestible, a kind of bravado, an excess of wordage which frustrates effect because it frustrates reading, inadequately imagined, barely organised brutality, clotted, unevenly handled, portentous, trying too hard, gaudy, too self-important, I can feel the author's constant presence like a salesperson who won't shut up and let you look for yourself.

I re-read my poems and, of course, it's all true. My better moments were attained when I relaxed and practised a little restraint. Bill's forte.

Relaxing wasn't easy, however. Some backstory: 1982. I was nineteen and going to be a lawyer due to the influence of the TV programme, *The Paper Chase*. I got an A for Legal Systems, but had quite enjoyed Modern Literature after a brief tanty: I threw Samuel Beckett across the room. So I considered a double major.

Seeing Original Composition in the prospectus I can't say exactly why I chose it. My literary endeavours extended to song lyrics, e.g. 'When I was young I had many loves / my family, my friends, my horse / Now I have one main love / And you are its source.' Sung to the tune of Rod Stewart's 'Tonight's the Night'—try it some time if you're looking for a challenge. And two bona fide poems.

Treestumps
Tombstones in a graveyard

Which I thought was just profoundly brilliant, and profound. The second poem I read to a friend at Vic House. He paid me the highest compliment by saying, 'It sounds like poetry.' Rough translation—he couldn't understand it.

Anyway, I needed to submit six poems. So I sifted through my biscuit box of broken dreams for anything deeper than a 'be mine tonight' sentiment, tarted up some inklings and sent them in. The clincher would be my response to the question, 'Why do you want to do this course?' Answer: In case law gets boring, and to have fun with words. How I got in I'll never know. I had alternative courses already mapped out, but destiny was to have me join Bill's coterie. Which, at the time, I would have imagined was some sort of jumbled-up wardrobe—fairly close to the truth when you saw everyone, but let's not get into literary dress sense.

I didn't know Bill from a bar of soap. Well, similar complexions. I joke now but at the time it was terrifying. There were real writers in the group. People who had been published and won awards. People who knew it wasn't just trucks that articulated.

Now it gets tricky. People always ask you, 'So how does Bill actually teach?' I don't quite know. Perhaps his greatest achievement is to create a nurturing environment. Which in a petri-dish cube in the Von Zedlitz building, with a jackhammer Woody Woodpeckering the adjacent wall, is a monumental achievement.

The big thing for me was the lack of judgement, or should I say, lack of judging. No good, bad, rewrite, tick, cross, see me later. If my abilities had been correctly appraised I'm sure I'd have dropped out and concentrated on going head to head with the Professor Kingsfield wannabe of the Law Department. Instead we had exercises. What a relief, homework I could understand.

My favourite exercise was writing a letter to a relative in which every line was a lie—something I'd wanted to do for years. Very quickly I was writing some fantastical thing, which I couldn't possibly stumble upon by myself, while staring into a one-bar heater in Aro Street. The exercises made writing a form of work: revolutionary thinking. I'd had some naive concept of magic and the Muse floating around. This was quickly dispelled and I started taking the task seriously.

Still, in Bill's class I was probably taking myself a little too seriously. An initial climate of earnestness prevailed. The real breakthrough came when someone actually said they didn't understand/like someone else's work. Everyone had harboured these heretic thoughts, but had been too afraid to cast the first stone in case it rebounded with greater force. At last the paper knives were out and true critical discussion could take place.

It would have been nice to have this from the start, but trust is time-intensive. I have heard of some years where critical faculties (good title for a uni drama) were unleashed in the first session. Ugly. Definitely not on the first date. Getting someone you trust to give you feedback is a necessity though. These days I use several people to critique my play drafts, and I appreciate their candidness—making sure I have some dirt on them in case they get carried away.

Solidarity. Writing is generally solitary, so discovering that other writers went through the same wringer was most heartening. Post-Bill some acolytes continued to meet, providing each other with a halfway house before they were blended into the great unwashed. I periodically write with other people—gym buddies to egg me on and pull me in new directions. The main drawback is you get only half the royalty cheque. The big plus is that arguing with someone else is much better stress management than another cup of coffee.

Probably the most influential exercise I did was a short story, where we were given three facts: a boy with a teddy bear appears, a ladder breaks and something is painted green. I cooked up a story about a boy stowing away on Noah's ark. It wasn't particularly good but I did write a lot of dialogue. I particularly enjoyed the scene where the boy was put on trial by the animals. I guess it was my first attempt at writing drama. I was finding a form I liked—not an easy task.

There was no specific stage-writing in the course, but I was beginning to value words. What Bill and the group had was an economy and care about use and placement. Interestingly enough, I've come back to writing poetry because of these things. And you can get closure on a page. Something much more elusive over two hours in theatre.

As the year wore on I got rather obsessive about words actually. Compiling a list of every word seen on a bus trip between Palmerston North and Wellington. My John Cage concrete art phase. But the most important words of 1983 would be:

SCENE: *A young man phones home.*

DAVID   The law's going okay, Mum, but I've dropped Contracts.

    Pause.

    Yes, I can pick it up again. I'm doing Shakespeare instead.

    Pause.

    No, I don't want to be a schoolteacher. I'm doing drama next year.

    Silence.

In 1985, in order to get the bursary, I did have to pick up Contracts again. I did just enough to get the final payment then stopped going to class. Supposedly this meant I'd failed terms, but my name was down to sit. So I went and wrote a story about how I'd come to be writing a story in a legal exam. It was my declaration of independence.

I liked the story so much I didn't want to hand it in. Thus I was in the unique position of smuggling paper out of an exam. I left one page with the note, 'Merry Christmas, Professor McLachlan. Don't worry about the missing pages, I wrote a story and ripped it out.' I got an E.

Without Bill Manhire I probably would have got something considerably higher. He's to blame. He's deprived New Zealand of another frustrated, and over-creative, lawyer. Original Composition had changed my life. Thank you . . .

Now Bill specifically said no sycophancy so I'll stop that there. ('Shooting a Sycophant'—an Orwell short story?) He also said, in his generous way, that he'd like this to be a manual for other writers. So I'll include some other things I find useful.

I have a large diary. Where I'm at is what I write, so it's nice to get those psychoses down. I make an effort to record a surprise a day. It doesn't have to be anything major, but all stories arise from one incident of the unexpected. The more story germs you have on tap the better. For example, I recently had some lovely whites dyed pink in the wash by a bleeding red T-shirt. Apart from a chance to vent my full gamut of expletives, it also set me to thinking. What if one's entire wardrobe was dyed pink and one couldn't afford another? What if your colour therapist says you're really a winter? Thus the unfortunate occurrence can be used for the good. Positive psychic energy.

Don't write dialogue first when working on a play. Rewrite the story until you get it right. Lines will come, note them, but avoid getting into a conversation. You'll end up with four-hour-long plays and it's painful cutting them in half. Believe me, I've been there.

Structure is all. Linda Seger's book on movies, *Making a Good Script Great*, translates well to stage. Very useful when you're watching something dire, as you can dissect it on her terms and salvage something from the evening. Seger on 'raising the stakes' is particularly valuable. Basically, throw everything at your hero, as much acid as possible. The struggle will be greater and we'll care more. That's what it's all about.

Read everything and anything. Ideas are everywhere. Newspapers have plenty of sensational plots, and can be a great source of lines. My current fave is Martina Navratilova on commitment in sport:

MARTINA It's like ham and eggs. The chicken has contributed but the
pig is really committed.

Comedy has one basic rule: someone hops into a car expecting
to go forwards and goes backwards. Always look for reversals of
expectation. John Vorhaus' *Comic Toolbox* is a useful guide.

Experiment in other forms and media. Much the same as Bill's
exercises can take you into unknown territory, so can working in a
totally foreign discipline. Learn the tambourine, whittle, design ad
campaigns. It's fun and you'll be surprised how it will illuminate your
chosen field. I particularly like sculpture. Thinking of a piece of writing
in a 3-D, textural way helps me work out problems in the shape of a
work. And I'm sure my 'Christ as a totara fencepost' and 'Tanalised
Christ resurrected' will one day be major installations.

As a final exercise for playwrights, I'd like to advocate one I
purloined from Sebastian Barry, the writer of *The Steward of Christen-
dom*. Nick Cave always said I was a name-dropper.

SEBASTIAN You are called to answer to the Gods of Theatre. Where
do you go? Who's there? Why have you been called?
Do it.

Long pause.

Sebastian thinks that what you describe is your personal theatre. The
stage in your cerebral cortex, where all your plays premiere before
being released on an unsuspecting public. I think it's a good gauge of
your concept of theatre and where you stand in it.

I described an ancient wooden globe open to the sky. It's very
hot. Greece. Spain. The Hawke's Bay. I walk barefoot through a large
entrance way. There's dirt on the ground. Blood. Cowshit. Maybe a
bullfight took place recently. There are huge gates that may release a
bull at any moment. I walk to the centre and can only make out a few
scattered spectators. They take no notice of me. They eat lunch, read
papers and play board games. I clear my throat and blabber on about
how I got into writing. It's a vain attempt to justify myself and I end

up shouting myself hoarse to no avail. I fall silent. I suspect one of the spectators is Bill Manhire. He's tucking into an omelette. Cheese and mushroom with a sprinkling of parsley. I ask for a bit. He says, 'Cook your own.'

Marton

We're at the Golf Club discussing satanic cults.
They had a special day for the young people
who committed suicide under the Marton bridge.
As if we haven't got enough tragedies in cars.
We had bodgies and widgies, but they were harmless.
The line dancers were upset
because the stage was uneven.
It was just plain dangerous.
The man in the ice-cream van thought the line dancing
music was the best he had heard all day.
All of these young people are growing up without melody.
They just like improvising noise. And when they sing
you can't make out the words.
Anyone would think they were in pain.
Did you go? God, no!
They've got four televisions in the TAB
and I could still hear it.
The Karate Club put on a display. But they'd forgotten to organise
something to kick.
There's been four youth groups set up since the war.
They've all started with a hiss and a roar.
One boy was eating his girlfriend.
There were little kids there.
The Mayor made a plea to the young folk of the Rangitikei:
'Please stop dying.'
I sit on the verandah and watch them walk home from school,
smoking and swearing. I wouldn't cross the road

to kick them up the arse.
I blame the parents.
I'm glad someone said that.
The TV came and talked to Gypsy
only because he had tattoos on his face
and some other guy, no one knew,
who was totally out of it,
lying in the grass in his leathers.
There were ordinary people there too.
It's supposed to become an annual thing.

Chris Orsman

Chris Orsman did the Original Composition course in 1993. His first book of poems, *Ornamental Gorse*, appeared in 1994 and the following year won the NZSA Best First Book Award. The two poems printed here are from *Ornamental Gorse* (for more information about 'Dubrovnik', see p.286); Orsman's new book, *South*, is a long poem sequence about Scott's doomed expedition to the South Pole.

Dubrovnik

May–June 1989

An Incident at a Café

He becomes a friend
merely by greeting you
in the *Dubro Yutro* café
near the city gates:

'You are perhaps English?'

It's not a bad guess:
there's the *International
Herald Tribune* on the table
and a packet of American
cigarettes. We talk.

He is a 'fantasist'
and a writer of distinction.
He waves a newspaper;
there's a page with a photograph
missing: it seems he operates

a clipping service for himself.
He explains that he knows everyone,
this is how he catches up
(serrating the page a little
with nail scissors,
snipping a nostril hair).

Try me, he says, name a writer!
Tolkien?
A great German!
Azimov?
Ah, the Russians were our friends once!
Margaret Mahy?
Yes, yes, I know her well!
A fine writer. A Black American!

The waiter comes with coffee.

Some Reflections

You come down a road
that is merely caulking
on a leaky coast, baffled
by the gales of the equinox;
seas of aquamarine and indigo
clasp the 'Pearl of the Adriatic'.

You do not find in this city
the 'misshapen pearl' of the Baroque:
you find a translucence so that
there seems, even on cloudy days,
a hidden source of light somewhere
buried in the pink and grey stones
of the place; and the balconies
of the mountain-side echo out
an impending height and weight,
poised like that painting:

'The Great Day of His Wrath'.

At the Pensione

My landlady at the *Pensione
Adriatico* is Mrs Panic—a name
that suits her in English.
Her husband is a troglodyte
who drinks schnapps in the cellar
and emerges now and then
with grievances while she works
her fingers to the bone.

There were signs of her doing this
everywhere: steaming buckets
left outside the toilet, the stain
of whitewash in the passage,
an empty stepladder.

Looking for the Saints

Patrons are in their churches
and the streets are travertine
and marble; winter still hangs
from the wrists of the trees
in the Placa; lichen is flecked
with the blue of the Good Thief's
eye; the city discards its prose
and stands amid counterpointed
highlight in its own illumination:

city of terracotta and Roman
justice buried in the harbour walls,
the civil candour of abacus
and trachelion and fluting
warmed by a lizard's blood
this side of Easter.

Saint Vlaho speaks to me
from his niche in the Cathedral:
patron of influenza, he once
pulled a fishbone from a peasant's
throat; he guards the city,
in the West he's known as Blaise.

The Harbour

My photograph of the harbour
beneath the city walls: a pier
of limestone at an oblique angle
to the shore, the tiled and gabled
houses with names like hearthstones,
a sea wall made of travertine

rising gently to a natural alcove
with wooden seats and a metal bin
where I smoked and drank mineral
water while the fishermen
picked out their nets, and cats
nosed among the men.

I was happy there.

A Lament

Saint Vlaho,
where are you now?
Did you foresee
ichthyosaurus rising
in the gorge of Yugoslavia?
or a fossil lashing the
sea walls of Dubrovnik?

Ornamental Gorse

It's ornamental where it's been
self-sown across the hogback,

obsequious and buttery,
cocking a snook at scars,

yellowing our quaint history
of occupation and reprise.

The spiny tangential crotch,
gullied and decorative,

I love from a distance,
a panorama over water

from lakeside to peninsula
where it's delicate in hollows,

or a topiary under heavens
cropped by the south wind.

I offer this crown of thorns,
for the pity of my countrymen

unconvinced of the beauty
of their reluctant emblem: this

burnt, hacked, blitzed
exotic.

Kate Camp

Kate Camp was a member of the 1995 workshop. Her poem 'Postcard' was the first exercise piece she brought to class. See 'Postcards' in 'The Exercise Chapter', p.290.

In Your Absence

In your absence
I stubbed out my arm.

Parcelled myself off
to various chaps.

I put the dog's head in a bucket
and she barked my shin.

I put my head down, received
brief papery epiphanies.

Enjoying a thermos of tea
in the Australian Garden

I thought—this is very fine, and—
No one is coming to rescue me.

Postcard

Hope weather is good etc all is well and dog is wagging.

I thought, being beautiful, nothing could hurt you.

In Greece men hiss from doorways.
The mountains are high and particularly chilly.
Everything is slow slow.
The coffee is very bitter.

If you had married, goats may have nibbled your train.
A shepherd removed a hunk of cheese from his pocket.
The marble of your apartment would be valueless as plastic.
No one would understand but stare instead.

In the Hokianga with my mysteries—
Goodbye Pussy, Swing Brother Swing—
I am a small world away.
Still I say—all strength

And you were too good
And you were too good
And you were too good for him anyway.

Through Hardship to the Stars

for Mark

It is a pleasure to order spices,
and good policy to empty out unknown powders.
I smile at a jar; once I was happy to write *flour* on its label.
Then, eyes moved in the head, skin wore off,
recipes were stained through overuse.

At the k-k-k-kitchen door
you tell me I'm your patron saint
and recite your Hamilton high school motto:
Latin blah blah blah:
Through Hardship to the Stars.

In the pantry sugar is crunching under cans
a jar of gherkins requires urgent attention
nutmeg is trailing from its packet.
So I send you off with a red apple
and return to my powders,
resisting the urge to alphabetise;
cardamom, cayenne, cinnamon, cloves.

1 - 4 - U

Alan Wesley of the 1-4-U restaurant, Hawera
has Groper, Snapper, Flounder, Tarakihi and Bluenose
which he can cook for you one of six ways—
Deep Fried, Pan Fried, Baked, Grilled, Crumbed or Curried
and you can forget the thick, heavy curried fish Mum used to make
because he mixes the curry himself and it's light as a feather.

Alan has tried to introduce a variety of salads,
which the locals are taking to slowly.
Pasta salad, rice salad, bean salad and Waldorf salad.
He's travelled the world, been a London cabby, seen these things.
I ask, can he arrange a visit to the Elvis museum in Argyle Street?
He has never been there—no interest in gold records and so on
though he likes music, likes all kinds of music—he tries
and is disappointed—the Elvis man is in a council meeting.

Edging his chair closer, Alan explains he can arrange activities—
hunting, fishing, rafting and horse treks.
He offers a brief resumé of his life to date.
On and on we eat and he gives advice—
on pressure cooking chicken with onions,
defrosting frozen fish in the pan,
and always dealing with the butcher personally.
Having paid by cash, cheque, credit card or eft-pos we go
knowing if we strike any problems we can call him any time
car repairs, tyre repairs, place to stay, local knowledge,
brain haemorrhage, stiff knee, golf tee, lemon tree, cup of tea,
road map, spinal tap, hooray, cheerio, toodle-oo 1-4-U.

Virginia Were

Virginia Were took the Original Composition course in 1986. 'We Listen for You on the Radio', already much anthologised, appeared in her prize-winning 1989 collection of poems and prose works, *Juliet Bravo Juliet*. She now lives in Auckland.

We Listen for You on the Radio

We know that there is
a yacht out there
struck into our map,
a star disabled north of Cape Reinga.
The cyclone blows it backwards
so that the land is
two hundred miles away; more than that.

You are out there
and the sea
will find its way into your ears
and mouth, it
fills your eyes with salt.
And *land* is somewhere.
You hold it in front of your eyes

in the small place that is safety
and walking down the street,
slow walking soft *light*,
your lover curled into the
small of your back,
a child clinging to the tips
of your fingers,

and the apples falling from the tree,
rotting in the yellow grass.
You can't see the horizon and
your life passes in the
time it takes to fall from
the top of a wave
and rise to the next,

and you fall fall fall
an eternity of apples
falling,
and the breaking of
branches.
The face of the next wave
is the face of your lover.

You have never seen
anything like it (these waves).
The sea will swallow you
if you don't get it right,
straight up the face, tremble
on the eyelash of the wave—
down the nose and into the hungry

mouth where it is hollowed,
still.
(Your child)
The branch snapped
and she fell
cried and you were there
with comfort and you

bound and soothed, held her
in your arms.
(The ribs are sprung,
the water finds its way in)
and we hear your voice crackle
out of phase down the radio,
the child and I.

(If you had two arms you would
hold us both.)
We cling to each other
even as you cling to the back
of your life,
cling to the few words that tell us
you are somewhere out there alive,

with three broken ribs,
running hills and valleys
our photograph safe inside your oilskin.
That you are alive,
eking out a can of spaghetti
some biscuits,
plumbing the wet chart

the face of land, the face
of each new wave mountain.
Time stops, three more days
of gale force winds
crawl on their bellies towards
you.
We don't know if you can

hear us, we can hear you.
We watch the tiny star which gives
your position make its way
down the TV screen on the
six o'clock news.
Your face is a little square
on the front page of *The Sun*.

The ends of bone crunch each other.
The radio threads you in
to us, then there is silence.
We would have the land moved
for you,
peeling back contours, licking
them and sticking an entire island

down,
its outline for you to step off
onto *land*.

Fiona Kidman

In 1977, Fiona Kidman was appointed in the footsteps of Christine Cole Catley and Michael King as a tutor of creative writing for Victoria's University Extension (now Continuing Education), a position she held on and off over sixteen years; and in 1988 she was the University's writer-in-residence. She is one of New Zealand's best-known and most influential writers, and continues to teach creative writing as a private practitioner.

Holding on to My Sleeve

They walk into the room, sit down at their desks, pick up their pens and turn expectantly towards you, waiting for some transforming scrap of wisdom.

'Write down five interesting things about yourself,' I might say to them. 'And then, choose three that you want to tell the rest of the group when you introduce yourselves.'

An uneasy shuffling begins as this new group of students begins to write. I felt so angry with you, some will say, later on, I didn't come for that. I didn't believe there was anything interesting to write down. Most of all, they are likely to say, I didn't come here to spill my guts in front of people.

And neither they should. That is not what my classes are about. They are not about therapy. But few writing teachers deny that writing begins within the student, that until you have turned a sheer instinct about the power of words into decipherable language, the journey you will take with each student has not begun. We begin at the beginning; we learn to reach inwards before we reach out.

So, within forty minutes of arriving at the class, the new student has focused on five aspects of their own character, choosing ones which are the ingredients of a story. More than that, in a group of twenty, they will have heard, if they are listeners, fifty-seven things about the other characters in the room. You can see dawning recognition, identification, interest awakening.

This is not the only tool I use, but it is a useful one. I would not be bold enough to say that this is the instant when I can tell whether a person is going to become a writer or not. Sometimes I have to travel their journey with them for a long time, often they have to go on on their own, and I don't learn for five or ten years, or longer, how they fared. But I believe true writers amongst the group know for themselves. They might not recognise the moment until much later, caught short with anger or surprise as they often are at the time.

Soon after this exercise comes another. Here is a list of about ten key phrases—a piece of jewellery; a family picnic; a cooking disaster; lost love—the list is never the same. Now, turn to the person next to you, and tell them a story for five minutes, straight off the top of your head, about one of these subjects. At the end of five minutes, on a signal, it will be the other person's turn to tell you their story.

For ten minutes the air is thick with voices and laughter.

'Very well,' I say, 'now pick up your pens and write down, as fast as you can, the story you have just told about yourself.'

Still no words of wisdom, no notes written down, no how-to-do-it tricks from up my sleeve. But something has happened to create a change in the way things were when the students walked into the room. They have written down a story based on their experience. It's the beginning of what Marguerite Duras has described as 'the black block' being transformed into a shape that can be read. The 'black block' is the process of mining the things we have inside ourselves, that have happened 'in the sleep of [our lives], in its organic rumination', unbeknown to us. Once we begin to see inside the 'black block' we are never the same again. It is my fervent hope, when I face that class, that radical shifts in perception and self-awareness are about to begin.

Can you really teach people to write? That question, so familiar, so haunting, yet it almost defies answer. But, unless you can confront it, you have no right to stand in front of a class, no mandate to present yourself as a teacher of creative writing.

I have told several versions of the story I am about to relate, but in this context, it bears re-telling. When I was a very young woman I left home for a week, against everyone else's better judgement, to attend a residential creative writing course for women, being held at Auckland University. It meant arranging childcare with friends and relatives, and generally disturbing the routine of a quiet suburban life. As well, it was a proclamation that I considered myself a bit different; perhaps, although it wasn't said straight to my face, that I thought I was a cut above myself, perceiving myself as a writer. It wasn't long before that notion was shaken—there were a number of tutors, and from one of them I learned on the first day that writing is something men do, and women 'have' as a hobby. I heard a great deal that was silly and prejudiced, in all sorts of ways, and we didn't do any writing at all, that week. And yet, I went back home with an overpowering determination to go on writing. Where did it come from?

In part, from the professor of English who convened the course. He was at once erudite and down to earth; he inspired without condescending, he shared his passion for books and good writing, and liberally sprinkling his conversation with titles and quotations that we could jot down for future reference. I thought he was handsome, too, and in the passionate hungry state I was in for information and direction, I was in love with him for the whole of the week. When I was finally drowsing into restless sleep around three each morning, I would half-dream, half-fantasise about walking downtown and finding him there. It would turn out that he had been secretly noticing me all week and—we would go off somewhere together. I scribbled all sorts of sensual scenes at the back of my notebook. This, incidentally, is how I write sex—I don't, as some people suppose, write down the techniques of supposed lovers, rather, I imagine certain scenes which are as erotically pleasing as I suppose most people's secret fantasies are. The difference with mine is that I write them into my fiction. This is one of the main reasons, I tell my students, that writers are considered mad. You must understand, especially if you are a woman, that you will have to live with the image of madness and badness, if you write about sex, violence or politics. It is a choice that I live with. But, as a person who wants to live in the real world, you will almost certainly have to learn to define for yourself certain boundaries that you cross at your peril. Only you can know what risks you are prepared to expose yourself to.

But back to that long-ago course. The late professor was a model of decorum from where I stood, and I can see now that what I was in love with was the driving need in myself to write, and that from him flowed energy.

There were other invaluable ingredients besides his influence; first, the companionship of sixty or so other women, who all wanted to write. Some of them already did, and there was only one aloof 'star' amongst them. She spoke only to the tutors, and I swore I would never be like her when I became a 'name' writer, which I had every intention of becoming. The other women made me feel that I was not alone, goofy or misguided in my ambitions. I also received practical advice about alternatives to immediately becoming a fully-fledged writer of fiction. There were options, like journalism, which might be remunerative and put my name before the public, while I developed skills as a creative writer. This was very much the course I would follow.

Despite a number of failings, and sometimes in spite of itself, this course provided me with some broad principles which have been the mainstay of my own teaching practice for many years. Inspiration, commitment to a belief in oneself as a writer, a heightened love of language, and straightforward practical advice. Not everyone who goes to a course will learn to be a writer. Some will come simply to discover an unpalatable truth that may save them a great deal of heartache later on, that they will never be one. You don't tell them this, of course, because you may be wrong, and they will delight in putting egg on your face in later years, and, if you are me, you don't like destroying people anyway. But neither do you encourage belief in imminent success. Some of the worst times I have had in the wake of teaching have been confrontations with disappointed students who believe that I have promised them the moon with a few words of faint praise. If you are any good as a teacher, they will leave with some rewards—like a heightened appreciation of books and writing.

However, I do believe, absolutely, that it is possible to unlock talent in talented people, to unleash their inherent imaginative power, and to provide instruction in craft that will make sense of the hallucinatory dream processes which have convinced them they are writers. It is for these people that I teach.

What features are particular to my teaching? Well, I am increasingly interested in a conceptual approach to a whole piece of work, the design if you like, a consideration of all the elements—character, place, period, familial relationships, and so on, that constitute the whole fabric. I don't think this can be taught in a hurry. The components of a design unfold over a period of time, with practice in between. This is where group work is invaluable. A small exercise in characterisation, for instance, can be workshopped amongst a number of people. My students learn early how to comment constructively on each other's work. They are provided with, and develop for themselves, a list of discussion points about an aspect they are studying. When a group is in session these lists become guidelines for commenting on the work, as opposed to, 'Well, I don't reckon that's so hot' or 'Gosh, that's marvellous'. They have to be able to say why, on both counts.

Nothing is compulsory in my courses. You may say 'pass' on anything, including reading things out to each other, and that is the only unbreakable rule about attendance, that the decision to pass is respected and unquestioned by the rest of the group. You may 'pass' on working in a group if you wish, too, although few accept the option on a regular basis. For people who are in the midst of a piece of work and running short of time in their regular working lives, group time can provide a space for them to pursue individual goals.

Which brings me to comment that no course is complete, in my view, without talking about ways to manage time. Writing is a fragile activity, connected with one's personal happiness. I don't mean that when we write we make happy images, or even that we have to be happy in order to write. What I mean, more or less, is that writers can only achieve what passes for happiness in any life by writing. Not to write is a burden and a punishment. And yet, in the light of all the messages we get about the difficulties of the writing life, we find excuses not to do it. We live with the 'black block' frozen inside us, while we make money, raise children, live out our other lives. We don't have time, we tell ourselves, and each other; it's too hard; too lonely; we cannot face rejection, and so on.

The first step that people often take to change this situation is to take a course. As we have seen, they place in their teachers' hands a hope which may never be realised, especially if they are still thinking about writing without having devoted time to seeing what they can do. But the teacher can say, look, how much are you asking of yourself, and how long have you given yourself to achieve what you want? And often the answer comes back something like this: I want to write a bestseller, and I guess it'll take a few months, and if you could just give me a few quick tips to get around the hard bits (and the names of some sympathetic publishers), it should be okay. It's just that I've got so much to say and I don't seem to be able to get it down.

So then you say, well, look, how much can you write in a morning? If the answer is, I can't write for a whole morning (this is assuming a session in which absolute truth prevails!), you might like to ask the student how much he can write in five minutes, ten minutes, an hour. By this time, having done the earlier exercises, or a version of them, he will have some idea of just what is possible. And from there, you can suggest programmes that are realistic and can be achieved within the framework of the person's current lifestyle and responsibilities. At the beginning, few students see writing as their only activity in the immediate future. It is important to help them build realistic goals and to confront fears about loneliness and isolation. The group itself is often the immediate answer to this last problem—lots of the groups continue to meet after a course has ended. Most writers are friends with other writers, and what better place to discover colleagues?

But, in the end, there is more to it than that. After all, there is the act of writing that goes on beyond the ra ra of the group. And this is what, long ago, I found for myself, that the greatest taskmaster is the page itself. Annie Dillard addresses this issue squarely in *The Writing Life* when she speaks of 'the page, the page, that eternal blankness . . . the page which you cover slowly with the crabbed thread of your gut, . . . the page that will teach you to write'.

So it is for this, too, that I must prepare my students. Although

I don't always succeed, I aim to write with the students for some of the time, to be involved in the same act, to share the moment of creation. If we can achieve that much together, I have usually gone some way along the path to convincing these writers of the future that, although I can tell them what I know, there are no tricks and my sleeves are empty.

Thirteen Poets

The dates of individual writers' enrolments in the Original Composition course are indicated at the foot of each poem. The full text of Fleur Wickes' 'Jane Finds Her Music' is printed in *Sport 11*. One or two of these poets—Lynn Davidson in particular—are also accomplished fiction writers, while Allen O'Leary is best known as an actor and playwright. Emily McHalick's 'Twelve Views of Matron's Bosoms' is strictly a prose piece, but is based on a poetic model—see 'Blackbirds' in 'The Exercise Chapter', p.281.

Gabe McDonnell

Pass

This is hard. I could tell you who
you're not like.
                    You're not like Mel
whose hair grows more quickly than
she ever did or Phil
                    grown sick of this
city and the degree he didn't get, or
Felicity (found out
                    about her name and
sulked) or my mother who always says
Really? when she knows
                    it's true. You're
not like Clare who's not like anyone you
know. You're like
                    the woman I think of
when I hear your name but a little taller.

1996

Lynn Davidson

Poem for Tamara

You are half born.
Your head between my legs like
a plum in the fork of two branches.
Your brother eats chippies and watches
us struggle to be free of
each other.
Our midwife tells me what you are doing.
This is the first time we
have needed an interpreter.
So we have come back to language.

Now you are born.
Your curved girl-body
like a tiny lilac seal
pulsing on my chest.
We watch you paint
Chinese characters in the air
with your hands and feet.
Already you are reduced to
speaking all languages.

1981

Helen McGrath

Beginnings

Water at Oakura
when I was a wee baby
was kept in Gordon's gin bottles
and my muddled family
those discerning adult Scots
somehow gave the gin to me
popping cubes of ice and pink
in their guests' measured little drinks
of pure water

in my cot and only three
years old and gurgling drunkenly
down down the downward spiral
baby clochard in my boots
keep walking her the doctor said
do not ever let her stop
make the child just keep on going
if you don't she will be dead
photo splashed all over Truth
panic and the low tide endless

COTCASE FOR A NIGHT SHELTER
INFANTILE PRECOCITY
SEMICOMATOSE TODDLER
CAROUSING OUT HER LULLABIES
& CHERUBIC OBSCENITIES
BURBLING IN OBLIVION

each grandparent holding me
as I thumped along the beach
like a baby footballer
grandparents still walking me
when the dawn & doctor came
finding me still held
in their hands

1983

Kimberley Rothwell

She Takes His Hand

and stores it as her hostage.
The newness of his stump
surprises him.
He mourns the loss of his
familiar tool,
mourns
his immediate touch.

When he wakes,
he slices
the newness from his face
and goes to spend his day
under a false sun.
He leaves his smell
loitering
in the sink.

He puts his finger
under her chin
and lifts it so she
frowns at the sun.
He takes her eyes
and holds them prisoner
in his dark and dustless pocket,
where, with his one hand
he juggles them
through his fingers.

1994

Emma Neale

After the Diagnosis

Spreckles Elementary School, San Diego, 1980

'The heart is not very regular.
There is a definite nervous disorder.'
At ten years old
the stumbles start.

There is a definite nervous disorder
No. Sit straight and still as a line that holds its breath.
The stumbles start
to lick at you from inside.

No. Sit straight and still as a line that holds its breath.
The desire watches you, starts
to lick at you from inside.
You pick up the pen.

The desire watches you, starts
to help you be brave.
You pick up the pen
from where the spasm hit out with an arm.

To help you be brave,
count the ten seconds away
from where the spasm hit out with an arm.
The mind etches an arc of crimson, but

Count the ten seconds away.
They jerk to get free of you;
the mind etches an arc of crimson. But
a red sprawl is sent a-skid by the race of hand and head.

They jerk to get free of you,
hot salt triggers.
A red sprawl is sent a-skid by the race of hand and head;
you rage.

Hot salt triggers,
she is by your side.
You rage.
Your name is struck through the air of the classroom.

She is by your side
the quiet love is beaten
your name is struck through the air of the classroom.
Even when she understands,

The quiet love is beaten
at ten years old
even when she understands.
The heart is not very regular.

1990

Alexandra Gillespie

A Syllabic Letter
I address it to you Pa

I was three you died
where the blinds made a
dark room in the day
My father at the
table crying I
can't remember you

You had a paisley
shirt I wore it in
a play I saw it
in a photograph
with concrete, roses
me and I was two

Mum and Dad gave birth
to me that weekday
as you waited by
the phone to ring and
say first girl to friends
First one in your life

Pa I grew and spelled
each level I have
written poems and
made speeches, men say
you would like the way
I became but Pa

There were months that I
got sick cried a lot
Fell in love asking
for the right man left
my school I tell you
these important things

At the library they
painted you I see your
face in oil I touch
that part of you, you
beside god's hands you
wear a lawyer's wig

1993

Michael Mintrom

Borstal Girl

I am a hopeless case
a girl with a
very bad centre
a borstal trainee
bored stiff, a girl who is
feeling lonely

Life goes on and on
is a bore
is slack
is a big hassle

My mother
she's all right
I love her, but I can't show it

I'd like most
to go home
to try and behave myself
to be free

Secretly I want to wake up and
know the right thing to do
wish I could experience
life over again
would like to be dead
hate life
wish I hadn't got into trouble

1987

Fleur Wickes

from Jane Finds Her Music

Jane's Pleasant Surprise

Tom's good kids are fine
He asks after you
I would like to say
How you are But I
can't speak of it. La

la la la, la la
Had no Daddy had
an Uncle Shaun though
He did put his hand
up and down her skirt
each and every day
oh.

Jane Lives Alone

Jane wants to clean
the house, love it
in the sunshine.
Shout stop to her laughing
children bouncing balls
in the hallway.
Kiss her darling on the mouth
in the morning.

In a dairy on the corner
Jane plays a game with
the man behind the counter.
Tells him about Tom or Isaac
or her son who fell down
on the step and made bruises.

As well, she says,
there is a kick inside.
Kicks and quietness
that is the pattern
of my days these days.

H e y   J a n e

I was walking,
some kids said
Hey Jane. I
looked back,
it was some
other Jane.
I could be any
Jane. With you
gone and me
alone, it's just
like that.

1993

Julie Leibrich

The Plate

1

There was a snow-storm the day I found you.
Assembly Rooms, opposite Bashful Alley.
A snip at £8.50!
The minute she saw me reach for my purse
(unseemly speed)
she knew she had misjudged your beauty.

2

Timeless colours
born of blackened kilns
in Staffordshire
nameless painter
maybe the hand
of a child.

3

In Kiangsi Province, in the time of the Ch'ien Lung, they said that the
princess for whom the peonies were grown never had a lover.

4

Cold on my face
despite the afternoon sun
you always keep your cool.

5

You love to come down for a party.
It reminds you of your youth
when Sheridan played in London.

6

Catalogue entry 152
Early stone plate. Newstone body. Octagonal design.
Chinoiserie pattern. Stylised peonies. Excellent hand-painting.
Use of full palette. Raised enamelling on petals.
Identity: Josiah Spode, Stoke on Trent, c.1805.
Status: In collection (not for sale).

7

Bleak Saturday you became an object someone thought
to teach me a lesson with. Macho man.
Big time stuff. Converting his rage to pain.
First yours. Then mine.
Later, passed it off as a way to catch my attention. Not impressed.
A girl who collects china can't afford to have a lover who throws plates.

8

Today, I planted peonies in my garden in remembrance of love.

1993

Emily McHalick

Twelve Views of Matron's Bosoms

View 1

'Iv ya take moi fannel, Iwl kiwl ya. Iwl kiwl ya.'
'You're not going to kill anybody, Daniel, go and watch some TV. I'm taking your flannel because it has got to be washed because it's Tuesday and all flannels get washed on Tuesday.'
'Eyem mad. Eyem mad. Eyem gonna kiwl.' Daniel slams the dishwasher rack on the stainless-steel bench. 'Eyem gonna kiwl.'

View 2

'Mr and Mrs Wright? Your child is not normal.'
'What do you mean?'
'I mean that by the age of five he may be able to unwrap a sweet.'
'What do you mean?'
'The best we can hope for is that he'll ride a bike at ten years old, but
don't get your hopes up. Now which institution will you put him in?
Here's the range.'

'Was it that brutal?'
'Yes.'
'Did the doctor really say that?'
'No. I can't even remember what the words were. It was being avoided
that was brutal, it took days before the doctor spoke to us, and you
could tell something was wrong simply because you were told nothing
at all.'

View 3

It was Daniel's thirtieth birthday on Friday, now it is Monday, the
cleaning lady says,
> 'If he wants to keep his cards out he can stick them on the wall.
> He knows I've got to dust on the top of his dressing table and it's
> no good putting his cards there because I've got forty rooms to
> do and I haven't got time to go taking them off and putting
> them back up again. They're in his drawer and as far as I'm
> concerned that's where they're staying.'

View 4

Daniel is having his toenails cut in the duty office. This is the first
time I meet him. He is pretending to be posing for cameras and I
almost see the flashes going off, he wears a pair of broken sunglasses
and the duty orderly grips his foot harder. She bends over his feet,
completely absorbed in the task, and uses her entire strength to cut
through their thickness. Consequently toenail clippings fly across
the room ricocheting off cupboards and walls. One hits me just under
the eye.

View 5

Naked, Daniel has the body of a child. His stomach sticks out and his navel sticks out even further. He also has two purple scars slashed across his back and rough calluses on his hands and feet.
'How did he get the scars?'
'He was about six or seven and he was being teased.'

View 6

'Go and shave.'
'Eyem not uh chield.'
'Go and shave.'
'NUUH.'
'I've told you, go and shave.'
The afternoon duty orderly says,
> 'You can't understand a word he says. Of course you've got to treat them like children because they bloody well are children, some of them. I've been working in places like this for twenty years and I know that if you treat them like children you've got a far better chance of being understood.'

View 7

We sit together on Daniel's bed. On his record player he plays the Rubinoos' version of 'I Think We're Alone Now',
> '. . . dah dah dah uh ha I th-think we're alone now uh th-there doesn't seem ta be uh anyone na a-around hound hound hound hound dah dah dah uh . . .'
We sit on his blue bedspread under his yellow floral curtains, moving our thighs in time to the music.

View 8

The duty nurse cannot hear what Daniel is saying. That is not quite true, once when she was peering up into his face, saying,
> '. . . what? . . . I didn't catch that . . . Sorry? . . . pardon? . . . what? . . . I didn't catch that . . . Sorry? . . . pardon? . . .'

He bent down to her level, looked her straight in the eye and said,
'You're fucking deaf.'
It was the clearest sentence I ever heard him say.
The duty nurse cried and resigned.

View 9

The matron instructs Daniel that he is not to hug people, especially if
they are people he does not know, and if he continues to do so he will
not be allowed out ever again.

View 10

Daniel is not allowed breakfast because he slept in.
Daniel is not allowed afternoon tea because he came back late from
his walk.
Daniel is not allowed to watch the end of his movie because the chef
wants to watch the rugby.
Daniel is not allowed dessert because he swore at the chef.

View 11

Daniel smiles at me because I pretend not to notice him buying low-
alcohol beer at the dairy. He leans up against the post outside, clicks
his tongue and nods his head at people going by, and waves at the fire
engine.

View 12

Daniel has been sent up north to another home. Why? Because late at
night when the units were locked up he climbed out his bedroom
window, walked to the end of the path where he could see in matron's
bedroom window. It was not perverted or creepy, it was just to see her
wonderful bosoms.

1988

Allen O'Leary

For the Old

the terminally ill,
and Mrs Smith
who hovers
an inch above the flower bed, more or less
looking the moon in the eye.

—You can do it, Mrs Smith.

Yes, she knows, nods
falls asleep.

—Mrs Smith, anywhere
you would like
to go?

✧

the day-
struck lawn, a picture
window, nurse
and the caretaker
who points.

What a pleasure
to see her, smooth, floating
there
halfway between camera
and the screen.
A naked sign.

✧

Because I'm the orderly
I get
to put her out.

Also, messages.

Or if they're wrong
I brush away the blue chalk
with my hands.

1986

Alex Scobie

To Himself

Marcus Aurelius sits stirrupless
On his charger, awkward, reluctant
To confront the barbarians
Who could smell the flowers of decay
On the other bank of the Danube,
Distraught at the prospect of the empire
In the hands of his only son
Who gaped at the world through lion's jaws,
And with body oiled, ate beans and onions
With rancid gladiators, whoring away
The night with Syrians—appetites
Sharpened by the closeness of death.

How could he have fathered such a
Monster? The mob said a gladiator
Debauched his wife in his absence.

Germans threatened the empire from without;
Commodus menaced it from within.
How could a philosopher solve his dilemma?
The emperor meditated an escape to a Stoic heaven;
The horse, unguided by its reins, carried
The sick emperor further into the forest.

1993

Stephanie Miller

Shepherding

Her pillow is soft
and she's nearly asleep.
She's thinking about Rodney.
He arrived in town today
and he needs a place to stay
but her son has put his knee
through a window
and severed an artery
and needs the spare bed
for ten days.
So what can she do about Rodney?
A bedsit, perhaps?

And she's thinking about words.
She has a poem
in pieces, on her mind—
sheep dip, sheep deep, deep sheep.
She should write it down
before the phone rings.
Too late.
She must leave to meet Rodney.

The cat is heavy on her feet
as they drive to Thorndon.
It had its flea treatment today—
cat nip, nip cat, cat dip.

They pass a large dog
outside a shaky building
and climb to the first floor.
There's a slope on the house
and a hole in the bathroom window.

Rodney turns a tap.
'Does the shower work?' he asks
'It does if you put a plug in it,'
says a faceless lady
surveying a faded room.
Tinakori Road roars in
through the hole in the glass.
'We'll try Brooklyn,' he replies.

The car winds around Karepa Street.
They peer at letterboxes.
See, the house is on the upside—
downside, upside, rightside.
Rodney is inside
beckoning from a window.
'I tried the door and it opened.
I like it, I'll take it,
we'll drive down and call them
from your place'—
down sheep, leap sheep, steep sheep.

But the landlord wants a long lease.
Rodney sips a coffee
and stares at the knee.
How about Hawker Street?

She waits in the car.
The building is upside
purple, wrong side.
Wallpaper waves from the windows.
She is watching for Norman Bates.

Rodney returns.
'It's a doss house for drug addicts,' he declares,
'let's see the hostel.'
He fastens his seat belt
and they drive to the Bay.

They stop off for crutches—
the knee, the sheep, the neap.
'There'll be a pair of crutches
with the capsules of Flucloxacillin
on the bench in the kitchen, this evening,'
she thinks. 'Where will I trim the meat
for the evening meal?'

'You're looking stressed,' says Rodney.
The sun is strong and the car is hot.
She needs to know the plural of neep.
'Will the stew stretch to six?'
'I would need a car if I lived out here,' he replies.

The driveway is deserted.
They peer into a communal kitchen.
There are cupboards the size of cubicles.
They look through bedroom windows.
They see cubicles the size of cupboards.
And the heavy silence of empty space.
'This won't do. I need people
and cinemas, and cafes,' declares Rodney,
'and I can't handle a permanent view
of the sea.'

The sea—
A sea of sheep
a nip of neap
and a cat deep
in a dip, asleep.

They drive towards the city.
'This is a day going nowhere,' she tells herself restlessly.
'It's pure Kafka,' says Rodney.
'I like it.'

1996

Elizabeth Knox

Elizabeth Knox did the Original Composition course in 1984, and during the workshop began her first novel, *After Z-Hour*, which won the PEN Best First Book Award for fiction. Her other novels are *Treasure* and *Glamour and the Sea*; she has also written a sequence of auto-biographical novellas. The piece which follows is an extract from *After Z-Hour*—six people have been stranded in a house during a storm, and the voice of a ghost, a World War I soldier named Mark, enters the narrative.

Mark

Went over on a pitching ship, its every deck packed. Slept on deck in the tropics.

No longer on parade, out of the eyes of civilians, tired of the itchy wool. Poorly equipped, but wasn't to know.

Not put off by the papers and casualty lists. Led on by the patriotic verses, to take the place of brothers who were slain. Scared the war could end with no share in the glory. Privileges like medals, mouthfuls of slang and song.

It was not odd for seventeen-year-olds to enlist. Not enough to be done on the farm. The world shelved, all those books about great deeds and distant places. Only Emma and the boys at home with four horses and eighty miles to a city.

Befriended. Andy, with his shoe shop in Ashburton. Alan, laughing at the children in Menil-la-Tour, clacking over the cobbles in hand-carved pattens. And when the column paused on the road, walking over to the stone wall to listen to a cuckoo calling clear and dark amid the blue shadows of a beech wood.

The chateaux shut up behind their walls, fountains silent and walks abandoned by the mademoiselles in striped silks, carrying frilled parasols.

The front thundering far away over the wheat fields.

Aid stations, jangling ambulances, ragged columns of wounded.

Nightfall in the trenches, the long graves with road names. At home in small timber, sandbag and earth caverns.

First things first: the friendliness, most important to be good to each other. Anzac no nonsense and suffering in silence. The day after the night we took the machinegun post, congratulations came down the line to the Tommies beside us. The silent exchange of guilty and bitter glances, our 'no nonsense' all to their credit.

Death all around and the smell of death. Figures in the mud between their trenches and ours, hanging heavy in the wire. Swelling up and then falling in on themselves, flesh folding around the ribs like wet, shrinking leather. Bodies blown out of quicklime graves. Noise, whirling shells, raining dirt and hot metal, hour after hour. Crouching under fire holding our hats, because the major was a muddler who we couldn't understand. 'I say, the fire's pretty hot.' (Oh yes, pass *that* vital message down the line.)

'Can you spare some men?' All hands to pass on the stretchers. Alan's leg smashed, his grey face wet and shining. Home for sure, for him.

Morning, mud, the puddles mucous green, charred signpost trees, white sky and pustular sun. No landscapes in the Kiwi and Koala cartoons, just ourselves—game buggers. Invaded by strange energy on the orders, 'Fix bayonets—rapid fire.' We were soldiers, but not an army (no drill in these cramped conditions, Major).

Over the top: *proved their steel and earned the name of heroes / In their baptismal fire . . .* Wind of bullets, shells bursting, slithering scampering advance over a stinking half acre.

Used to play soldier out in the home paddock, lying face down among the thistles. Emma in the gun's sights, walking sedately in her white apron, seeking out the eggs of the ranging hens. It was a carved wooden gun, nuggeted black and filthy to hold.

One night at the foot of a hill with a wooded crest—living, unsmashed land—Andy said, 'There's nothing on this hillside but us and them.' It wasn't true. The Major said, 'Dig in.' Gunfire coming. Over the ridge two Germans were talking; 'Jabbering,' Andy said, but they were talking about a saddler in Königsberg.

Alan, a one-legged man, drowned in cold salt water and burning oil, when the hospital ship was torpedoed on its way home. Rose never believed it, left the light on for her straying soldier, burning through the clustering trees, the windbreak around her father's house. Come home.

'D'ya need a hand, cobber?' Cold hands fumbling with the helmet's strap. Blue fog drifting through the trees. There, under one tree, in the crook of its roots, a white speck. Do you see it? A white flaw in a portrait of a bare, dark wood. A star, a flower, a tiny white winter violet. Promising the scent of icy rivers and fresh faraway gardens. For that it is worth standing up out of the mud in a wind of bullets.

Alan, his grey face glossy, his cheeks slack, screaming, 'God help me! Help me, help me—' But *I* am not God.

Aber Gott und ich sind tod. Yet I was safe. Here. Home.

When they wheeled me out on to the grass at Oatlands the sun came out from behind the clouds and warmed my body, healing it by immersion in a balm of brightness. No lover, mother or nurse has a touch like the sun. I had no more blisters, blindness or breathlessness. Green came walking over the lawn, his arm in a sling. He said, 'It swelled up, all nasty with pus. They removed a two-inch piece of shrapnel. It's on the mend.' Then, 'Now tell me, Thornton, did you hear what happened to Given?'

(The hour has come, the hour which freezes me, which asks and asks and asks.)

They would hand out paper headed, *Chaplain's Office, New Zealand Expeditionary Forces.* I'd take three sheets and think of Green and Given, a table between them in the dugout, reading. Given's face intent and serious, Green viciously scribbling out with a dark, greasy pencil. Envy bounding out from behind his duty. And I'd wonder: 'What can I write that will be read and won't provoke him? I don't want him to come along tomorrow evening and say "Kitchener wants" me to stand sentry duty for the third night in a row, or worse still, go out with the wiring party. What can I write that won't worry Emma? Shall I say that after all this, the world will be better, because everyone will try harder? It's true, but I'm still anxious about these deep furrows and strange seeds.'

(What happened was that a bullet caught him across the face, broke his nose and tore out his eyes.)

When the blisters were gone they told me to write a letter, gave me a page with the hospital letterhead. I picked up the book beside my bed and leafed through it. Taking these words from the text I wrote: 'All the visions and consolations of my youth are dead. We know little and are bad learners: so we have to lie. Ice is around me, my hand is burned with ice. Weariness has at last to lie down and sleep, even on the snow.'

August 1916

Dear Emma,

My Dear, this country is beautiful. So quiet, full of leafy woods lying in little valleys, roads flanked by stone walls and small shrines surrounded by trees. The roads are all straight, often lined with elms and poplars.

The closer one gets to the front the fewer women and children there are to be seen, eventually only old men working the fields within the sound of the guns.

A while back Alan and I interviewed some men offloaded from a Red Cross train at Le Havre. They were waiting patiently, a few smoking, scarcely moving, conserving their strength. There were we, so full of vim, thinking we'd be able to make a difference as soon as we went up the line, and there were they, having seen action, a good deal wiser than we! Puffing out our chests we swaggered over to ask questions, as was our right. They were Canadians, not little chaps like the Tommies, but tall and slow-spoken. 'Well, what is it like?' we wanted to know. 'Not bad,' one fellow said, then let us inspect a German helmet he had as a souvenir. Talking to these cheerful men I became sure: *We are not going to lose this war.* The chap with the helmet told us we could finish it for them.

I have even seen some Russians; they made tea for us at the bivouac on the way up. They are really very friendly and hearty. I can't think what they are doing behind our lines.

I hope you are not still angry at me for volunteering. It was a matter of self-preservation, because, if I hadn't, I would have been ashamed. And without my self-respect I would have no power to act. Being 'heroic' is really the simplest option . . .

September 1916

. . . When Andy and I were on sentry duty last night, nestled down behind the parapet, the Lieutenant brought us the remainder of a tin of peaches. Wonderful! The officers have a mess cart which carries all sorts of goodies, including wine—while we have to make do with boiled beef, biscuits and the inevitable plum and apple jam. Though sometimes we live out of our haversacks, often we are cooked for: potatoes, boiled beef, onions et cetera—with occasionally something savoury scrounged. For a while it was asparagus, which grows wild over much of the countryside. However, that's now all gone to seed.

By the time this letter reaches you it will be winter here. There is no sense of exchange, or continuity, or even of contact in our letters. I write to you in far away future time. A fellow from SuVolk was telling me it takes **** for one of his letters to reach his wife. The letters between them are like a conversation.

Recently we were up near an old chateau. I spent the night lying on the stone floor of an ancient barn, looking up at some coloured flares and the moon floating in a streak of cloud. Ruins against the dark sky; fallen masonry, the gaps of windows in the walls, and the twisted ironwork of some ornamental gates.

The next morning the countryside looked so strange, we could see a merry little wood just beyond where the strafing was, the field directly before it a mess of jumbled earth. In the distance the guns lazily thumping away.

Emma, I don't think you should keep going on about how I was all fired up, as though that is bad in itself, or bad in *me*. Certainly the war is a 'common concern', but that doesn't mean I need not have gone. Firstly, it is unfair to quote at me the pompous things I used to say when I fancied myself the next Keats. Secondly, because they *are* common property, our feelings will always be used to fuel the fires of common concern. In some cases the most we can ever hope for is to choose which particular blaze we are to be thrown into! Maybe it was wrong I was fired up, but I hope to be just as combustible at seventy as I was at seventeen . . .

October 1916

. . . It is quiet here now; we are standing by **** sitting on our packs where we have stopped. Some aeroplanes just droned over and I watched little black clouds flowering among them—Archie shells.

Later: They are strafing now. Doug and I had been sent off with a whole collection of rattling canteens to a well on the hillside. Then it started, our guns hammering their infantry, the barrage gaining strength, the guns setting each other off like a pack of howling dogs.

The noise of a battery is terrible. When it first sounds it tears you in half. It is unbearable, it shakes the brains out of your head.

We could see the land below; cloven trees and dry trenches, clouds of dust where the shells were falling, aeroplane shadows crossing no-man's-land, and one blimp gliding over it all, like a small whale.

We filled up and hurried back down. Now they are answering our fire. Crumping. Not at all an apt word . . .

November 1916

. . . I wish I knew what we were expected to do next. It has been a bad week. The weather is becoming wintry. It has been pouring with rain and we have been, half the time, hip-deep in mud. It's a bloody nuisance being expected to pump out the trench for days while water slowly drains back into it. Then it rains again.

Doug was killed yesterday during a strafe. A shell landed in the trench, buried itself in the mud, spinning and hissing, and exploded. One killed, one seriously wounded, four slightly wounded. I picked myself up, scattering a few fragments of shrapnel—my coat is scorched where they fell . . .

July 1917

'. . . it doesn't matter what I think or what I do. I still haven't learned, and maybe will never learn, to separate what I love and have hope for, from what I cannot afford to love or have hope for. I don't see how I can be expected to go on saying, on one hand, 'I can't countenance this,' and on the other, 'but I can't *help* it.' One half of my heart in a sermon, and the other in the drill.

I have been on burial detail for part of the week. It's not too bad —lashings of quicklime. Funny thing is that, after a while bodies become quite boring and routine. Not horrible, just unpleasant. Death is the same. Someone dies to whom you talked over mess, and it is difficult to make it mean anything. A slightly sad change of circumstances, that's all . . .

November 1917

. . . November. The sleet has given way to frost and freezing mist. Through it all a cold little shrunken sun.

Sorry I can't write properly, it is very cold and my fingers are fat, puce-coloured sausages. But the post goes and this goes with it.

I got your letter of 24.8.17. I can understand you feeling that it is ridiculous that I am here and in danger, that I could die and you might not know about it for months. Perhaps it wouldn't seem so ridiculous if you were surrounded by streets full of neighbours with sons, brothers, husbands and fathers over here with everyone around you as anxious as you are, your anxiety would seem less important. Yet since you seldom see anyone, but the Michaelsons and the Harpers, who can't quite feel as you do, you cannot accept my being over here as the sad necessity it is.

And still Emma, I'll tell you this, right now my being here seems silly and useless to me. I keep thinking back to the old chap in Christchurch telling me, 'It's young men like you who are going to save the Empire.' The boy who heard that was all aglow with self-importance, thinking he could make a difference. Because we come to the world fresh we foolishly suppose that with our new lives new possibilities are born. It isn't true. The short range of possibilities are already worked out. We can change nothing, we can expect nothing. However long it takes the world will teach us our places, by preaching *itself* against *ourselves* . . .

December 1917

. . . I think I'm growing up. I wish this page were cleaner and fresher when it reaches you. I wish I could be sure it will reach you. This word, and this. Of course they *must* censor them.

I hope I haven't been too much of a bother to you since mother died: I suppose I was a typical younger brother and played on your forbearance. You are my family, the farm is my family too. If I came home tomorrow I'd let you be Ralph instead of Peterkin. D'Artagnan died in the Low Countries, but I'd rather come home. I long to see the trees in full flood and the wind whitely streaking the hillside.

Winter in the trenches, what a prospect. Andy consoles me by saying he hopes it will be our last. It will certainly be the last for some of us.

With best wishes,
I remain,
Your affectionate brother,
Mark

The third night. First the mud froze, the wreckage—earth, trees, men, machines—hardened, the field healing itself under a glittering skin, a cosmetic frost. Four of us peered over the parapet, Alf and Bill holding reels of wire, Calvin and I with pliers. Everything was quiet, the crescent moon was behind the clouds.

Calvin scrambled over the top and we followed, heading towards the crumbling abandoned trench a quarter of a mile ahead of our lines. It was hard going. The ground was a mass of shell holes, lying edge to edge. From time to time one of us would slip into a hole and have to be hauled out by the others.

'It's a damn shame the way the Captain always shoves you in it, Mark,' Alf said.

'Never mind.'

'Well, you're no shirker.'

'I love a good wiring party.' I touched his arm.

Calvin stopped and looked anxiously around. 'I think it's a bit further over to our left.'

'I reckon you're right.'

We squelched along a little way, then Alf exclaimed, 'Here it is!' He jumped in. 'Righto, Bill, give me a hand—'

Side by side they began to lay a double-strand entanglement. Calvin went ahead of them; I kept low, duck-walking along the edge of the trench.

'Blast, this handle's sticky with ice!'

'Frost doth as actively burn—'

'Shut up, Mark!'

I could see only shadows, a haze of breath, the vague gleam of the wire.

'Hang on—I think I smell gas.' We stopped, snuffling the air, then simultaneously unclipped our masks and pulled them on. Once my head was muffled I became nervous and impatient to get this stunt over with.

Alf and Bill were shambling over a heap of earth where the trench wall had collapsed, emerging into what faint light there was, two giant spiders spinning out wire web. Ahead of them Calvin came to the beginning of what remained of the trench, paused, then jumped down into it. Something exploded. A golden wall billowed out at me, flinging me back into our entanglement, the pressure of the blow centred at the base of my throat.

My gas mask was damaged; I couldn't breathe. I tore it off— smelling cordite, blood and mustard gas. There was a wound in my throat, at the junction of my collar bones. When I began to choke it welled blood. I covered it with my hand . . .

When I came to I felt nauseous, my eyes were streaming and my face itched. It had begun to snow. Droplets of vapour had frozen on the wire. It was glazed with ice, silvered and beautiful. I couldn't lift my head to look around, and there was not a sound from Alf, Bill and Calvin.

Not a sound. At home it seldom snowed. I couldn't get used to this dumb show of drifting flakes. Rain says, 'this, this, this, this . . .' Snow says nothing.

Adam Shelton

Adam Shelton was a member of the 1994 workshop. He works as a journalist, and in 1997 is the holder of the Louis Johnson New Writers' Bursary, awarded annually by Creative New Zealand. On 'The Old Man and the Ghazal', see 'Translation', p.290 of 'The Exercise Chapter'; on 'Russell My Pet', see p.287.

The Old Man and the Ghazal

The highlight of my week is watching the Lotto balls on TV tumble down the chute. The green and yellow and red flashes of colour are a feast to my eyes. I sit on the edge of my seat swearing at the balls, go balls, go balls. Go Balls Go. One day I'll win that bugger.

That's the big one for me because since I lost my job I don't have the money to go places, to see people. I can't be bothered.

Dorothy is in hospital with her cancer again so I get down there every day and drop off at the RSA on the way home, but I don't feel like me any more. A man gets depressed doing nothing. You lose your zip, your ping, and I'll tell you what, when Dorothy was at home the old pecker wouldn't stand up. I mean I am sixty-five but she's a great lady and the old bugger should have some life left in him yet.

Now Dottie, when she was young she was something. I have a photo of me and her on my Norton, both in leathers ready for a trip, and she's holding me tightly around the waist and I have a grin like a flaming Cheshire cat. I like that photo. Dottie says I look like a hoodlum. I think I look special. I look like I'm going somewhere.

That's still me really, inside, a biker, a risk taker. We went everywhere on that bike. Very little money, a small tent to sleep in at night, racing past cars, playing chicken with trucks, Dottie screaming and whispering softly in my ear, me hoicking into the wind and having it thrown back into my face. I sold the bike when our boy arrived; get something sensible, said Dorothy.

But that's still me. It's just, just that money and things and the family they got to me. And you can't spend your life on a bike. I still have that photo, and I show it to anyone who wants to see, anyone who has time to stop and look.

I'm getting on I suppose, slowing down, I don't have much zip any more but I'm comfortable here, and with Dorothy in the hospital well I have space now I never had. And I do visit her every day and sometimes if the drugs are on the ebb she knows I'm there.

I'd love to win Lotto for Dottie. Now that'd be something.

You know our boy, he's in Israel on a commune. Last month, a letter arrives and it's got a poem with it. The poem looks like that graffiti on the railway station and our boy says in his letter it's a guzzle, dad, a nineteenth-century Urdu poem from Pakistan, and I asked Dorothy what's he doing reading Urdu poetry from Pakistan in Israel. Does he have a job?

Urdu poetry. If you want to look at the guzzle, well, here it is.

سب کہاں، کچھ لالہ و گل میں نمایاں ہوگئیں   خاك میں، كیا صورتیں ہونگی كہ، پنہاں ہوگئیں!

تھیں بَنات النعش گردوں دن كو پردے میں نہاں   شب كو ان كے جی میں كیا آئی كہ عُریاں ہوگئیں؟

نیند اُس كی ہے، دماغ اُس كا ہے، راتیں اُس كی ہیں   تیری زلفیں جس كے بازو پر پریشاں ہوگئیں

ہم مُوَحِّد ہیں، ہمارا كیش ہے ترك رُسوم   ملتیں جب مٹ گئیں، اجزای ایماں ہوگئیں

یوں ہی گر روتا رہا غالب، تو اے اہل جہاں   دیكھنا ان بستیوں كو تم كہ ویراں ہوگئیں

Makes no sense to me. But our boy says the most important thing is just to look at it and get the feeling for it because after a while it moves into you and calms you down, and you let it mean what you want it to mean, and he says its spirit soothes you and I think it'll do you good, Dad.

Dorothy says he's not on drugs, but I'm wondering.

So I've tried looking at this poem and the best I can think is that it's grand they've invented a paint that you can't write graffiti on top of. I know that's not what I should be thinking; our boy's told me:

think of your heart, Dad, think of love, think of your heart. And I'm thinking, I think of my heart every day, boy, on the climb home from the RSA. Don't tell me about my heart.

Anyway, our boy tells me the poem speaks of a son's feelings for his father who is away at war. The son is moping, he says, over the chances he has missed to tell the father that he loves him, and he wonders if the father will make it home from the war, and somewhere in a desert the father is lopping the heads off Arabs with a sword.

I suppose, if you stand back and really look at it, you can see the father and the son. The son on the left and the father on the right. Both different, but very similar, the same form but different scars and bruises, and to my eyes the father looks a bit more battered and the son a bit straighter but they're there, together. And the longer you look at them the less important their differences become till they just sort of blend in with each other.

But I'm tired now, and there are better things than poetry to think about. I just hope he's on top of things, and if I win Lotto this week I'm going to be on the phone to him, and down to the hospital with flowers for Dottie, and off to the club to buy beers. That'll wind them all up. I'm going to sit down now, I don't have the heart for all this excitement. Here, have a look at this photo—that's Dottie and me on the Norton—let me rest a bit, till my breath comes back.

Russell My Pet

I

I don't have many things. Nothing you could define me by. I don't have those bits and pieces people have that let you know who they are. I have my panel van, and there was Russell, but I don't have much. Look at me and you would be pushing it to work me out. I keep things close to me, in my van, and in myself.

Russell got around though, around the neighbourhood. I had to get after him a bit, more than was good for me, knocking on people's doors and asking have you seen him, Russell. Last week, on Monday, I did the rounds and at first was given six potatoes from across the road and a couple of invitations to drop by some time. But no Russell.

I had my pockets stuffed full of nuts and bananas, that come-home-Russell food he loved. It was a hot day and the fruit was turning to jam in my pockets and my mind too seemed to be dissolving in the heat. I needed to lie down, but I needed to find Russell first before anything happened to him.

Sometimes he went to Bill and Esme Cotton's. They had a cockatiel, Sarah Jane, that they let fly around the kitchen, and Russell would sit on the floor against the sink cupboards shrieking like a baby and Sarah Jane would shriek back, and Esme would yell at Russell to keep away from the fridge and Bill might yell at Esme he isn't doing any harm leave the poor ape alone. But not today.

Bill stood on his porch staring at the brick wall of his neighbour's carport.

'Bill.'

'John.'

Esme appeared behind Bill. She smiled at me like you do to neighbours, and as if she knew things about me I was yet to find out.

'I saw Russell take off earlier. You have to keep track of him better. We know him, and the others around here are getting used to him, but people don't like an ape in their garden, frightening the children,' she said. 'You're not firm enough with that ape.'

'Russell's harmless,' I said.

I left them staring at the back of my neck. I walked through the suburbs looking for Russell. I stared through people's windows and over people's fences. I saw plastic bags drying on clotheslines and I saw a man wearing stockings caressing his chest in front of his bedroom mirror. But Russell for all his size and noise had vanished. I walked home. Bill was on his porch.

'John.'

'Bill.'

I was planning to ring the police and the animal shelter. I was working on the right words to explain a missing ape.

'John.'

'Bill. What.'

'Did you see the police go past? Four cars. Esme said something about an intruder, on the news, around here. Did you find Russell?'

'No, Bill.'

'Could be,' said Bill.

'He's harmless,' I said. But I took off back into what I now saw as the suburban jungle and the cliché became a picture in my head with Russell whooping and stomping in an unfamiliar backyard surrounded by taunting suburban natives.

When something happens around here it can take on a proportion unhealthily distorted from its scale, and all energy focuses on it, and there is a pull of voices and feelings and bodies in its direction. Like water squealing down a plughole, everything rushes towards the event.

So it wasn't too hard to find. It was impossible to miss in this stagnating pond, the police with their guns behind their cars, prone in the gutter, behind fences. Their guns were aimed at a property with shrubs trimmed like show poodles and lawn edges as straight as a narrow mind, and in the middle of it all the mighty Russell, my unkempt uncouth friend, pulling dahlias from a flower bed and throwing them at a woman and the growing crowd. I yell, Russell, come here, come here, Russell boy. But Russell was always his own ape. He was a good boy but he did things his own way, in his own time. He did not respond.

So I did the only thing I knew he would respond to, if he was going to respond at all. I took off my shirt and started hitting myself on the chest, making monkey noises. My fists forcing the noise from my lungs. Yelling and the crowd shuffling behind me. I was shouting and the crowd was staring at me and Russell was stuck somewhere in his own mind, back in the jungle, hanging out.

Then someone shot him in the head. A cop. And he fell over dead. And the crowd let out a noise like air from dirty bellows.

'Fucking ape,' said a cop.

'Yeah, leave our women alone,' said a man.

I had lost my only friend.

2

Russell arrived in our family because my father had a low sperm count. I was the first born, the first of many it was hoped as Mum had always aimed for a team, a gaggle, a school of us. And after I was born, Mum and Dad had a lot of sex, good sex, Dad said to me once, as if to highlight his role, good sex but fruitless. No more children.

After many attempts to increase the family, doctors gave Mum and Dad the news, the low sperm count, the low chance of any more children, and Dad, who by all accounts took the news well, ran to a petshop. If he couldn't father children the house could still be full of noise and games, Mum told me Dad had said. She was thinking of the sort of games you have with a kitten and a piece of paper tied to string. She was surprised when Dad came home with an ape.

'He's called Russell. That's because apes live in trees,' said my father, and there was no more discussion on the matter.

'Doesn't he look just like a human,' said my father as Russell rolled on the floor leaving coarse black hairs in the carpet fibres and monkey drool on the arm of the sofa.

Mum held me tightly against her chest.

'You're mad,' she said. 'Keep him away from the baby.'

Dad rolled on the carpet scratching his armpits, making soft gentle monkey noises.

3

There are great stories to be told about Russell.

Stories of how my father tried to teach Russell to catch ball, to brush his teeth in the morning, to stand up when women entered the room.

Of how, on the day my mother left my father and me, Russell opened the front door as Mum struggled down the hall towards it with a suitcase.

Of how, when Russell reached ape adolescence and my father did a drunk monkey imitation in front of his workmates and Russell, Russell screamed and jumped on him and smashed his head open on the paving stones of the patio.

There is the story of how, with no family left, Russell became my friend, my companion.

All these stories would be buffed and polished into family myth by now if there was anyone left to share them.

Louise Wrightson

Louise Wrightson did the Original Composition course in 1996, and in 1997 won the New Zealand Poetry Society's International Poetry Competition. For a glimpse of her poetry, see 'The Pantoum' section in 'The Exercise Chapter', p.288.

Inés

I

Inés is having dinner with her son, a chef. They are eating potatoes carved into mushrooms and sautéed in turmeric. A light dusting of nutmeg adds to the effect. Her son thinks fungi are very overrated, except for truffles. He knows a wealthy woman who often orders them in his restaurant. She just sits, looking at the plate. I haven't come to eat—she said quietly to him one night, touching his sleeve—I've come to inhale. The woman smelt exquisite.

That night Inés dreams of a giant mushroom. It is eighty hectares—the exact dimension of the bush reserve near her house. It rains in the night and the mushroom grows. The bush reserve becomes famous. It is balanced on top of the mushroom and is quite hard to get to.

II

Inés is in bed with her husband. He confides that once he believed in magic. He was a boy magician. His father's friend took him to a bookshop. The book he wanted was very expensive. His father's friend asked for a rubber and a pencil. They turned their backs, rubbed out the price and wrote a new one. Then they gave the rubber and the pencil back to the shop assistant. She thanked them and sold them the book.

That night Inés dreams her husband is sawn in half. One half—the top half—refuses to get out of bed. It shouts—Time is money! Getting and spending! I'm sick of it! The bottom half goes to work as usual, wearing polished black shoes and grey trousers.

III

Inés is shopping at the supermarket. She hears a faint voice calling for help. A young boy has his head stuck in a clothing donation bin. Inés tells him not to panic. If he got his head in, he can get it out. She suggests standing on tiptoe. His head slides out easily through the slot. The young boy grins at Inés, puts on his hat and does a joyful little jig.

That night Inés dreams she is in labour. It is difficult to give birth. The head of her second son keeps appearing and retracting.

IV

Inés is in a crowded tearoom. She buys a pot of tea and a chocolate bar. The only seat is beside a man with dreadlocks. He unwraps the chocolate bar and takes a large bite. Inés stares at him in astonishment. She has done assertiveness training, so she takes a larger bite. The man glares. Inés takes a bite from his muffin too. She leaves with her head high. Outside the tearoom, she opens her bag to get the car keys and finds her chocolate bar.

That night Inés dreams she is lost in the bush reserve. She has been missing for four days. Her hair is matted. She is naked, pregnant and very hungry. All she has to eat is a chocolate bar. Her son and half of her husband—the bottom half—are searching for her.

Ingrid Horrocks

Ingrid Horrocks was a member of the 1996 workshop. 'Wonderful Things' is a prose poem from her course folio, which used a mixture of prose and poetry to explore aspects of Japanese culture and society; it subsequently won the Macmillan Brown Prize.

Wonderful Things

—Finding a letter in the letterbox. Instead of taking it inside you walk through the park. You find a nashi tree. Picking one nashi you sit beneath the tree. Only then, with juice dribbling down your chin, do you take the letter from your pocket and open it.

—A temple without a sign. The last red leaves float on the pond. There is an old man sweeping but he does not utter any wise words.

—Cycling along a lane above rice paddies to the sound of dragonflies. Watching the people bent in the field under lampshade hats.

—A red lantern restaurant filled with old men smoking. The woman, in a grey kimono, explains the menu, but her Japanese is thick and you cannot understand. You ask her to choose. While you are waiting for the food, Kirin beer arrives on your table and a man nods and crinkles his face at you.

—Chopsticks flashing between a child's fat fingers.

—A man getting off a crowded train. You have been standing and swaying forever and now you sink into his seat. The heater suddenly blows onto your legs. You sleep.

—Being told that you sleep talk in Japanese.

—Coming out of the subway, finding that snow has begun to fall but has not yet whitened the cars. You put your mittens on and walk home. When you ring the bell your little brother rushes out of the yellow warmth and asks—have you seen the snow?

—Taking your shoes off at the door and stretching your legs under the kotatsu as you drink tea. At first your toes hurt but soon you can wiggle them luxuriously.

—A bath that is so hot you want to put cold in but you resist. You enter slowly, bit by bit.

J.H. Macdonald

J.H. Macdonald took the Original Composition course in 1988, where he wrote 'On the Burning Deck' for his end-of-course folio. This subsequently became the first part of his novel, *The Free World*, published recently in New Zealand, and also in Australia where he now lives. The following piece is the opening section of 'On the Burning Deck'.

from On the Burning Deck

4TH AUGUST, 1986

These gardens are secluded, crepuscular and romantic, with flame trees and Bird of Paradise plants to imply the real tropics, and leafless English oaks that contradict them. At this hour the birds are returning to their trees and drown out the noise of rush-hour traffic.

I push Olga in her wheelchair up onto the terrace of the mansion. Alec is there already lounging against the balustrade. A taffeta waterproof over her shoulders, Olga sits like a wooden god enthroned.

There is a group of Campbell's magnolia in here, planted by the wife of some high colonial official late last century, and even though midwinter has barely passed, they are in full flower. Since there seems to be a break in the almost incessant rain, we are making a party of coming over to admire them before dinner. It is the viewing season. Alec came ahead with his dog. He brings him across for exercise every evening, treating the place as if he were a keyholder to a London square. The gardens belong to the old Government House and have been absorbed by the University, and Alec took the right as professor emeritus.

I can't decide about the magnolia. Their flowers are a coarse music-hall pink but the swollen buds you might take for sparrows, small grey birds, so lifelike are they perched on the elaborate, Chinese branches.

Front is pixilated. He stands stock still, alert to every doggy possibility quivering in the dusk, then bolts beneath the Moreton Bay figs at the end of the lawn. A moment or two later he reappears — pedigree, investigative—at the foot of a clump of giant bamboo.

Olga is talking endlessly to Alec. I am out of earshot, but I can see that he is getting restless. He puts his hand into the pocket of his jacket for his cigarette case.

I whistle Front up, 'End of game, Front,' and we go back towards the terrace.

I can hear Olga now, 'And after all that, how is it that one can never find the exact word to describe the expression on a person's face? And that is not quite what I wanted to say either. I mean the history of a face too.'

Alec stops leaning on the balustrade and stands up. 'The things you talk about, Olga, are simply not there.' He begins along the terrace.

'Alec,' Olga calls out, 'remember the pooper-scooper.' Olga can't reach down far enough to pick it up. When Alec turns back she says quietly, 'The dog is yours, and you cannot expect your secretary to carry that thing.'

Alec walks ahead, and I follow pushing. The chair needs a bit of manoeuvring over the single step when we go inside. Their flat is in an old block. The fanlight gives the name in ruby glass: *Valmouth*. Olga and Alec live on the top floor in an apartment made out of several of the original small flats. We have to wait in the lobby for the lift.

Alec says, 'I mean there's no logical connection between what you see and what you want to read into it, Olga.' Olga ignores him. The lift mechanism makes a noise, and through the grille I see it begin to pull the slack loop of cable up as the cage descends.

Alec bends down and speaks to Front. 'Doggy. And doggy, what if human beings all had tails like you, eh?' Front promptly sits down in expectation of something: a pat, a titbit. 'What if that were the case? Poker, diplomacy, human intercourse itself, would not be possible.'

Olga laughs. She turns her wheelchair in a complete circle so as to come to rest facing Alec. She raises a finger in admonition. 'Watch out, riverboat gambler,' she says. 'Tonight's the night the lights went out all over Europe.'

The lift arrives. There isn't enough room for a wheelchair and another person, so Olga goes up first and sends it back for Alec and me.

I have been Alec's nominal assistant now for almost six weeks. There is very little to do. Alec has hardly any correspondence any more and seems to prefer to spend most of the day by himself. He stays in his studio where he makes buildings for an immense model city he is devising. Nevertheless he wants me round in the flat, as we have arranged, should he need me. Sometimes he calls me in to help adjust something in the city, or add a new building. The model is much bigger than a ping-pong table, and we use a boathook. Or at least I do. Alec is not strong enough in the shoulders now to keep the thing steady, and he could easily drop it on the model. We edge the toy edifices out onto the streets and gently nudge them along. When I get them within reach, I can sweep them up with a longhandled brush and shovel. Adding things is the reverse. You just put them down in a convenient street, as close to the eventual site as you can reach, and push them the rest of the way with the hook.

Alec is as nervous as a cat while we are making these alterations to his imaginary city. When I do not quite follow what he has in mind, he gets slightly impatient. 'I do believe, Nicholas, that I shall have to reinstate the system I used with my previous assistants. I will bring the big plan up to date again, and then I can simply give you the drawings and the address. I will go to Olga's room and talk to her while you put the changes into effect.' All the streets on the model have names in Alec's mind, and all these little blocks of wood like cigarette packets are tall houses with street numbers and occupants. He never gets round to doing anything about the map though. It's almost as if he would rather keep it all in his head.

There is a trapdoor in the middle of the city where Alec has made a park. This part seems to be finalised because Alec has glued the miniature trees to the top of the trap so they don't fall off when you open it up and put your head out. But maybe you just have to do that with toy cities. Now and then, to move things Alec wants moved, I have to crawl under the table and come out through the trapdoor in the centre of the city. I can almost see the people in the streets. I have an idea then why he has made it.

Olga's room always has flowers. People bring them to her. Really quite a lot of people come to see Olga. They sit in her room and talk and talk. Dr Lindenbaum pays more house calls than are strictly necessary, for example. Then there are callers in the late afternoon. They gush at me in the hall when I let them out, 'Isn't she wonderful? Such an appetite for life at her age.'

I have to answer the door. Alec skulks in his studio at that hour of the day.

Olga likes her flowers to be lavish. She likes branches of them in her room if she can get them. The university groundsman cut down an armful of magnolia and gave them to Alec, for Olga. 'Did you ask him for them?' Olga said when Alec brought them in.

'It took me a bit by surprise,' Alec said. He told Olga that the groundsman had called out to him and asked after her. He had seen us come across the night before. So Alec told the groundsman it was our blossom-viewing party. He thought for a moment, then said abruptly that he'd cut some down for her, and went away and fetched his pruning shears. 'I couldn't say no,' Alec finished.

'Lean man, very bright blue eyes?' Olga asked. Alec said he thought so. Couldn't be sure.

'He's been in those grounds for almost forty years, man and boy,' Olga said. 'He used to wolf whistle at me. It was our standing joke.'

Alec allows himself three cigarettes a day: one with lunch, one after dinner, and one for emergencies. He doesn't always use the emergency one and saves them up for Wednesday and Saturday. Alec does the cooking, and he has people to dinner on those days. Sunday evening is given over to watching television since there might be something 'presentable' to watch that night. On Wednesday, Alec's friend Geoff Butler generally comes to dinner. Geoff Butler was once

Alec's student. Now he is fifty-five, and they share an interest in wine and food. And they talk about public life. There is a Mrs Butler. The permanent invitation to her has never been dropped, but it is never spoken of. On Saturday Miss Rose comes. Miss Rose lives in one of the flats downstairs. She met Olga when they were both mixed up in the theatre. Miss Rose was the wardrobe mistress sometimes, and sometimes the prompt.

Olga can be a snob. She will not accept that the woman who delivers books to house-bound readers for the public library simply brings the books and takes them away again. She comes once a fortnight, and they have elevenses. It is easiest for the volunteer to find a parking place at that time. The reason is not clear.

Olga says that she is such a nice, intelligent woman, who is very good at choosing books. The volunteer is rather ordinary and suburban. Olga blandly flatters her on her judgement and sensitivity in bringing exactly the books that Olga wants to read, and ignores her embarrassment. Olga's tastes are actually not that specific. She munches steadily through biographies that cover the period of her life. Granted she does have a preference for careers in arts, letters, theatre, music, but politics, the profession of arms, anything touching this century will do. She isn't interested in Frederick the Great, but she is very interested in what Cyril Connolly thinks about Frederick the Great.

A woman comes to clean the flat four mornings a week. She and Olga are thick as thieves. She is the salt of the earth. It is probably a good thing that they are cronies. Her cleaning is pretty perfunctory, but Mrs Wells does a lot of things for Olga that she can't do for herself any more. Olga can't reach up to hang things in the wardrobe, and she leaves them out for Mrs Wells to put away. Olga wears a mandarin dressing gown all morning, and Mrs Wells helps her get dressed before she leaves at midday.

I don't have lunch with Olga and Alec. I try to get out for a couple of hours when they are having their naps, so I have a snack afterwards. You've got to get a break or you start to feel as old as they are.

But this job suits me. It gives me time. I get a room and board, and a small allowance: pocket money. At least since Alec's an economist, he has realistic ideas about what you need for pocket money.

And it's a nice room, up under the roof away from the main part of their flat. There's a desk and a bookcase, and I can look over the parapet, away down the harbour to the islands in the distance. They do want me in the flat a lot of the time, but that's alright. It's just wanting me there, not wanting me to be doing anything in particular, and I have plenty of time to get on with my own interests.

I knew about Alec and Olga long before I came here. They're well known.

What do I say? Alec is Emeritus Goodman Professor of Economic History at the University. He held a personal chair for many years, which was finally permanently endowed just before his retirement. His great work was the writing of *A History of the Refrigerated Meat Trade*, which went, of course, far beyond the scope of its title to discuss extensively the social as well as the economic development of the country. Having, and this is infrequent, an element of vision allied to practicality, he used to be very much in demand as an adviser to the very highest levels of government. And he and Olga moved easily in the artistic circles that contributed so much to nationalist cultural life here post-war (which is slightly odd because they consider themselves citizens of the world). I can half-remember hearing his name on the radio as a kid. He used to broadcast too, once. Talks. I wouldn't have understood a word, I suppose.

I expected there would be more to this position than simply being Alec's secretary. Anyway I couldn't bear the idea of trudging to work at a set time every day with all the other sheep, and trudging home again, and not having anything especially useful to do in between. Just some stupid job.

I have taken to conducting long conversations with Olga in her room during the second part of the afternoon. She is happy to talk. Then the three of us take tea in there at five o'clock, and afterward Alec goes to cook dinner. 'It keeps him alive,' says Olga.

At first Alec took me with him whenever he went out for provisions. Now he tends to stay in, and I go out more and more on errands by myself. He still takes Front out every day. Olga goes with him in her wheelchair on the days 'when her legs feel like it'.

Dinner takes place in Alec's studio. It is a vast space that he has carved out of two floors at the top of the building. The outside wall is made of glass bricks. The base for the toy city takes up most of the floor space in the high part of the studio, and there is a sleeping gallery where Alec and Front have their lair. Below that there is an alcove lined with books that is used as a living area. There is a long sofa covered with a piece of folk weaving, and the round table that we eat at.

Olga's room is quite different from the studio, which is a sort of modern monastery. Her room is full of what she calls her 'souvenirs'. She has a fondness for objects that are Victorian and surrealist at the same time, like small vases in the form of hands. There is an engraving in an ebony frame by the door that I look at as I go in and out. It shows red-coated Marines getting out of a rowing boat beached on a tropic strand, and advancing toward figures in grass skirts. Underneath it is entitled *Interview with the Chief of the Gambier Islands*. 'That is my souvenir of West Africa,' Olga says, 'not that I have ever been there.'

Bill Manhire

This chapter gathers together some of the exercises I have used in the Original Composition course. Some I have invented, some I have stolen. Cross references are given to contributions which have their origins in exercise suggestions.

The Exercise Chapter

Blackbirds

This exercise is based on Wallace Stevens' famous poem, 'Thirteen Ways of Looking at a Blackbird', which is exactly what its title says: thirteen short, numbered poems which glimpse or evoke or somehow react to a blackbird. The overall effect is to make an ordinary thing seem quite mysterious.

I

Among twenty snowy mountains,
The only moving thing
Was the eye of the blackbird.

V

I do not know which to prefer,
The beauty of inflections
Or the beauty of innuendoes,
The blackbird whistling
Or just after.

IX

When the blackbird flew out of sight
It marked the edge
Of one of many circles.

XIII

It was evening all afternoon.
It was snowing
And it was going to snow.
The blackbird sat
In the cedar-limbs.

Early in the workshop programme, I give students a copy of Stevens'
poem—all thirteen sections—and ask them to use it as a model for a
poem of their own: 'X Ways of Looking at Y'. The resulting poem
might be 'Seven Ways of Looking at a Vacuum Cleaner', or 'Ten Ways
of Looking at an Anzac Day Parade', or even 'Twelve Views of Matron's
Bosoms'.

It is not just that the structure of Wallace Stevens' poem makes
the day-to-day world seem more interesting than usual; it also implies
that there might be more ways of thinking about it than are actually
there on the page—a fourteenth, maybe, or a fifteenth. Knowledge is
partial and fragmentary, and depends on perspective. A single thing is
composed of a range of different things; how can we know anything
completely? Thus as the poem unfolds, section after section, you get a
sense of exploration. The text is finding out about something; it is not
trying to offer you some complacent, final piece of wisdom.

It helps if poets aren't too complacent about the things they think
they know. The Stevens poem teaches the importance of care and
focus and particularity, and it also leaves the writer room to move
during the process of composition. The words can be found and
accumulated over quite a long period. Some sections may come quickly,
some may slowly inch their way into existence. You may end up with
twenty ways of looking at something, but find yourself reducing them
to seven. Then, as well as selection, there is the task of ordering the

various sections. Because the poem has no predetermined beginning and end, you must try to decide which section would be best first, which last. And, after the beginning and ending are settled, you need to arrange the pieces in between. Do you want to imply a narrative, or a deepening of perception? Or do you want to play up the possibilities of contradiction? Is your poem predominantly about a particular thing, or about the process of a mind thinking about that thing?

And so on. The exercise idea, which isn't original to me, always seems to produce fine work, and it generously rewards attentiveness, uncertainty and patience. It encourages humility and a concern for craft, and it works strongly against the egotism which sometimes unbalances aspiring poets. Many of the pieces in *Mutes & Earthquakes* have a sort of 'Blackbirds' structure behind them; some which use it quite explicitly are Dinah Hawken's 'Talking to a Tree Fern' (p.47), Adrienne Jansen's 'The Rain and the Spade' (p.63), Julie Leibrich's 'The Plate' (p.245), and Emily McHalick's 'Twelve Views of Matron's Bosoms' (p.246).

Syllabic Ancestors

This is another poetry exercise, one which can produce astonishing work. The general idea is that a poem is written as a personal letter to a specific person, usually an ancestor. Sometimes I vary the idea: the poem might be written to someone in a photograph; sometimes it has to be composed of lies (see David Geary's essay, p.206). Here is my current version of the exercise, which involves the use of syllabic form.

> Write a poem in the form of a letter. Address someone directly, but leave out the 'Dear X' and the 'Yours sincerely'. There are two controls.

> 1. Address your poem to a parent or grandparent or great grandparent—someone you feel close to, but perhaps a little remote from in terms of immediate information and knowledge.

- Tell them about yourself—how your life has gone, how you hope it might go (even what you plan to have for breakfast tomorrow—i.e. don't drift off to the misty heights).

- And consider (or ask them) how *their* life has gone. (Be specific, be anecdotal; don't be vague.)

Please include each of these elements, but in whatever proportions feel right to you. Acknowledge the relationship. Try to touch on things that puzzle you, but don't necessarily try to solve the puzzle.

2.   Write your poem in syllabic metre. That is, maintain a regular syllable count in each line. An *odd* number of syllables usually works best—seven or nine.

Sometimes I show people Thom Gunn's poem, 'Considering the Snail', both as a technical model (it has seven syllables in each line), and as an example of how syllabics can give a particular character to a poem, in this case a sort of steady, deliberate, forward movement.

> The snail pushes through a green
> night, for the grass is heavy
> with water and meets over
> the bright path he makes, where rain
> has darkened the earth's dark. He
> moves in a wood of desire . . .

Syllabic form can impose some unlikely but wonderfully effective line-breaks ('a green/night', 'rain/has darkened', 'He/moves'). But it's a great deal harder to carry off than it seems. How do you introduce words of more than one or two syllables without resorting to hyphens at the ends of lines? Sometimes there's a bit of cheating. Here is a poem addressed to her grandmother by Fiona McLean (see also p.324) which fiddles the syllable count a couple of times, but doesn't ever falter.

Beyond the Pale

You knew what to do
with small children and
husbands lacking oomph.
You steeled family
with your steady gaze.

I touch my mother
with your hands; your eyes
dark in my mirror;
your spiderweb genes
tangling my helix.

I could tell you of
a minefield of glances,
a war of small hurts.
You could not say this
in so many words.

The breast that suckled,
the blackness that crept,
are now quite rotted,
fled into the wet earth.
The silence of soil.

You want to sleep now
but I keep calling
baying for your blood.
You know you cannot
go until I say.

One advantage of this exercise is that it stops the poet addressing
the universe in a set of large and cosmic gestures. It requires a kind of
intimate straightforwardness of voice. And like 'Blackbirds' it insists
that a poem is an instrument for finding something out, a means of

discovery, and not some grand, reductive declaration of something the poet already knew before she started writing.

See also Alexandra Gillespie's poem on p.240.

Five Things

At first sight this exercise is particularly arbitrary and bullying, since it looks intent on taking total charge of the writer's subject matter. A bland uniformity seems to be threatened, yet the happy effect is that students become wonderfully inventive, and sound more than usually themselves, more than usually true to their individual voices. Certainly Emily Perkins ('Dark Room', p.202) and Chris Orsman ('Dubrovnik', p.215) came up with very distinctive solutions to the following instructions.

Write a piece of prose which makes room for:
- A child standing in water
- The *Oxford Dictionary of Saints*
- Someone claiming to be a close friend of Margaret Mahy
- A newspaper from which a photograph is missing
- A stepladder (but no one's on it)

These items can appear in any order and in any manner you like, but they should all be present.

Sometimes I substitute a visual image for one of the listed items. This sort of thing, for example:

Or this:

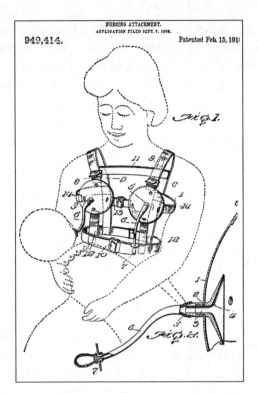

Two other contributions to *Mutes & Earthquakes* have their origins in the 'Five Things' exercise (though the details differ from those in the list above). See Hinemoana Baker's 'Hiruhārama' (p.91) and Fiona McLean's 'Written in Blood' (p.324).

My Pet

Some of those ancient classroom writing exercises weren't so bad. E. Annie Proulx's recent novel, *Accordion Crimes*, is essentially an elaboration of 'A Day in the Life of a Penny'. This is an exercise adapted from one set by the contemporary American writer, Alison Lurie. I change it a little from year to year. Here is the current version.

Write a composition on the subject 'My Pet'.

The crucial requirement is that this must be a pet you have never owned. It can be anything from a kitten to a dinosaur, from a fly to a dragon. Describe what your pet looks like, how you acquired it, what it eats and where it sleeps, what tricks it can do, and how it gets on with your family, friends, neighbours or people at work. What are its politics? Does it have strong religious beliefs?

Write your piece in three parts, numbered 1, 2 and 3; or with individual titles.

One of your three sections should concentrate on telling a story.

See Adam Shelton's 'Russell My Pet', p.266.

Poetic Form: The Pantoum

There is no such thing as free verse. New poets need to work with forms, but with forms which aren't familiar or forbidding—as the sonnet, for all its popularity, often is. (Hence the use of syllabics in the ancestor exercise, p.283 above.) The pantoum is originally a Malay form, loosely Europeanised by nineteenth-century French writers. In Malaysia the *pantun* is a set of quatrains rhyming a-b-a-b; in each verse the first and second couplets develop different themes and motifs. The European pantoum, however, relies on formal repetitions, a little like the villanelle or the sestina.

The American poet, John Ashbery, once explained his own pleasure in writing sestinas by referring to the experience of riding a bicycle downhill. After a while, he said, you don't know whether your feet are pushing the pedals, or the pedals are pushing your feet. The pantoum can offer writers a similar experience. (For a sestina, see James Brown's 'Waterford II', p.58; see also Dinah Hawken's essay, p.38. Two New Zealand poets who have particularly practised the sestina are James K. Baxter and Andrew Johnston.)

In its English version, the pantoum repeats its lines in a thoroughly systematic way. The second and fourth lines of one stanza become the first and third lines of the following stanza, and so on, with the form eventually coming full circle in the final quatrain, where the first and third lines of stanza one appear again—in reverse order—as the second and fourth lines. Thus the poem begins and ends with the same line— like a snake with its tail in its mouth. In English it's best not to rhyme. Louise Wrightson's 'Otari', which first appeared in *Metro*, is a fine example of the form.

Otari

A dark wind roars in the pines
The river runs over the stones
I am listening, lying alone
A morepork calls out to the stars.

The river runs over the stones
The rimu are creaking like masts
A morepork calls out to the stars
The frogs kak kak kak in the rushes.

The rimu are creaking like masts
The high tension wires are singing
The frogs kak kak kak in the rushes
The rain tat-tat-toos on the leaves.

The high tension wires are singing
The waterfalls burst and splatter
The rain tat-tat-toos on the leaves
The foxgloves are heavy and soft.

The waterfalls burst and splatter
A tui is sounding the morning
The foxgloves are heavy and soft
You used to lie here beside me.

A tui is sounding the morning
I am listening, lying alone
You used to lie here beside me
A dark wind roars in the pines.

For further examples of the pantoum, see Alison Wong's 'The river bears our name' (p.112), Emma Neale's 'After the Diagnosis' (p.239) and James Brown's 'Cashpoint: A Pantoum' (p.56). (For James Brown's poem, see also 'Found Poems', p.292 below.)

Postcards

The idea is to write some sort of story composed of postcards. Like 'Syllabic Ancestors' this exercise controls the 'address' of the text: someone particular is being spoken to. I usually ask for the piece to be composed in three numbered sections. Each section must include three distinct elements: a description of the stamp, a description of the picture on the card, and the message on the card. There is the opportunity to tell a real story (three postcards inevitably prompt the familiar structure of beginning, middle and end); and there are also opportunities for interesting contrasts between the different exercise elements—especially between image and message. I haven't included any examples in *Mutes & Earthquakes*, though Gabrielle Muir (see p.95) was an award winner in the Mobil-*Dominion Sunday Times* Short Story Competition in 1991 with an entry called 'Three Postcards'.

One of many possible variants is the exercise Damien Wilkins set in 1995. Writers were to imagine they had received a postcard containing some shocking or surprising news. The exercise was to reply to the postcard without revealing directly what the news had been. There were two components—describing the picture part of the postcard, and then giving the writing. Kate Camp's poem, 'Postcard', on p.221, is her response to the second part of this exercise.

Translation

Sometimes I ask students to translate from a language they don't know. This exercise seems to offer a great deal of freedom, but in fact there is often a great deal to keep in mind. The very look of a text in, say, Russian can be extraordinarily suggestive to readers who don't speak Russian, and there are also various kinds of symmetry and repetition which, a glance tells you, could inform an English translation.

Later on, of course, after all the English versions are done, it may

ДОЖДЬ

Я слышу
прошили тишь
капли
дождя

Будь я глухим
по́ры на коже моей
раскрылись бы
и впитали тебя

Я
узнал бы тебя
по влажным твоим поцелуям
будь я слепым

по особому
запаху
опаленной солнцем
земли

по дроби твоей
барабанной
когда
затихают ветра

Но если бы я
не видел
не слышал не осязал
не вдыхал бы тебя
ты все же
творил бы меня
размывал меня
хранил меня
дождь

be interesting to learn that the text in question happens to be a Russian translation of one of the small classics of New Zealand literature, Hone Tuwhare's 'Rain'.

I have used a number of other languages in this way, including a Chinese version of my own poem, 'The Old Man's Example'. My favourite translation exercise involves the Urdu poetic form, the *ghazal*. I reproduce for the class a couple of examples from *Ghazals of Ghalib*, a book edited by Aijaz Ahmad in 1971. The editor describes the ghazal form in detail (it is essentially a short form written in five self-contained couplets), prints many examples of the ghazals written by the nineteenth-century poet, Ghalib, and puts alongside them a range of translations by contemporary American poets such as Adrienne Rich, W. S. Merwin and Mark Strand. Usually I give the workshop two ghazals to translate. The first comes with Aijaz Ahmad's literal translation and notes—i.e. all the information that he gave to his commissioned poets. The second is just the text:

خاک میں، کیا صورتیں ہوں گی کہ، پنہاں ہوگئیں!   سب کہاں، کچھ لالہ و گل میں نمایاں ہوگئیں

شب کو ان کے جی میں کیا آئی کہ عُریاں ہوگئیں؟   تھیں بنات النعش گردوں دن کو پردے میں نہاں

تیری زلفیں جس کے بازو پر پریشاں ہوگئیں   نیند اُس کی ہے، دماغ اُس کا ہے، راتیں اُس کی ہیں

ملّتیں جب مٹ گئیں، اجزائے ایماں ہوگئیں   ہم مُوَحِّد ہیں، ہمارا کیش ہے ترکِ رُسوم

دیکھنا ان بستیوں کو تم کہ ویراں ہوگئیں   یوں ہی گر روتا رہا غالب، تو اے اہلِ جہاں

Then I wait to see what happens.

In 1994, thanks to Nikhat Shameem (see p.200), we learnt that ghazal is pronounced 'guzzle'. I had imagined that the word had all the lyrical lift and lightness of a gazelle. The fact that we were now dealing with the *guzzle* form gave Adam Shelton the opportunity he needed, and instead of producing a piece of poetry he wrote a very short story, 'The Old Man and the Ghazal' (see p.264). For another imaginative reworking of the ghazal idea, see Johanna Mary's piece of surreal pseudo-scholarship, 'The Desert and the Sown: A New Proto-Hurdu Tablet', which appeared in *Sport 9*.

The Canadian poet Phyllis Webb has written many ghazals, and Dinah Hawken's 'A New Word' (p.49) is influenced by ghazal form.

Found Poems

As T. S. Eliot said, immature poets imitate, while mature poets steal. His own poem *The Waste Land* is full of thefts. I usually set a found poem exercise quite early in the workshop programme, and ask for the poetic spoils to be brought along to our final meeting. With found poems, writers have to be alert to the world, hunting for the words that are there already. What writers notice can be far more important than what they think. (I thoroughly approve of David Geary's bus trip between Palmerston North and Wellington, p.210). Usually I hand out the following poem to show what I mean. I've seen it attributed to several authors, most often to Julius Lester.

Parents

Linda failed to return home from a dance Friday night.
On Saturday
she admitted she had spent the night
with an Air Force lieutenant.
The Aults decided on a punishment
that would 'wake Linda up'.
They ordered her
to shoot the dog
she had owned about two years.
On Sunday,
the Aults and
Linda
took the dog into the desert
near their home.
They had the girl
dig a shallow grave.
Then
Mrs Ault
grasped the dog between her hands and
Mr Ault
gave his daughter
a .22 caliber pistol
and told her
to shoot the dog.

Instead,
the girl
put the pistol
to her right temple
and shot herself.

The police said
there were no charges
that could be filed
against the parents
except possibly

cruelty
to
animals.

My assumption is that Julius Lester found these words in the
court reports of an American newspaper. He arranged them in lines
and stanzas, and supplied a title—all devices which signal a poem yet
also shape particular meanings. A title like 'Parents' tells us to think
about parental responsibility, as does the fact that Mr Ault and Mrs
Ault get a whole line each: there they are, isolated and guilty, visible
in the poem in ways that perhaps weren't apparent in the original
court report. Strictly speaking, the words haven't changed at all; but
the change of context, along with the change of genre, has transformed
them entirely. They mean something quite different.

Writers invent the world, but they also edit it and scavenge in it.
Many of the contributions to *Mutes & Earthquakes*—stories as well as
poems—contain found material. Sometimes the simple narrative of a
set of events can have the effect of found poetry (see Jenny Bornholdt's
'Then Murray came', p.52, or Stephanie Miller's 'Shepherding', p.252;
see, too, the Grace Paley List Assignment, p.298). There are three
'genuine' found poems in this anthology. Wanda Barker's 'On tracks
to be with angels' (p.124) was found in the *Dominion* and published
subsequently in *Printout*; Michael Mintrom's 'Borstal Girl' (p.242) is
composed out of a multiple-choice sentence-completion questionnaire

in a book called *Youth in Crisis*; while James Brown's 'Cashpoint: A Pantoum' (p.56) deftly explains its own point of origin.

Group Work

Most of the exercise work in the Victoria workshops is done between classes. A topic is set, and the work is reported a week later. Sometimes, though, we do something in class. Cut-up work of various kinds can be interesting. For example: each person brings a sheet of their own writing to class; another person cuts it into several pieces with scissors, then rearranges it; then someone else again starts obliterating words to make a new text. Often the effect of all the deliberate disordering is to intensify the effect of the original. Here is an example from the 1991 workshop. (I don't remember now just which three writers were involved in producing it.)

Will You Remember This

Shall I tell you the problem?
    I discovered love in love: I have such difficulty. The memories true and not true, all clarity, all conscience—living in London, even when I was seventeen, catching sight of him, his face lit up, stabbed—then as now.
    It was a word, the year was almost over. His skin stays, I think I can still feel it. By that time I was in love, hungry and sleeping badly—it must have been natural. I collapsed, being in love with him. 'Precious things,' Americans call it. America is so big, vast in the bloodstream—men's names, colours . . .
    The first time I remember seeing him was the first time I can remember. He made me dissolve. *Oh speak to someone else at once.* I don't understand, when I was four I couldn't help it.
    I adored Wellington—there were two of them, vivid, which is arguably the point. I wanted the dictionary: immersion, vitality, vastness. I fell headlong. We were living in winter, bewildered: I didn't notice Sunday morning. You can get lost in there, lost in things, in that boy.

Sometimes we work on a group poem. One way is to settle on a structure, and then for each person to write a single line using that structure. Eventually, after a process of ordering, a poem exists. Here's one called 'Homage to Kenneth Koch'—mainly because the 'I used to . . . but now I . . .' line structure picks up one of his suggestions.

> I used to tear, but now I crumble.
> I used to dream about clouds
> but now I live inside them.
> I used to care for what they say
> But now I've resigned.
> I used to do my bit for society
> But Herbie refuses to go
> to any more slack do's at Plunket.
> I used to stutter sound
> but now I stutter whole words.
> I used to climb walls and sing of apple trees
> but now I sit in the middle
> of a soft white room.
> I used to grow my hair
> but now I wear it short.
> I used to be young but now I avoid time.
> I used to know nothing
> but now I am deceived.
> I used to, to, to . . . But now?
> I used to hop-scotch and skip
> but now I'm inert.
> I used to be brilliant but now I'm cured.

Another good joint exercise is the surrealist game of 'Definitions or Question and Answer'. One person writes a question on a piece of paper, folds the paper so as to conceal what has been written, and then passes it on to another member of the group who writes an answer. The process produces some fascinating explanations of the universe:

Where did the violin find its music?
A woman with ladders in her stockings.

Why do the people riot?
One spoon of sugar.

Why is there only one word for rain?
Because the statue moved.

Here is a whole short poem made out of questions and answers. The Wai-te-ata Press published a literary calendar which gave a page each to work by members of the 1996 (and last) Original Composition workshop. My own last-minute, entirely stolen, contribution was made out of a question-and-answer session.

Sonnet at the Speed of Light

What is the most beautiful obsession?
Too much pressure and too little clarity.

What is a rainbow? Two men talking
but their hands are still.

What is the secret you are most ashamed to reveal?
Light in the night like a moon.

If a train left Ontario and travelled at 105 miles per hour . . .
Just what the hell do you think you are aiming at?

Then what is a library of books?
The secret I am most ashamed to reveal.

And what does an oboe sound like underwater?
A door shutting. A door shutting.

And what is the sound of a pillow?
A tablespoon of flour.

A few more to end with . . .

Dialogue

Most fiction-writing workshops use some sort of dialogue exercise. Barbara Anderson has said somewhere that the first time she felt she was really writing was when she was set a dialogue exercise by an editor from Radio New Zealand's drama section who was a guest at the Original Composition workshop. (And see the note to 'Up the River with Mrs Gallant', p.25.)

John Gardner has a good dialogue exercise which involves each character having a secret. The secrets may not be directly expressed, says Gardner, but they must be there for the reader to intuit. 'Purpose: to give two characters individual ways of speaking, and to make dialogue crackle with feelings not directly expressed.'

Here is my own most recent dialogue exercise:

> Write a two-handed story entirely (or as entirely as you can manage) in dialogue.
>
> No stage directions. (This isn't a play.)
>
> One of the characters should be someone you like or admire or somehow approve of; the other should be someone you don't particularly care for.
>
> Don't indicate in any obvious way which is which.
>
> If you want a particular setting, then I suggest Antarctica.

Grace Paley's List Exercise

> An assignment called the List Assignment. Because inside the natural form of day beginning and ending, supper with the family, an evening at the Draft Board, there are the facts of noise, conflict, echo. [Often] the most imaginative, inventive work has happened in these factual accounts.

I sometimes add one or two further controls. For example: 'Include one or two patches of dialogue; include a recipe.'

Your Mother's Kitchen

This one is stolen from Rita Dove.

> Write a poem about your mother's kitchen. (It helps if you actually draw the kitchen first, with crayons!) Put the oven in it, and also something green, and something dead. You are not in this poem, but some female relation—aunt, sister, close friend—must walk into the kitchen during the course of the poem.

One from John Gardner

> Describe a lake as seen by a young man who has just committed murder. Do not mention the murder.

(See Nikhat Shameem, p.200, for a short piece prompted by an exercise of this sort.)

Writing Between the Lines

This is a poetry writing exercise made especially for word processors.

> Choose a poem of between ten and twenty lines, a poem which is more or less new to you, but by a generally admired and preferably contemporary poet. Type out the poem, triple-spaced. Then, between the lines, fill in a new line, based on or suggested by the original line. Once you have finished, erase the words of the original, and begin to work seriously on the poem which remains.

This exercise is by J.D. McLatchy (see Dinah Hawken, p.38), who suggests that the completed poem be thought of as the first part of a longer poem; the thing to do next is to write 'a companion section—Part II, and entirely your own—that extends the first part by continuing or departing from or in some other way varying the themes and images of the first'.

McLatchy warns that some poets are better for this exercise than others. The American poets he suggests are Robert Hass and Louise Glück. New Zealand poets likely to work well as a starting point for 'writing between the lines' include Lauris Edmond, Michael Jackson, Bernadette Hall, Gregory O'Brien, Andrew Johnston, Iain Lonie, Fleur Adcock and—though his voice could be overpowering—James K. Baxter.

For exercises and writing suggestions, see the essays elsewhere in this book by David Geary, Fiona Kidman, Damien Wilkins, Joy Cowley and Dinah Hawken.

Further Reading

The best 'further reading' is the work of other novelists, poets and story writers. There are many bad books on writing, and many rather pointless ones: *Attention-Grabbing Query and Cover Letters*, for example, or *How to Write and Sell Confessions (Tested Techniques for Today's Confession Market!)*, or—the one that seems to cover the lot— *How to Write like an Expert about Anything*. But there are also some excellent and genuinely helpful books. Here are my current favourites: dates, authors and titles—but not publishers, as there are often various editions.

Two very encouraging books to start with: Dorothea Brande's *Becoming a Writer*, a classic which was first published in 1934, and Ann Lamott's *Bird by Bird: Some Instructions on Writing and Life* (1994)—both titles help you get started, and then suggest how to keep going. Peter Elbow's *Writing with Power* (1984) is also a demystifying general introduction to a range of different kinds of writing (his chapter on poetry is called 'Poetry as No Big Deal').

The best books on poetry writing are probably those by Kenneth Koch, who covers the whole age range: *Rose Where Did You Get That Red: Teaching Great Poetry to Children* (1973), *I Never Told Anybody: Teaching Poetry Writing in a Nursing Home* (1977), and *Wishes, Lies, and Dreams: Teaching Children to Write Poetry* (1980).

A very lively and helpful poetry book, *The Practice of Poetry* (1992), is edited by two American poets, Robin Behn and Chase Twichell. As its subtitle—*Writing Exercises from Poets Who Teach*—makes clear, it is a compilation (nearly 300 pages) of exercise ideas from a wide range of poet-teachers. (I found Rita Dove's poetry exercise, p.299 above, in this book.)

A similar—though less successful—compilation for novelists and story writers is *What If? Writing Exercises for Fiction Writers* (1990), edited by Anne Bernays and Pamela Painter.

Two excellent fiction-writing titles are John Gardner's famous 1984 text, *The Art of Fiction: Notes on Craft for Young Writers*, and Jerome Stern's alphabetically devised *Making Shapely Fiction* (1991), which, as one of the cover puffs rightly declares, is 'full of wisdom with a light touch'.

The standard fiction-writing manual in North America is probably Janet Burroway's *Writing Fiction: A Guide to Narrative Craft*, which is now into its third or fourth edition. Closer to home there is Australian novelist Kate Grenville's *The Writing Book: A Workbook for Fiction Writers*, first published in 1990.

Sarah Quigley

Sarah Quigley did the Original Composition course in 1996, while she was completing an Oxford DPhil on the poet Charles Brasch. 'Falling' won the 1996 NZ *Listener* / Parker short fiction competition. Penguin will publish her first book of short stories.

Falling

You don't know why but you suspect it's because he's your best friend's boyfriend. Even the words are one big yawn. Bands have sung them, poets have written them, half the world has lived them, and now you're thinking them.

This makes you very angry.

He's not even someone you'd like to like. He has smooth hair, you like rough hair. He says he picked up Public-School-Speak after living in London, but he was only there for eight months and most of the time he lived with a girl called Anna whose Dutch accent was thicker than a McDonald's shake.

And that's another thing, he's the type who talks about his exes. He notices your Audrey Hepburn face, the violet veins in your wrists which remind him of Tolstoy novels. Then, just when you think you're the only one with almond-shaped eyes, he tells you who bought him the paua ring which he never takes off even in bed.

Is this bad taste or is it sexy?

The Dutch have a saying: When the cat's away, the mice will dance on the table. (You also have a clog-wearing friend, also called Anna: Coincidence # 1 .) You know that as soon as Rebekah leaves for Japan at the end of the month, you'll be heading for that table ready for the rumba. Will he? You're not sure. The look he flung at you across Rebekah's vodka-filled head last night raises ambiguities you thought could never be held in your one-dimensional head.

Because you're simple, you've always been simple, that's just the way it is. But you think the time might have come to develop some complexities, some perplexing complexes to make you less readable and harder to put down.

Just in time.

It's not only a bad pun, it's not true. Because Justin never hurries. The first time you remember seeing him was the afternoon when you and Rebekah went to see *Dead Man*. Jim Jarmusch has genius, Johnny Depp has good timing, Justin has both.

Rebekah's fretting. Will he turn up or will she have to avoid still-life class for the rest of the term and get a D? She's so jumpy, she's clocking up clichés by the second. She trips up the stairs, she steps on someone's cardigan and shuffles it halfway along the row. She balances the *Mission Impossible* bucket of popcorn on her armrest, then rests her arm on it. You say it doesn't matter, but you haven't had lunch and you feel like a piranha.

Dead Man starts. The hand-held camera shots make your empty stomach queasy. It's all in black and white, *Dead Arty*. A Tarantino shoot-out gives it boy appeal—but where's the boy? Rebekah's hands are unravelling your favourite green jersey.

As the camera swoops and lurches in on Johnny Depp, you do your own swoop-and-lurch. There's a Johnny lookalike standing broodily at the door. His face is white, his leather jacket is black, and most people turn to look at him. Against the rolling prairie his profile looks suitably wolf-like.

Ignoring the usher's torch, he strides up the stairs towards you. Your mother always told you not to sit on the aisle because you get jabbed with needles and forced to join a religious cult. You're so glad you don't listen to your mother. He's beside you, he speaks. You get a jab somewhere in the stomach region, but it's pleasurable pain.

'Hey,' he says. You shift on a sea of popcorn. Far far away, Johnny D has been shot in the leg.

'Rebekah?' he says. 'That you?'

You crunch out of your row to let him sit beside your best friend.

His entrance, your exit. You feel a jab somewhere near the heart, a hundred times more painful than tetanus or hepatitis shots. Obviously you're not immune to jealousy.

That was Justin, arriving too late into your life. Rebekah has genius, you have bad timing.

It's the end of September and you have your hands full. You're swotting for exams, looking for a holiday job with sunbathing hours, and hoping to seduce your best friend's boyfriend without buying a ticket for a long-term guilt trip. It's a big ask.

Rebekah writes. She's cold and she's discovered she's allergic to buckwheat noodles. There are two other English speakers in the whole town and one of them's sixty. Justin hasn't written and she wishes she was in the Krazy Lounge having a tuna melt with you.

You wish she would stay away forever. You wish you were nicer.

Just in case.

He says he might call round on his way home from night-class. You've offered to show him photos of Rebekah in full kimono-kit, now you have to set the scene.

You have a shower, wash your hair, and dry it straight. It takes you forty-five minutes to do this but you look more sophisticated. You also look like you've spent forty-five minutes on your hair. You stick your head back under the tap and aim for casual.

What if he comes into the bathroom to piss? It's too tidy. It's anally tidy. You fling a towel on the floor. Its folds look unnatural so you fling it again. After five flings it looks passable, and you have too many other things to put in disarray anyway.

You scatter a few things about: toothbrush, hairbrush, tampons. Too contrived? Too in-your-face I'm-a-Woman? Put the tampons back in the bottom drawer, leave the toothbrush, hairbrush.

Your room is suddenly too obvious for words. How could you ever have thought an Indian bedspread hung from the ceiling was a good idea? But it's too late for major redecorating. Your room looks out over the Terrace, curvy lights around the waterfront: at least your view is arty. (Apparently his flat has the harbour too: Coincidence # 2.)

You open the window. Too noisy. Close it: too stuffy. Open it a few inches and stick a brick in the gap, which straight away slides into the night. Two floors down, then the roof of a car. Shit. You pull the cane blind down, switch off the light, flatten against the wall. Imagine him arriving. Spring away from the wall, switch on the light.

You wrestle the cork out of the Cab Sav your brother gave you last Christmas. (After eleven months you just found it under your bed, along with a photo of you, Rebekah and Justin drinking red wine through straws: Coincidence # 3.) You have an excellent idea. You pour a third of the bottle down the sink, put an extra glass on the table. Someone else has just left, he can help finish the bottle. Very casual.

You fill your own glass and swig it down to a believable level. You arrange yourself on the sofa, with one leg stretched out. You pick up your new Milan Kundera and give it a quick batter against the coffee table.

Half an hour later you have cramp but you'd better not abandon your pose just yet. It's only ten o'clock, and maybe the class is running over time. You keep Milan Kundera open at page 253 but you're finding it hard to follow the story, flicking between page 253 and Chapter One. You hear the door downstairs bang (you left it open, you're not uptight). There are footsteps on the stairs. They go past your room and up to the next floor. You refill your glass.

By midnight, you have finished the wine and you can't remember a word of what you've read. Slightly savagely, you pick up your props and put them away, neatly. You've wasted an evening on the bastard, not to mention good reading material. Well, that's it, you're older and wiser.

At four o'clock the next day you're letting yourself in when you hear the phone ringing. A few of the others from his art class went for a drink, he didn't remember till the pub closed, he knew you would've gone out by then. But he might call in tonight on his way to his mate's, OK?

You might be in, you're not sure, call anyway.

You ring Anna and cancel the movies: you're not feeling too good. (This is true: you feel nervy and tense.) You run five blocks in the rain to Liquorland and buy a suitably cheap but not too cheap red wine. You have a shower, wash your hair.

You haven't seen him for a week and a half. You're feeling pretty desperate and anyway you need to borrow a tent for New Year and Rebekah said he's got one.

He's been thinking about ringing you because he needs a model for next week's assignment and he thought he might shoot your face. He calls you Emily B in a mocking kind of way.

You say you're pretty busy at the moment but you'll have a look at your diary. You pick up Kundera, rustle him a bit, and then say that, actually, you're free tonight. (Joni Mitchell's in the background and you were playing her two days ago: Coincidence # 4.)

'Just your face,' he says mockingly. 'Emily B.'

When you arrive, he's smoking a joint with his neighbour. A girl, but she's pale and spidery so you can afford to be nice to her. She stares at you with light blue eyes and says, 'As long as it's just your face.' They both laugh, she leaves.

He rolls another joint, offers it to you. You don't really want any, you've already had a few vodkas to get you out your front door, but you like the thought of his lips where yours have been so you have a quick drag and exhale fast.

'OK Emily B,' he says and he pours you a whisky. You knock it back because you think it might stop your hands shaking. You sit on a stool by the window where the gold MASSAGE PARLOUR sign will bring out the gold in your hair. He moves you to the dingy armchair in the corner.

'Heard from Rebekah?' you say. You pinch your wrist, viciously, to stop any more good lines.

'Nope,' he says, and he looks at you hard. He doesn't say much more, he just clicks away and moves your chin around a bit, and pours you some more whisky. He's putting away a few himself but it doesn't seem to affect him. You look at some photos to the left of his ear: pointy female nudes, from the neck down. Not voyeuristic, not contrived. Not Rebekah.

He passes the joint with one hand, holds his flash up in the other. His shadow-arm reaches right across the room to touch your shadow-head. You start to feel very strange but if you just hold onto the ridges on the arms of the chair you'll be OK. 'How's it going?' you manage. Your fingernails cling to the ridges in an edge-of-the-precipice way.

'All right,' he says.

He comes up close and looks way into your eyes, further than anyone's ever seen before. 'How's you, Emily B?' he asks. You can see your reflection but nothing else is very clear.

He moves your chin up and pulls you towards him. You lose your grip on the chair. You know this isn't good. You stand up and vomit all over the carpet.

Rebekah's back. Two months of chilblains meant she got to know the pharmacist round the corner (English speaker # 2). He's American. As soon as he gets back to Portland, Oregon, he'll buy her a ticket for the end of the first semester.

'So how's your life?' she asks.

You tell her in a casual voice that there's a dearth of men in Wellington. There's been no one remotely interesting/interested all summer. Your heart sings. You know once you tell Justin you had a bad dose of shellfish you can start again from when he lifts your chin and leave out the bit where you lie on his carpet with sick in your hair.

She says she hears you sat for Justin. She asks if you met his neighbour.

You vaguely remember: thin, peaky, kind of Gothic.

'Got her claws in the day after I left,' she says. 'Bitch. Bastard.'

You go with her for a tuna melt at the Krazy Lounge. There's a new waiter who looks a bit like Keanu and looks a bit at you.

Barbara Else

Barbara Else was a member of the 1988 workshop. The following piece is from the opening of her bestselling novel, *The Warrior Queen* (1995); it first appeared in 1992 as a short story in *Metro*. With her husband Chris Else, Barbara Else runs Total Fiction Services, a manuscript assessment service and literary agency.

Hot Chips

Kate's in bed in a hotel, looking at her homework. She's forty-one years old, doing homework on holiday. The words on the paper are in Cyrillic script and there's a picture of a coin. It must be a Russian coin, she thinks. Kate no longer knows why it's important for her to do homework at her age but she supposes she had a good reason when she decided to take Russian.

She looks at the paper. The meaning is trapped in the words, the strangely formed letters, and won't come out. The first capital letter looks like a parrot.

Maybe she'd rather go to the Taronga Park Zoo. She might enjoy the boat trip. Zoos are places to visit when you're away from home. But she doesn't want to go there on her own.

Neither of the others will go with her. Jessica says she's too old for zoos: Mum, they're cruel, and I don't think they're Green! Besides, she's made a friend in the hotel and the girls spend time together, going into shops, smiling at gorgeous guys, smothering laughs behind their hands, making sure they're noticed as they deserve to be, elegant and awkward, young, exuberant.

Richard's here too, but not on holiday. Kate doesn't think Richard ever has a holiday as normal people understand the word, though once or twice a year he has time off for scheduled enjoyment. On this trip, Richard's at a conference. He drew up the agenda: it took weeks of faxes back and forth across the Tasman Sea, long evenings in his study while his bald patch got mottled and his remaining hair stood up all fluffy. Each day he says: **Aren't you enjoying yourself? This took a lot of organising on my part. It's not asking much to expect a word of thanks.** And he looks really hurt.

They are three people crushed into a small hotel room because someone's secretary screwed up the travel arrangements. Thank God there's a secretary to take the blame, thinks Kate: it's a big conference and something had to get screwed. It won't be me, in this small room with a teenage daughter sleeping in the fold-out bed which she doesn't fold away during the day. Why should she? It's her space. Kate's glad Jessica has a space to herself.

Haven't I said 'thank you'? she thinks. I'm sure I would have remembered to say 'thank you' somehow or other. Damn, I wish I had remembered. She wishes she could remember if she'd said it or not, or if Richard's just being a pain.

He's gone down to breakfast. He got out of bed and stalked around like a thunder clap with no clothes on. He doesn't stalk around naked at home: he wears pyjamas and holds the pants fiercely closed. Kate knew what he was thinking: **I'm paying for this room, I'll do just what I like for once.**

His bottom, tight and plump as a football, marched into the bathroom. Jessica glanced at Kate. Kate glanced at her too. The looks flicked away. When Richard's around, sometimes the rest of the family pack everything their looks say into suitcases which they store behind their eyes; they leave them there, unopened. Though right then Jess lifted a long thin teenage arm and pointed at the top of her own head. She giggled, not looking at her mother. Kate pulled the sheet up so Richard wouldn't hear her laugh too. The Barometer, Jess meant. Richard's bald patch, blotchy red which means full organising mode so stand back please, dogs and small children at the rear for safety, well back, thank you.

Kate knows she doesn't look grateful she's on holiday. The smog in Sydney this year is making headlines. She's got the worst cold she's had for years and the worst period pains she's ever had. They were the worst last month too. Each month Richard says: **Sorry, I was going** to do something about that. I'll speak to Martin. There's a new drug on the market that's supposed to do wonders. I could prescribe it myself but you ought to see Martin first. We should do this properly. But I'll do it for you. If that's what you want.

If she says please, that would be great, he'll Frown (the Frown that comes with a capital F). He'll say, we really ought to do it properly. If she says no, that's OK, he'll forget to talk to Martin till next month. Kate always says it's OK. It's only a problem for two days. Two out of thirty-odd is fine.

And Kate looks at it this way: because each month he says he was going to do something, it's proof he cares about her. He just gets tied up in his work. And each month, because she doesn't fuss and nag, it's proof she cares about him. It's nice, to still care about each other after more than twenty years. And Richard does think that things should be done properly. She's glad someone in the household does things properly. I'm glad it doesn't have to be me, she thinks.

Richard likes her to have holidays. He likes her to come to conferences. He likes her to dress up and go with him to the functions in the evening. During the day she can shop. He likes to see what she buys: **That must have been cheaper than back home. You're well set up now, aren't you.**

Books are the only things cheaper than back home. Kate has bought a book of short stories by Elizabeth Jolley. She hasn't shown it to Richard, though she isn't sure if Elizabeth Jolley is feminist or just intelligent.

She's bought a red dress covered in wild patches of orange and yellow, edged with satin and with ribbons on the sleeves. It's a bold, gypsy dress, exotic. It was amazingly expensive but she coveted it and so she bought it. She'll probably wear it, once, maybe twice. She bought a plain black dress which will be useful if she has to go to a funeral one day. She bought a purple silk shirt long enough to wear with nothing underneath if she ever wants to. She nearly bought a scarf.

She has bought presents for the ones she loves back home. A pair of embroidered braces and two CDs for her trendy son, Owen. A book on 'Good Ocker Meals Fast' and a bark painting for her brilliant older daughter Alice, as well as a T-shirt and some tights. She has bought a necklace and a red leather bag for her arty sister. The necklace is made of coins—they might be Russian coins—and funny links shaped like the letter Z. She bought a palette of eye makeup for her niece who's just a bit younger than Jessica. She found a pair of earrings, eucalyptus leaves dipped in gold, for her best friend Libby. She has walked up and down the Walks in the Queen Victoria Building; the Prince of Wales Walk, the Grand Walk and all the other Walks. She bought an almond croissant and a cappuccino and watched the tourists gather for the pageant in the Royal Clock when it struck the hour. Everyone laughed when Charles II had his head cut off. She tried on bathing suits and giggled when they made her look like something in the crazy mirror at a carnival. The shop assistant asked if she was all right.

Kate's been to the shops every day for four days. There are two more days before they go home. The other wives seem to love shopping but Kate thinks she'll scream if she has to go into one more huge department store, one more teeny wee boutique. She could go on a bus trip, but she did them all when they came to a conference here last year.

She looks at her homework again. She likes the Cyrillic parrot. Maybe this paper tells her in Russian how much it costs to buy one. She liked the parrots at the Melbourne Zoo when they were at a conference there three years ago. One of them clambered along the bars and bobbed up and down. She bobbed back. In a broad Australian accent it said, *Do you wanna dreenk? Do you wanna dreenk?* She did.

The bird cage in the Melbourne Zoo was exactly like a bird cage— big and round, metal bars curving together at the top. Kate sang to the parrot that talked to her: *Only a bird in geelded cage.* A red smudge from the iron bars came off on the blouse she'd bought once in Italy.

Damn, thinks Kate, I've forgotten to bring the textbook I need to do my homework properly. It's not really homework, it's preparatory reading. The first lecture's in two weeks. She nearly told Richard she couldn't come with him this time because of the reading she wanted to do, and anyway it wasn't a good idea to keep Jessica out of the sixth form for the first week of the year. But it wouldn't have been fair to him. He's so responsible himself and loves getting cross when other people are irresponsible, like when they don't do their homework. Then he can square his shoulders under the burden, which is hard with his bull neck, but when he tries to do that Kate thinks he looks hilariously gorgeous.

If her stomach's better tomorrow she might go to the Public Library and see if they've got the book she needs. That would give Richard something to laugh about. Kate likes his chuckle. **The library? On holiday? You should go to the beach. Jessica and you should go to the beach, go on the ferry to Manly.**

Jessica has told him she hates the beach. Has done since she was eleven years old: get real, Dad. Who wants a tan these days, what are you, stuck in the sixties? All Jessica wants is to shop till she drops.

Richard comes back from breakfast. He checks again that he's thoroughly close-shaven. He looks for his conference pack. Jessica's using it as a lap table, writing postcards.

'When you're ready, Budgie,' he says. Without looking at him, Jess holds the pack up. Jess hates it when he calls her that, but he's got off lightly this time: he must realise, for he blinks at Kate. She blinks back. Jessica rolls away over the fold-out bed to finish the cards with her head stuck under the dressing table. Richard picks up his jacket. As he strides out again he tells Kate to be ready by seven, it's dinner at the revolving restaurant and he wants her to sit next to the new president.

'Your new black dress is very elegant, wear that,' he says.

I'd rather wear the red one, she thinks.

At conferences, in the evenings, Kate is the parrot on the shoulder of a Captain's jacket. *Awk.*

The menu is usually handwritten. In gold or green. Last night it said:

Medallions of kangaroo triumphant, presented on a cushion of raspberry coulis.

Kebabs of buffalo, anointed with a blessing of garlic screened with a curtain of fennel.

They farm buffalo in Australia! And serve it in restaurants! Kate expected it to taste like old dry wood but it absolutely melts!

Another wife, usually called Miranda, usually peers across the table through the shimmer of the candelabra and says brittle things about where she's travelled to lately. Last night, the Miranda was

Beverly, one of the Australian wives. She said: *Deed you go to the Eenternational Meeting? Mexeeco Ceety was fabulous. The leather. Tooled leather. I came back laden. Belts, and bags, and a hat, a tooled leather hat! I'm going with Peter to the Paris meeting. Oh my God. Gucci.*

The Captain's jacket said what it usually says at dinner parties: **Kate loved Italy but I had to keep her away from the silversmiths on the Ponte Vecchio ha ha.**

The men all said what they always say: **Ha ha.**

The women echoed: *Ha ha ha.*

It's the same every time. Except last night Kate decided to dance up and down on her Captain's sloping rugby-thick shoulders, and talked about her Russian homework. That caused a crack in the brittle conversation.

Awk.

At least Martin Daney threw her a wink. Everyone else gave those slow nods that make their necks longer, so they looked like ducks peering into a bottle. But Martin laughed, with Kate and at everyone else. Martin's here without his wife. He's having a great time. His laugh drives Richard nuts. It always has, since they were in medical school together. Martin always comes off best, in everything Richard hopes he'll be best at. So Kate is careful not to laugh too much with Martin. She'd rather sit next to Martin tonight than Don Donovan, the new president, who's weatherbeaten with a leer.

Two more days before they can go home.

Maybe her cold will be better tomorrow. Her stomach should be better. Kate won't go to the zoo, today or tomorrow. Jess is right. It's unfashionable to like zoos, to watch the beautiful creatures, caged and quietly angry with eyes that carry secret thoughts of everything and nothing, not reasoned thought but thoughts that are pure feeling, closed off, secret. Today, Kate will go shopping and eat hot chips.

In the subway near the hotel is a place which sells the best hot chips in the world. Fat hot chips, salty. The best in the *universe.*

Salt's bad for her. It clogs her arteries. Mainly it's bad because if Richard sees her have salt, he does his big F.

She's bought hot chips every day and relished every grain of salt, ripping the bag open to lick in the corners. The stall keeper looks like

314 Mutes & Earthquakes

one of his chips, square-set and nicely browned. He has a black moustache and white apron. He could be Russian. Maybe his name is Cyril, she thinks. Maybe his till is full of Russian coins.

✧

Kate takes two Panadol and goes shopping until lunch time. She buys more tissues for her cold. It's hell to have a cold in this hot weather, in the smog. She looks at all the shops she looked at yesterday. Then she goes underground. Cyril looks cross when he sees her. He has an excellent line in frowns, too: he and Richard could swap notes, thinks Kate. She wonders if he stalks round naked at home. A naked (saltless) hot chip. He might disapprove of her buying chips so often, even though it means more cash in his till. She rises on her toes to look over the counter, to see if the drawer has a section for Russian coins and squiggly links like the letter Z. Cyril gives her a very black look. Kate thinks she might have a temperature. Or maybe it's too many Panadol. She remembers to say 'thank you' for the chips and sidesteps to the next stall for an avocado sandwich.

She walks through the underground arcade to the moving stairs that take her to the hotel. She holds the bag of hot chips to her chest. In the foyer, the Suitcase Boy glances at her. He can smell my chips, she thinks. In the lift she presses the button for floor nine.

The maid has cleaned the room. Jessica is long gone. Kate puts the safety chain across the door. She takes off her shoes. She takes off her blouse and her trousers. Then she takes off her underwear, except her knickers, and heaps all the pillows against the head of the queen-sized bed. She sits cross-legged in the middle of the mattress, leans back and tucks one heel into her crotch.

She lays the avocado sandwich on the quilt for later and opens up the bag of chips. Kate closes her eyes. *Ah, Cyril,* she breathes. *My Katerina!* he breathes back. The hot rising scent, deep, delicious. She eats the chips slowly, feeling the edges on her tongue. She is savoury, crisp, sizzling.

Jenny Pattrick

Jenny Pattrick took the Original Composition course in 1993, when her highly successful radio series, *A Matter for Grace*, first began to take shape as her end-of-course folio. 'Wild Turkey' has also been broadcast on radio, and is one of a new group of stories which have a shared setting and cast of characters.

Wild Turkey

The youngest Kingi child watches from behind the gate.

'No use going up,' she says, 'Dad's not there.'

Vera, who believes in dark forces, and considers this child to belong to them, averts her eyes as she steers towards the shed.

'Don't go in there,' says the child. 'There's something dead.' Her eyes are fierce behind a tangled curtain of hair. 'Something horrible,' she says.

'Thanks for the tip,' says Vera, 'Where's your Dad then?'

'Back behind.' The child gestures. 'He's covered in blood,' she adds. 'And the baby might die.'

'Happy days,' says Vera. Humming 'Christ the Lord is Risen Today' against possible effects of the evil eye, she swings open the gate and child, goes through, swings them both shut. Vera's tattered oilskin, ancient army surplus, drags in the mud at one corner; her grubby grey locks straggle out from under a sou'wester of the same vintage. Round the back Augusta is screaming.

'Please God they both die,' mutters Vera. 'So we can all get some peace.' But she doesn't mean it.

George is indeed up to his elbows in blood. He waves a dripping hand at Vera. 'Breech,' he says. 'Grab her head, will you?'

Vera plants her gumboots firmly in the mud, puts a headlock on

Augusta. George, at the other end, heaves on the emerging little hooves.

'You will raise donkeys,' puffs Vera. 'Unnatural breed.'

George feels inside for the other legs. 'Damn,' he says.

Augusta bares her yellow teeth and brays to the skies. A flock of starlings bursts from the macrocarpa, an auspicious omen. The slippery bundle comes free with a rush, depositing George and the newborn donkey in the mud.

'Well,' says Vera, standing back to let the mother take over, 'one more hee-haw in the bloody dawn chorus.'

'You can't fool me,' says George. 'You're as nuts about them as I am.'

'Rubbish,' says Vera, but her tough old heart is melting at the sight of Augusta licking her newborn, at the little donkey's rickety efforts to rise.

George runs his arms under the tap, thumps the boards of the shed. 'Got something in here for you,' he says. 'Christmas present. What do you say to a wild turkey?'

Vera's lumpy face cracks wide. 'Wild turkey?' she screams. 'I haven't tasted that in twenty years. Straight up?'

'Straight up. Had a shoot up at my brother's last night. Big flock of them taking over his paddocks. Eat more grass than his damn herd. We bagged twenty for the Christmas hangi. Thought you might like one too.'

'Would I ever!'

George opens the shed door. Little Lovey skips and screams behind him, making the most of the horror. Vera clicks her tongue in admiration. She walks round the black mountain of feathers. A scrawny red head dangles at one end, two great yellow feet claw the air stiffly.

'My God, George, it's almost as big as me!' says Vera.

George takes the tomahawk from the bench, removes the head with one blow.

Lovey shrieks. 'Can I have it? Can I have it?'

George throws it out the door and Lovey runs to pick it up, to poke, with a curious finger, at the staring eyes.

George slits the crop, removes a ball of grass as big as a rock melon, and tosses that out the door too. The child chases it, whooping like a banshee, kicking it forward till it rolls under Augusta's hooves. Lovey offers the ball of grass to the new mother, who accepts, munching with relish. Vera looks away with distaste at this unusual recycling. And yet, she acknowledges, why not? I am going to eat the turkey itself.

Next George draws the stinking innards down into a bucket. Vera doesn't notice the smell. She's planning a gorgeous aromatic stuffing.

'Right, Vera, she's all yours,' says George. He hoists the bird onto her shoulder. The severed neck, dangling down her back, nearly reaches the ground; the wings, spreading wide, turn her into an evil, hump-backed angel.

'Witch! Witch!' sings little Lovey, dancing round Vera and whacking her with the wobbling turkey head.

'Witch yourself,' says Vera, with a certain fervour. She believes six-year-old Lovey is already a talented member of the black sisterhood.

Vera's stubby legs sag under the weight, but she is independent to the core, as George knows well. Patronise Vera, offer her a helping hand, and she'd bite your head off. She staggers the few yards across the road to her own ruin of a cottage.

'Bloody hell,' she says, her eyes like lamps. 'Wait till Bull hears about this.'

Most people in Piwari leave the tiny community for Christmas. The two Kingi families take off north, which accounts for half the population; Sam Collins, the mill-owner, in the new two-storeyed house near the road, goes to Taupo; the three McAneny sisters, who have lived together in the same crumbling home for twenty years (no one knows what brought them to Piwari in the first place), catch the Intercity for some unknown destination south; and a few nomadic hippies, squatting in empty houses, usually return to comfortable families elsewhere for a decent feed. That leaves Vera and Bull.

Both have lived in Piwari all their lives. They went to the same school; both worked till they retired in Ohakune, he in the drapery, she cleaner at the pub. For five years of his life Bull was a famous All Black, then he came back to the drapery and went on as before, unremembered, a recluse. Both he and Vera, as only children, inherited their parents' homes, his down by the railway-line, a neat bungalow, white boards with yellow trim and dark green roof, kept immaculate inside and out, with plastic bottles of water on the lawn to deter dogs; hers next to the bush reserve, a ramshackle heap of borer and rust, roof iron held down by old tires, two long-dead cars in the backyard, stacks and stacks of old newspapers inside, but outside a vegetable garden to match Bull's in production if not in orderliness. No one knows how old they are; no one can say why they never married.

Every day of the week, except Sunday, Vera cooks a hot meal in her kitchen, tucks the dishes into an old pram, and wheels the food down to Bull's place, where they eat it together. The sight of gritty old Vera and her rattling pram stumping past at six pm reassures other Piwari people that the world is still turning.

Back home Vera ties a piece of old sash-cord round the turkey's scaly legs, suspends him from the tank stand, and starts plucking. Two hours later she's still going and the yard is awash with drifting, shifting feathers. Who would imagine a bird possessed so many? Vera curses the weakness in her aging fingers. She tries pliers on the biggest of the wing feathers but even so a few remain, black flags on a lovely snowy carcass. She trots inside for the wire-cutters and snips them off at skin level.

Across the road Augusta brays.

That night, after a dinner of savoury mince, mashed potatoes, Bull's carrots and Vera's silverbeet, wheeled down as usual in the pram, Vera tells Bull about the turkey.

'I don't know about *that*,' says Bull. Bull is a big man, you could fit two of Vera into his frame, but he has always been cautious, even on the rugby field. 'I don't know about *wild*,' he says.

Vera snorts. 'Wild is ambrosia, Bull, wild is the aristocrat of your turkeys.'

'That's as may be, Vera, but with wild how do you know what they've been eating, tell me that! They could have been anywhere!' Bull shakes his slabby head at the thought of black flocks of turkeys, gobbling in nasty places.

'And another thing, Bull,' says Vera, uneasy now, but plunging on, 'I want you to come to me for Christmas dinner this year.'

'What!' says Bull. 'But I've decorated the Christmas tree!'

'Well I can see that *now*, can't I? It's lovely. And tomorrow. And on Christmas morning if you like, I'll bring some scones down.'

Bull is incredulous. This is a major break with tradition. He argues, he sulks, he crashes the dishes in the sink. Vera, dismayed by the onslaught, holds firm to her principles. You can't wheel a large roast turkey down the road in a pram, it wouldn't be proper, besides which it wouldn't fit. Besides which her living room is perfectly comfortable in its own way, there is absolutely no reason why they shouldn't eat there sometimes. Besides which they are neither of them getting any younger and it is a danger to life and limb wheeling a loaded pram over potholes day after day.

Bull goes quiet. 'I thought you liked coming,' he says. 'I thought you liked the change of scene.'

'Well I *do*, you know I do, Bull, but what about a bit of a change for you just once in a while? I'm not saying every day, just Christmas dinner.'

She adds, after a stubborn pause, 'And once in a while.'

Bull shoves his fists in the pockets of his brown corduroy jacket. This evening, like every evening except Sunday, he has come in from the garden at five-fifteen, showered, squeezed into a freshly ironed shirt, his good trousers and jacket, polished his already shining shoes, poured out two good whiskeys and sat waiting in his quiet and spotless living room listening for the rattling pram.

'You always come to me for Christmas dinner,' says Bull, looking at the floor, the window, anywhere but at Vera.

'I always come to you for every dinner,' says Vera, 'I come to you with every dinner. But not on Saturday. Not with wild turkey and that's my final word.'

Next day, Christmas Eve, Vera wheels down cold meat and salad, nothing fancy, so that their appetites won't be blunted for the big day. Piwari is empty. Augusta and the little donkey look lonely and cold in their big paddock, but rain is setting in so Vera doesn't stop for a chat.

The meal is amicable enough, the subject on both their minds is not mentioned. But in the end it can't be avoided. As Bull helps Vera into her oilskin and gumboots, he says. 'I could bring up the wheel-barrow, tomorrow night, help you carry down the food.'

Vera sets her mouth in a straight line, ignores his embarrassment. 'Bull, if you can wheel the barrow up, you can come inside to eat. My house may not be an oil painting, but it won't bite you. What if it's a night like this? Eh? I'm not ruining wild turkey. No, Bull, I want you to come to me.'

'I can't,' says Bull, barely audible.

'Won't,' says Vera, close to tears. 'I'll eat it myself then.'

Christmas Day is windy and wet. Vera decides not to take scones down to Bull. The storm, sweeping up from the south, brings a curtain of hail, most unseasonal, which batters down her scarlet runners and breaks the tomato shoots. Vera curses the storm, the cold and all stubborn men.

Stuffing the turkey revives her spirits, though. She listens to carols on the radio, humming along while she crumbles bread, rubs in a little butter, breaks in two eggs, chops onions and garlic from the garden, adds a jar of preserved mushrooms, kept since Easter when the fields were full of them. The turkey's gizzard is huge, tough to get the knife through, but Vera won't give in, she loves giblets. Her mouth waters as she fries them in a little chicken fat and adds them to the stuffing. During the frying she hears odd little thumps at the back door, but thinks nothing of it. Wind, she supposes and goes to see if it is properly latched.

It is not wind. Vera's back door opens onto a little decrepit porch. One end of the porch is open, the other is half boarded to shelter the door to her toilet. Blocking the toilet door is the very solid frame of Augusta, lying on her side, with the baby tucked snug against her creamy belly.

'Bloody hell,' says Vera, who has been putting off going till the stuffing was made. She flaps at Augusta, shouts, tries dragging at her ears. Augusta won't budge. Vera beats the donkey with a stick, but gently. Augusta bats her beautiful eyes and looks the other way.

In the end Vera has to stomp across the road in the rain to the

Kingis' long-drop. The Kingis' shed door has been left latched open. George's three other donkeys are inside, dry and comfortable, munching on hay. Why on earth doesn't Augusta do the same?

Vera has to enter her house by the front door, quite the wrong sort of feeling, especially in wet weather. In the kitchen the great turkey carcass is waiting under its shroud of greased sheeting. Vera brings the oven to 325° Fahrenheit and manoeuvres the baking dish from bench to chair, from chair to oven. She can only just manage. There is a tense moment when the great jutting breastbone catches on the top element, but in the end the bird fits and the slow roasting commences.

As the dark, gamey smell of turkey rises in the kitchen, the bumps on the back door increase in volume. Vera had hoped that if she ignored Augusta, the donkey might drift off. She jerks open the back door in a rage. Augusta is there, on her feet now, nose to the door, butting away. She tries to trot past Vera, into the kitchen. This is outrageous! Vera shoves hard with the door, forcing it shut, though the weight of the animal is almost too much for her.

Something about the donkey's insistence is weird. Vera is flushed now, she feels trapped in her own home. First Bull and now Augusta, the day is turning sour on her. Bump bump bump, the donkey is at the door again. Postnatal dementia? wonders Vera. Has that little monster Lovey bewitched her? Vera remembers Lovey feeding the donkey grass from the turkey's crop, and again the thought turns her stomach. She has to sit down for a minute.

In the end it is all too much for her. Bundled against the weather, she leaves by the front door, half running, stumbling on the uneven road. The day is dark and bitterly cold but no light shows in any of the deserted houses, nor smoke above any chimney pot. Vera feels evil in the air. Bull's neat home, lawns and garden immaculate, is a haven of warmth and light. Bull stands in the doorway. He is dressed in his good clothes and has perhaps been standing there, behind the door, for some time.

Bull brings her inside, a courteous hand under her elbow, removes the coat as if it is mink, pours a sherry. He pretends not to notice her agitation. Vera gulps.

'Bull, you've got to come and help,' she says, 'I am under siege by the forces of darkness.'

Bull looks at her. He sips his sherry.

'That evil child Lovey,' says Vera, 'fed the turkey's crop to Augusta. The ball of grass, you know, from its neck, no doubt impregnated with some strange alluring digestive juices. Now the donkey is fixated on my bird. Wants to come inside. There is some dark communication going on between them, Bull, the donkey and my stuffed turkey.'

'Nonsense,' says Bull. The flat words are like music to Vera.

'I know it sounds crazy . . .' she says.

'Vera,' says Bull, 'get a grip on yourself. Donkeys are not attracted to meat. As you very well know.'

'If the donkey is bewitched, though?'

'That donkey is simply lonely, Vera. Lonely. Piwari is empty.'

Vera looks at Bull, sitting neatly, feet together in his crowded barren room.

'Except for us,' says Vera. She sips her sherry. 'Well,' she says, after a silence, 'you may well be right, Bull. I am superstitious, I'll grant you that.' She stands. Bull stands too, always the gentleman.

'I see,' says Vera, 'you have your good clothes on. Are you coming up for your dinner then?'

Bull clears his throat. 'I thought I might accept the invitation,' he says. 'If it's not too late.'

Vera beams. 'You'll have to take the place as it is,' she says. 'I've had no time to clean.'

Bull swallows, nods without speaking. He is tense as they leave his spotless world and step into the untidy night. Vera keeps chatting to gentle him along.

Vera takes Bull in through the front door. The smell of roast turkey, at least, is inviting. The kitchen is the only inhabited room in Vera's house. Vera spreads a newspaper for him on the best of her kitchen chairs. Bull lowers himself as if onto broken glass. When he is well through his first whiskey, and the potatoes are browning up nicely, Vera opens the back door. Demon possession is no longer in the air. It is simply two cold donkeys standing in the doorway.

'Room at the Inn,' says Vera, winking at Bull. Bull pales, closes his eyes for a moment, but holds his ground. Augusta and child enter, stepping neatly. Vera takes them through to the front parlour, where she has made a nest of old newspapers, discovering a mouse nest in the process. She scratches their soft grey noses and returns to the kitchen.

Bull is uncorking bubbly. 'Vera, *please*,' he says. 'Wash your hands before you do anything. You don't know where those donkeys have been.'

Vera smiles, runs her hands under the tap, raises her glass.

'Happy Christmas, Bull,' she says.

It may not have been the most relaxed of evenings, but as Vera said next evening to Bull, back at his place, over turkey leftovers, it was a good start.

The turkey itself was delicious.

Fiona McLean

Fiona McLean did the Original Composition course in 1994. She would probably call herself a poet rather than a prose writer. For one of her poems, see p.285. On 'Written in Blood', see 'Five Things' in 'The Exercise Chapter', p.286.

Written in Blood

It was the story of a journey, and she wasn't at all sure she liked it. It certainly became very messy in places, and seemed to lack symmetry. She couldn't help wondering what it was driving at.

So it was just the three of them, and they got in a car and drove. There was Sarah, who was too skinny, and James, who was too beautiful, and Byron, who just never left, after she had made James turn around and go back. Byron wasn't a hitch-hiker in the sense that he wanted to be picked up, he didn't stick out his thumb or anything; just walked down the Desert Road in a storm. But he was happy enough to take the ride and, although he dripped over everything, she thought, Good, maybe he'll help things, we can't argue any more. He didn't seem to notice the silence between the two of them, just told them about the town he came from with three petrol stations and one pub and no women.

She could remember the time James too had stood waiting for her, through rain and wind and timid sunshine. She emerged at five o'clock, squinting in the light, and drank in the sight of him, a Greek god of the elements, indifferent to nature, shedding the weather from his broad shoulders. She watched his lips move and never heard a word.

She went home and looked him up in a *Dictionary of Saints*. Saint James, also called James the Greater, also called 'son of thunder'.

Noted for his impetuous character and fiery temper. She wondered what he was like in bed.

After they turned right at Waiouru, the conversation lagged. She offered to take the wheel, as they sped past the tour buses at Tangiwai, but James ignored her. Byron was staring out the window, searching for a glimpse of mountain amidst all the cloud. She found herself biting her nails, chewing her cuticles in a desperate attempt to occupy the space. James once told her she looked like a stick insect, all eyes and no substance and no fingernails either, for God's sake. She had replied in kind, telling him she was more like a weta, the female weta whose bite is poisonous only in mating season, and fuck her bloody fingernails.

Then Byron spoke. He wanted to know if the two of them were married.

After the first year, she had noticed a change in his eyes. They moved slowly, no longer followed her around the room, no longer lingered when no one was looking. She wrote him a poem

> For you are rooted deep inside me
> as deep as the teeth within my gums
> grooved within my skull.

and he smiled so sweetly that she felt her stomach leave her body and writhe on the floor in ecstasy and they made love all night. And she averted her eyes when he looked over her shoulder at other women. And she failed to notice the desperation in his voice when he tried to stop her leaving early, as if he knew he could not help but be unfaithful without her in his field of vision. And she had left. Once, she dreamed that James was standing before her and she reached out to stroke his hair and his skull was so soft that it crumpled like an eggshell.

Byron raised his eyebrows at her as she glanced at him, curled up in the back seat, as she willed James to answer. They were strangely arched, kinking into a bow between his eyes, almost too contrived for a man. The Byronic hero, she thought, oh you are so witty, Sarah, all thundering brows and tormented gazes. Thunder and lightning and hail and blizzard and climatic fury. Disorder is in the air and the winds scream in victory.

She went shopping and bought tampons and chocolate and Panadol. She lay on the bed and bled blood into the white cotton sheets. She dreamt of giving birth to a grown man and of screaming a scream that no one could hear. She lay awake at night and cried crocodile tears and thought of the rivers of Africa.

Byron asked to keep going straight ahead at Raetihi. He said he wanted to drive down by the Wanganui River. He said he was spiritually joined to all water, and to this stretch in particular. He said it was in the nature of a homecoming. James didn't argue. The road became skinnier and the day grew black. Sarah folded her arms across her chest and hugged herself. It was very cold.

When she saw the river, murky in the rain, she thought, I have never seen this river before in my life. And she thought, Isn't it odd how we define a river by its banks rather than by the water that is in it. Maybe I have seen the Wanganui River before, floating around Wellington Harbour, maybe I have swallowed mouthfuls of the stuff. Maybe seventy per cent of me is the Wanganui River.

At Jerusalem, James stopped the car. The windscreen became a sheet of solid water. Jerusalem became invisible. Byron spoke and told them he was the son of James K. Baxter. James laughed. Byron said nothing. James said that Baxter was a saint among men. Byron said he wouldn't know, he'd never met the man. James said it was probably time to be going. Byron said nothing. Sarah thought about silence as a weapon.

As they joined State Highway 4, Byron told them that he was the great great great great grandson of Captain James Cook. Sarah remarked that the weather certainly was deteriorating. James pointed out that Byron was in fact black. Another silence descended over the car. They bypassed the city and headed for home.

As a child she had a bird that repeated everything she said. As a woman she dreamed of her child-self holding a golden birdcage with a cat inside, his eyes as green as grass. The cat had eaten her bird. She said to the cat, I love you. The cat replied, I love you too.

Ken Duncum

Ken Duncum took the Original Composition course in 1983, and is best known for his work for theatre (in particular *Blue Sky Boys*) and for screen (*Cover Story*). He was writing poetry back in 1983, and this extract from *Horseplay* brings a poet, James K. Baxter, into collision (and a sense of comradeship) with the novelist Ronald Hugh Morrieson.

final scene from Horseplay

Having met, got pissed, and brushed with murder, suicide and marriage one winter's night in Hawera in 1972, RONALD HUGH MORRIESON *and* JAMES K. BAXTER *finally reach some kind of accord as morning approaches.*

RON   This poetry racket, mate—there any money in it? If the readies are there I reckon I could give it a burl. Tried every other bloody thing.

JIM   Why not?

He picks up paper and pen.

I'll take down the words.

RON   Now? Out loud?

JIM   On the tongue.

RON   What'll I write about?

JIM   Whatever.

RON *shapes up self-consciously to begin.*

RON   Nah—I feel like a prize dork. I've never written anything with someone in the same room.

JIM [*writing*]   'Ode to—Hawera'.

RON   Shouldn't I kick off with a tree or a vase of flowers or something?

JIM A poet is not so much magician or dreamer. If he resembles
anything it's the emu, who digests stones and old boots.

RON I dunno, mate.

JIM [*writing*] 'I dunno, mate—'

RON Oh, now come on . . .

JIM 'Oh now come on . . .' I'm sending this to *Landfall* by first
post. With your name on it.

RON Right, ya bugger.

JIM Write, you bugger.

RON O . . . Hawera! Thou great . . .

His eye falls on the horse carcass wedged in the doorway.

. . . horse's arsehole! 'Horse's arsehole'? That's fucked! What
kind of poetry is that?

JIM Keep going!

RON You keep going!

JIM Hawera—horse's arsehole
What iron frost grips your knackers
Out of season? . . .

RON Just a minute, mate—if anyone's going to put the boot into
this town—[it'll be me!]

JIM 'Out—of—season . . .'

RON jumps in.

RON Dawn cracks like an egg into your main drag
Spilling the Rotary President butcher
Farting and whingeing out of his sister-in-law's bed

Slowly at first, gathering momentum, the poem starts to roll.

An hour from now he'll be scraping mouldy bread
Into the sausage mix, parting the plastic-strip flyscreen
Of another day, conning bored pregnant wives with green-
nosed kids
That he'd slip them some beef tea in bed
Soon as look at them—telling me pissy-eyed later on
'Mate—it's the fuckin' highlight of their day!'
Yeah, and morning breaking too on pub

And Post Office, eclipsing the blue all-night light
Of Davies Gas Station And Lubritorium
Where Jim who lost his boy in a shunting accident
Lies cold, shit-faced round a flagon of Blackberry Nip
While a quarter mile away, as still as a corpse,
His wife is staring at the faded wallpaper.
Then the whistle goes at the Treatment Station
As sharp and quivering in the chilly air
As a chord on a cool vibraphone.
From the hinterland to the coast the lazy wind blows
—so lazy it'd rather go through you than round you—
As the young cop with the seven-a-side moustache
Drives through town thinking of the electrically charged
    flesh
Of a girl at a dance, and the old cop, spindle-shanked
And herring-gutted, unshaven as an albino hedgehog
Heaves his brewer's goitre on top of his wife with the bung
    eye.
Sadness dives and collars me low, and the sun
Supposed to disperse the chimeras of the small hours
Only serves to sheet them home. Donkey deep, somewhere
Down the line this town turned dog on me, its narrow
    roads
Shooting away like arrows only ever returned me here,
    waking
With a labouring heart, enough dirty water on my chest
To sink a boat. Hawera, horse's arse, from metho kings
To bible-bangers yawns and stretches, dips its lips in
    Ovaltine,
Forgets its dead in the yellow cemetery. Today
In shaking sunshine with no zip in it, I'll punch arms
And slap backs, grinning away with murder in my heart
Good old Ron, booze artist, bullshitter and headmaster
Of the most hectic school of froth-blowers in the South
Taranaki—but there's the wheel of a Leyland ten-tonner
Leaning on my heart, a six-foot trench on my trail,
The whole town chipping in for a headstone. This hard case

Remembers nights, the moon in the gutter of the sky
With its parking lights on, brandy glowing like a beacon
In the belly, swooping home down the backroads
From the first time a woman wrapped her legs around me
Saying, 'Boy, that feels good'. And home was Ma—and that
    open grave
That sits drinking with me in the Imperial, leans across the
    table
To say, 'Just curl up in me, son—they'll plant you where
You can lay your head on her lap like you used to as a kid
Coming back on the train from Opunake beach.' And I
    want to—
I'm tired and I want to—but instead I stagger out into the
    empty street
Where a cannonball wouldn't startle a tomcat
With my brain screaming, 'Run, boy, run!
Change the scenery—shoot through—get lost! Fuck off
Out of it and away!'
But Hawera and me—deeper than blood
A boiled carrot and a hunk of corn brisket
What can I say?—as my grave catches up with me
On the street beside the TAB, lights my smoke
And arm in arm we head on our way—
Alright
Alright! ALRIGHT!!
I'll stay.

Pause. He turns to BAXTER.

Not going too fast was I, mate?

BAXTER *is deep asleep and has been for most of the poem.* RON *slips the piece of paper out of his fingers, looks at the few scrawled lines and, amused, screws it up. He goes to close the piano lid, the train whistle sounds from the station,* RON *listens, fingers a scale, then sits down and plays a jaunty jazz tune (Ain't Misbehavin') as the whistle fades into the distance. Light brightens outside the window and the birds start to sing. Fade.*

THE END

Vivienne Plumb

Bill's Last Class

It's like this:
in the lift
my stomach has that dropping feeling
same as back in the room.
But out in the night, on the street,
I fly.
Bon soir, mes amis.
I'm sorry but when the night turns pitch
I must fly,
the gravel spewing up from my heels.

At the cable stop,
Salamanca,
the one light shines
iridescent
through my red plastic pencil case.

There's the other one going up
says the man to his child.

Acknowledgements

For permission to reprint items included in this anthology, acknowledgements are made to copyright holders and places of publication as follows.

Rachel Bush: the author, *Sport* and Victoria University Press (*The Hungry Woman*). Barbara Anderson: the author and Victoria University Press (*I think we should go into the jungle*). Forbes Williams: the author and Victoria University Press (*Motel View*). Eirlys Hunter: the author. Dinah Hawken: the author, *Sport* and Victoria University Press (*It Has No Sound and is Blue*; *Water, Leaves, Stones*). Jenny Bornholdt: the author, *Soho Square*, *Sport* and Victoria University Press (*Moving House*; *Waiting Shelter*; *How We Met*). James Brown: the author, *Sport* and Victoria University Press (*Go Round Power Please*). Adrienne Jansen: the author, *Sport* and Whitireia Publishing / Daphne Brasell Associates (*How Things Are*). Damien Wilkins: the author. Alison Glenny: the author and *Sport*. Paola Bilbrough: the author and *Sport*. Kirsty Gunn: the author and Faber and Faber (*First Fictions: Introduction 11*). Hinemoana Baker: the author and *Sport*. Gabrielle Muir: the author and *Sport*. Lauren Holder: *Soho Square*. Anthony McCarten: the author. Laurel Stowell: the author. Alison Wong: the author and *Printout*. Saut Situmorang: *Sport*. Annora Gollop: the author and *Sport*. Betty Bremner: the author and the *Dominion*. Catriana Mulholland: the author and *Sevensome: New Poems by NZ Women*. Julia Wall: the author. Andrew Loughnan: the author. Caren Wilton: the author and *Printout*. Virginia Fenton: the author and *Sport*. Wanda Barker: the author and *Printout*. Jane Gardner: the author and *Sport*. Miro Bilbrough: the author. Joy Cowley: the author. Johanna Mary: the author and the *School Journal*. Jo Randerson: the author and *Sport*. Pat Quinn: the author and Penguin Books (*Subversive Acts*). Catherine Chidgey: the author, *Sport* and Victoria University Press (*In a Fishbone Church*). Vivienne Plumb: the author, *Between These Hills* and University of Otago Press (*The Wife who Spoke Japanese in Her Sleep*). Samara McDowell: the author and *Sport*. Nikhat Shameem: the author and *Sport*. Emily Perkins: the author and *Sport*. David Geary: the author and *Sport*. Chris Orsman: the author, *Sport* and Victoria University Press (*Ornamental Gorse*). Kate Camp: the author, *Landfall*, *Sport* and *Takahe*. Virginia Were: the author, *Sport* and Victoria University Press (*Juliet Bravo Juliet*). Fiona Kidman: the author. Gabe McDonnell: the author. Lynn Davidson: the author and *Sport*. Helen McGrath: the author. Kimberley Rothwell: the author and *Sport*. Emma Neale: the author and *Between These Hills*. Alexandra

Gillespie: the author and *Kapiti Poems*. Michael Mintrom: the author. Fleur Wickes: the author and *Sport*. Julie Leibrich: the author and *Kapiti Poems*. Emily McHalick: the author. Allen O'Leary: the author and *Friends and Family*. Alex Scobie: the author and *Sport*. Stephanie Miller: the author. Elizabeth Knox: the author and Victoria University Press (*After Z-Hour*). Adam Shelton: the author. Louise Wrightson: the author and *Sport*. Ingrid Horrocks: the author and *Landfall*. J.H. Macdonald: the author, *Sport* and Victoria University Press (*The Free World*). Sarah Quigley: the author and the *Listener*. Barbara Else: the author, *Metro* and Godwit Publishing (*The Warrior Queen*). Jenny Pattrick: the author and Radio New Zealand. Fiona McLean: the author and *Sport*. Ken Duncum: the author.